The
AUDACITY
of
HOPE

ALSO BY BARACK OBAMA

Dreams from My Father

The
AUDACITY
of
HOPE

——

*Thoughts on Reclaiming
the American Dream*

——

BARACK OBAMA

CROWN PUBLISHERS
NEW YORK

CROWN is a trademark and the Crown colophon is a registered
trademark of Random House, Inc.

Library of Congress Cataloging-in-Publication Data
Obama, Barack.
The audacity of hope : thoughts on reclaiming the American dream /
Barack Obama.—1st ed.
p. cm.
1. Obama, Barack. 2. Legislators—United States—Biography.
3. African American legislators—Biography. 4. United States.
Congress. Senate—Biography. 5. Obama, Barack—Philosophy.
6. National characteristics, American. 7. Ideals (Philosophy).
8. United States—Politics and government—Philosophy.
9. United States—Politics and government—2001– . I. Title.
E901.1.O23A3   2006
973'.04960730092—dc22   2006028967

ISBN-13: 978-0-307-23769-9
ISBN-10: 0-307-23769-9

Printed in the United States of America

Design by Lauren Dong

10   9   8   7   6

First Edition

To the women who raised me—

MY MATERNAL GRANDMOTHER, TUTU,
who's been a rock of stability throughout my life,

and

MY MOTHER,
whose loving spirit sustains me still

Contents

Prologue

IT'S BEEN ALMOST ten years since I first ran for political office. I was thirty-five at the time, four years out of law school, recently married, and generally impatient with life. A seat in the Illinois legislature had opened up, and several friends suggested that I run, thinking that my work as a civil rights lawyer, and contacts from my days as a community organizer, would make me a viable candidate. After discussing it with my wife, I entered the race and proceeded to do what every first-time candidate does: I talked to anyone who would listen. I went to block club meetings and church socials, beauty shops and barbershops. If two guys were standing on a corner, I would cross the street to hand them campaign literature. And everywhere I went, I'd get some version of the same two questions.

"Where'd you get that funny name?"

And then: "You seem like a nice enough guy. Why do you want to go into something dirty and nasty like politics?"

I was familiar with the question, a variant on the questions asked of me years earlier, when I'd first arrived in Chicago to work in low-income neighborhoods. It signaled a cynicism not simply with politics but with the very notion of a public life, a cynicism that—at least in the South Side neighborhoods I sought to represent—had been nourished by a generation of broken promises. In response, I would usually smile and nod and say that I understood the skepticism, but that there was—and always had been—another tradition to politics, a tradition that stretched from the days of the country's founding to the glory of the civil rights movement, a tradition based on the simple idea that we have a stake in one another, and that what binds us together is greater than what drives us apart, and that if enough people believe in the truth of that proposition and act on it, then we might not solve every problem, but we can get something meaningful done.

It was a pretty convincing speech, I thought. And although I'm not sure that the people who heard me deliver it were similarly impressed, enough of them appreciated my earnestness and youthful swagger that I made it to the Illinois legislature.

SIX YEARS LATER, when I decided to run for the United States Senate, I wasn't so sure of myself.

By all appearances, my choice of careers seemed to have worked out. After two terms during which I labored in the minority, Democrats had gained control of the state senate, and I had subsequently passed a slew of bills, from reforms of the Illinois death penalty system to an expansion of the state's health program for kids. I had continued to teach at the University of Chicago Law School, a job I enjoyed, and was frequently invited to speak around town. I had preserved my independence, my good name, and my marriage, all of which, statistically speaking, had been placed at risk the moment I set foot in the state capital.

But the years had also taken their toll. Some of it was just a function of my getting older, I suppose, for if you are paying attention, each successive year will make you more intimately acquainted with all of your flaws—the blind spots, the recurring habits of thought that may be genetic or may be environmental, but that will almost certainly worsen with time, as surely as the hitch in your walk turns to pain in your hip. In me, one of those flaws had proven to be a chronic restlessness; an inability to appreciate, no matter how well things were going, those blessings that were right there in front of me. It's a flaw that is endemic to modern life, I think—endemic, too, in the American character—and one that is nowhere more evident than in the field of politics. Whether politics actually encourages the trait or simply attracts those who possess it is unclear. Someone once said that every man is trying to either live up to his father's expectations or make up for his father's mistakes, and I suppose that may explain my particular malady as well as anything else.

In any event, it was as a consequence of that restlessness that I decided to challenge a sitting Democratic incumbent for his congressional seat in the 2000 election cycle. It was an ill-considered race, and I lost badly—the sort of drubbing that awakens you to the fact that life is not obliged to work out as you'd planned. A year and a half later, the scars of that loss sufficiently healed, I had lunch with a media consultant who had been encouraging me for some time to run for statewide office. As it happened, the lunch was scheduled for late September 2001.

"You realize, don't you, that the political dynamics have changed," he said as he picked at his salad.

"What do you mean?" I asked, knowing full well what he meant. We both looked down at the newspaper beside him. There, on the front page, was Osama bin Laden.

"Hell of a thing, isn't it?" he said, shaking his head. "Really bad luck. You can't change your name, of course. Voters are suspicious of that kind of thing. Maybe if you were at the start of your career, you know, you could use a nickname or something. But now . . ." His voice trailed off and he shrugged apologetically before signaling the waiter to bring us the check.

I suspected he was right, and that realization ate away at me. For the first time in my career, I began to experience the envy of seeing younger politicians succeed where I had failed, moving into higher offices, getting more things done. The pleasures of politics—the adrenaline of debate, the animal warmth of shaking hands and plunging into a crowd—began to pale against the meaner tasks of the job: the begging for money, the long drives home after the banquet had run two hours longer than scheduled, the bad food and stale air and clipped phone conversations with a wife who had stuck by me so far but was pretty fed up with raising our children alone and was beginning to question my priorities. Even the legislative work, the policy making that had gotten me to run in the first place, began to feel too incremental, too removed from the larger battles—over taxes, security, health care, and jobs—that were being waged on a national stage. I began to harbor doubts about the path I had chosen; I began feeling the way I imagine an actor or athlete must feel when, after years of commitment to a particular dream, after years of waiting tables between auditions or scratching out hits in the minor leagues, he realizes that he's gone just about as far as talent or fortune will take him. The dream will not happen, and he now faces the choice of accepting this fact like a grown-up and moving on to more sensible pursuits, or refusing the truth and ending up bitter, quarrelsome, and slightly pathetic.

DENIAL, ANGER, bargaining, despair—I'm not sure I went through all the stages prescribed by the experts. At some point, though, I arrived at acceptance—of my limits, and, in a way, my mortality. I refocused on my work in the state senate and took satisfaction from the reforms and initiatives that my position afforded. I spent more time at home, and watched my daughters grow, and properly cherished my wife, and thought about my long-term financial obligations. I exercised, and read novels, and came to appreciate how the earth rotated around the sun and the seasons came and went without any particular exertions on my part.

And it was this acceptance, I think, that allowed me to come up with the thoroughly cockeyed idea of running for the United States Senate. An up-or-out strategy was how I described it to my wife, one last shot to test out my ideas before I settled into a calmer, more stable, and better-paying existence. And she— perhaps more out of pity than conviction—agreed to this one last race, though she also suggested that given the orderly life she preferred for our family, I shouldn't necessarily count on her vote.

I let her take comfort in the long odds against me. The Republican incumbent, Peter Fitzgerald, had spent $19 million of his personal wealth to unseat the previous senator, Carol Moseley Braun. He wasn't widely popular; in fact he didn't really seem to enjoy politics all that much. But he still had unlimited money in his family, as well as a genuine integrity that had earned him grudging respect from the voters.

For a time Carol Moseley Braun reappeared, back from an ambassadorship in New Zealand and with thoughts of trying to reclaim her old seat; her possible candidacy put my own plans on hold. When she decided to run for the presidency instead, everyone else started looking at the Senate race. By the time Fitzgerald announced he would not seek reelection, I was staring at six primary opponents, including the sitting state comptroller; a businessman worth hundreds of millions of dollars; Chicago Mayor Richard Daley's former chief of staff; and a black, female health-care professional who the smart money assumed would split the black vote and doom whatever slim chances I'd had in the first place.

I didn't care. Freed from worry by low expectations, my credibility bolstered by several helpful endorsements, I threw myself into the race with an energy and joy that I'd thought I had lost. I hired four staffers, all of them smart, in their twenties or early thirties, and suitably cheap. We found a small office, printed letterhead, installed phone lines and several computers. Four or five hours a day, I called major Democratic donors and tried to get my calls returned. I held press conferences to which nobody came. We signed up for the annual St. Patrick's Day Parade and were assigned the parade's very last slot, so my ten volunteers and I found ourselves marching just a few paces ahead of the city's sanitation trucks, waving to the few stragglers who remained on the route while workers swept up garbage and peeled green shamrock stickers off the lampposts.

Mostly, though, I just traveled, often driving alone, first from ward to ward in Chicago, then from county to county and town to town, eventually up and down the state, past miles and miles of cornfields and beanfields and train tracks and silos. It wasn't an efficient process. Without the machinery of the state's Democratic Party organization, without any real mailing list or Internet operation, I had to rely on friends or acquaintances to open their houses to whoever might come, or to arrange for my visit to their church, union hall, bridge group, or Rotary Club. Sometimes, after several hours of driving, I would find just two or three people waiting for me around a kitchen table. I would have to assure the hosts that the turnout was fine and compliment them on the refreshments they'd prepared. Sometimes I would sit through a church service and the pastor would forget to recognize me, or the head of the union local would let me speak to his members just before announcing that the union had decided to endorse someone else.

But whether I was meeting with two people or fifty, whether I was in one of the well-shaded, stately homes of the North Shore, a walk-up apartment on the West Side, or a farmhouse outside Bloomington, whether people were friendly, indifferent, or occasionally hostile, I tried my best to keep my mouth shut and hear what they had to say. I listened to people talk about their jobs, their businesses, the local school; their anger at Bush and their anger at Democrats; their dogs, their back pain, their war service, and the things they remembered from childhood. Some had well-developed theories to explain the loss of manufacturing jobs or the high cost of health care. Some recited what they had heard on Rush Limbaugh or NPR. But most of them were too busy with work or their kids to pay much attention to politics, and they spoke instead of what they saw before them: a plant closed, a promotion, a high heating bill, a parent in a nursing home, a child's first step.

No blinding insights emerged from these months of conversation. If anything, what struck me was just how modest people's hopes were, and how much of what they believed seemed to hold constant across race, region, religion, and class. Most of them thought that anybody willing to work should be able to find a job that paid a living wage. They figured that people shouldn't have to file for bankruptcy because they got sick. They believed that every child should have a genuinely good education—that it shouldn't just be a bunch of talk—and that those same children should be able to go to college even if their parents weren't rich. They wanted to be safe, from criminals and from terrorists; they wanted clean air, clean water, and time with their kids. And when they got old, they wanted to be able to retire with some dignity and respect.

That was about it. It wasn't much. And although they understood that how they did in life depended mostly on their own efforts—although they didn't expect government to solve all their problems, and certainly didn't like seeing their tax dollars wasted—they figured that government should help.

I told them that they were right: government couldn't solve all their problems. But with a slight change in priorities we could make sure every child had a decent shot at life and meet the challenges we faced as a nation. More often than not, folks would nod in agreement and ask how they could get involved. And by the time I was back on the road, with a map on the passenger's seat, on my way to my next stop, I knew once again just why I'd gone into politics.

I felt like working harder than I'd ever worked in my life.

THIS BOOK GROWS directly out of those conversations on the campaign trail. Not only did my encounters with voters confirm the fundamental decency of the American people, they also reminded me that at the core of the American experience are a set of ideals that continue to stir our collective conscience; a common set of values that bind us together despite our differences; a running thread of hope that makes our improbable experiment in democracy work. These values and ideals find expression not just in the marble slabs of monuments or in the recitation of history books. They remain alive in the hearts and minds of most Americans—and can inspire us to pride, duty, and sacrifice.

I recognize the risks of talking this way. In an era of globalization and dizzying technological change, cutthroat politics and unremitting culture wars, we don't even seem to possess a shared language with which to discuss our ideals, much less the tools to arrive at some rough consensus about how, as a nation, we might work together to bring those ideals about. Most of us are wise to the ways of admen, pollsters, speechwriters, and pundits. We know how high-flying words can be deployed in the service of cynical aims, and how the noblest sentiments can be subverted in the name of power, expedience, greed, or intolerance. Even the standard high school history textbook notes the degree to which, from its very inception, the reality of American life has strayed from its myths. In such a climate, any assertion of shared ideals or common values might seem hopelessly naïve, if not downright dangerous—an attempt to gloss over serious differences in policy and performance or, worse, a means of muffling the complaints of those who feel ill served by our current institutional arrangements.

My argument, however, is that we have no choice. You don't need a poll to know that the vast majority of Americans—Republican, Democrat, and independent—are weary of the dead zone that politics has become, in which narrow interests vie for advantage and ideological minorities seek to impose their own versions of absolute truth. Whether we're from red states or blue states, we feel in our gut the lack of honesty, rigor, and common sense in our policy debates, and dislike what appears to be a continuous menu of false or cramped choices. Religious or secular, black, white, or brown, we sense—correctly—that the nation's most significant challenges are being ignored, and that if we don't change course soon, we may be the first generation in a very long time that leaves behind a weaker and more fractured America than the one we inherited. Perhaps more than any other time in our recent history, we need a new kind of politics, one that can excavate and build upon those shared understandings that pull us together as Americans.

That's the topic of this book: how we might begin the process of changing our politics and our civic life. This isn't to say that I know exactly how to do it. I don't. Although I discuss in each chapter a number of our most pressing policy challenges, and suggest in broad strokes the path I believe we should follow, my treatment of the issues is often partial and incomplete. I offer no unifying theory of American government, nor do these pages provide a manifesto for action, complete with charts and graphs, timetables and ten-point plans.

Instead what I offer is something more modest: personal reflections on those values and ideals that have led me to public life, some thoughts on the ways that our current political discourse unnecessarily divides us, and my own best assessment—based on my experience as a senator and lawyer, husband and father, Christian and skeptic—of the ways we can ground our politics in the notion of a common good.

Let me be more specific about how the book is organized. Chapter One takes stock of our recent political history and tries to explain some of the sources for today's bitter partisanship. In Chapter Two, I discuss those common values that might serve as

the foundation for a new political consensus. Chapter Three ex-
plores the Constitution not just as a source of individual rights,
but also as a means of organizing a democratic conversation
around our collective future. In Chapter Four, I try to convey
some of the institutional forces—money, media, interest groups,
and the legislative process—that stifle even the best-intentioned
politician. And in the remaining five chapters, I suggest how we
might move beyond our divisions to effectively tackle concrete
problems: the growing economic insecurity of many American
families, the racial and religious tensions within the body politic,
and the transnational threats—from terrorism to pandemic—
that gather beyond our shores.

I suspect that some readers may find my presentation of these
issues to be insufficiently balanced. To this accusation, I stand
guilty as charged. I am a Democrat, after all; my views on most
topics correspond more closely to the editorial pages of the *New
York Times* than those of the *Wall Street Journal.* I am angry
about policies that consistently favor the wealthy and powerful
over average Americans, and insist that government has an important role in opening up opportunity to all. I believe in evolution, scientific inquiry, and global warming; I believe in free
speech, whether politically correct or politically incorrect, and
I am suspicious of using government to impose anybody's religious
beliefs—including my own—on nonbelievers. Furthermore, I am
a prisoner of my own biography: I can't help but view the American experience through the lens of a black man of mixed heritage, forever mindful of how generations of people who looked
like me were subjugated and stigmatized, and the subtle and not
so subtle ways that race and class continue to shape our lives.

But that is not all that I am. I also think my party can be
smug, detached, and dogmatic at times. I believe in the free market, competition, and entrepreneurship, and think no small number of government programs don't work as advertised. I wish the
country had fewer lawyers and more engineers. I think America

has more often been a force for good than for ill in the world; I carry few illusions about our enemies, and revere the courage and competence of our military. I reject a politics that is based solely on racial identity, gender identity, sexual orientation, or victimhood generally. I think much of what ails the inner city involves a breakdown in culture that will not be cured by money alone, and that our values and spiritual life matter at least as much as our GDP.

Undoubtedly, some of these views will get me in trouble. I am new enough on the national political scene that I serve as a blank screen on which people of vastly different political stripes project their own views. As such, I am bound to disappoint some, if not all, of them. Which perhaps indicates a second, more intimate theme to this book—namely, how I, or anybody in public office, can avoid the pitfalls of fame, the hunger to please, the fear of loss, and thereby retain that kernel of truth, that singular voice within each of us that reminds us of our deepest commitments.

Recently, one of the reporters covering Capitol Hill stopped me on the way to my office and mentioned that she had enjoyed reading my first book. "I wonder," she said, "if you can be that interesting in the next one you write." By which she meant, I wonder if you can be honest now that you are a U.S. senator.

I wonder, too, sometimes. I hope writing this book helps me answer the question.

Chapter One

Republicans and
Democrats

O N MOST DAYS, I enter the Capitol through the basement. A small subway train carries me from the Hart
Building, where my office is located, through an underground tunnel lined with the flags and seals of the fifty states.
The train creaks to a halt and I make my way, past bustling
staffers, maintenance crews, and the occasional tour group, to
the bank of old elevators that takes me to the second floor. Stepping off, I weave around the swarm of press that normally gath-
ers there, say hello to the Capitol Police, and enter, through a
stately set of double doors, onto the floor of the U.S. Senate.

The Senate chamber is not the most beautiful space in the Capitol, but it is imposing nonetheless. The dun-colored walls are set
off by panels of blue damask and columns of finely veined marble.
Overhead, the ceiling forms a creamy white oval, with an American eagle etched in its center. Above the visitors' gallery, the busts
of the nation's first twenty vice presidents sit in solemn repose.

And in gentle steps, one hundred mahogany desks rise from
the well of the Senate in four horseshoe-shaped rows. Some of
these desks date back to 1819, and atop each desk is a tidy re-
ceptacle for inkwells and quills. Open the drawer of any desk,
and you will find within the names of the senators who once
used it—Taft and Long, Stennis and Kennedy—scratched or
penned in the senator's own hand. Sometimes, standing there in

the chamber, I can imagine Paul Douglas or Hubert Humphrey at one of these desks, urging yet again the adoption of civil rights legislation; or Joe McCarthy, a few desks over, thumbing through lists, preparing to name names; or LBJ prowling the aisles, grabbing lapels and gathering votes. Sometimes I will wander over to the desk where Daniel Webster once sat and imagine him rising before the packed gallery and his colleagues, his eyes blazing as he thunderously defends the Union against the forces of secession.

But these moments fade quickly. Except for the few minutes that it takes to vote, my colleagues and I don't spend much time on the Senate floor. Most of the decisions—about what bills to call and when to call them, about how amendments will be handled and how uncooperative senators will be made to cooperate—have been worked out well in advance by the majority leader, the relevant committee chairman, their staffs, and (depending on the degree of controversy involved and the magnanimity of the Republican handling the bill) their Democratic counterparts. By the time we reach the floor and the clerk starts calling the roll, each of the senators will have determined—in consultation with his or her staff, caucus leader, preferred lobbyists, interest groups, constituent mail, and ideological leanings— just how to position himself on the issue.

It makes for an efficient process, which is much appreciated by the members, who are juggling twelve- or thirteen-hour schedules and want to get back to their offices to meet constituents or return phone calls, to a nearby hotel to cultivate donors, or to the television studio for a live interview. If you stick around, though, you may see one lone senator standing at his desk after the others have left, seeking recognition to deliver a statement on the floor. It may be an explanation of a bill he's introducing, or it may be a broader commentary on some unmet national challenge. The speaker's voice may flare with passion; his arguments—about cuts to programs for the poor, or obstructionism on judicial appointments, or the need for energy independence—may be soundly constructed. But the speaker will be addressing a near-empty chamber: just the presiding officer, a few staffers, the Senate reporter, and C-SPAN's unblinking eye. The speaker will finish. A blue-uniformed page will silently gather the statement for the official record. Another senator may enter as the first one departs, and she will stand at her desk, seek recognition, and deliver her statement, repeating the ritual.

In the world's greatest deliberative body, no one is listening.

I REMEMBER January 4, 2005—the day that I and a third of the Senate were sworn in as members of the 109th Congress—as a beautiful blur. The sun was bright, the air unseasonably warm. From Illinois, Hawaii, London, and Kenya, my family and friends crowded into the Senate visitors' gallery to cheer as my new colleagues and I stood beside the marble dais and raised our right hands to take the oath of office. In the Old Senate Chamber, I joined my wife, Michelle, and our two daughters for a reenactment of the ceremony and picture-taking with Vice President Cheney (true to form, then six-year-old Malia demurely shook the vice president's hand, while then three-year-old Sasha decided instead to slap palms with the man before twirling around to wave for the cameras). Afterward, I watched the girls skip down the east Capitol steps, their pink and red dresses lifting gently in the air, the Supreme Court's white columns a majestic backdrop for their games. Michelle and I took their hands, and together the four of us walked to the Library of Congress, where we met a few hundred well-wishers who had traveled in for the day, and spent the next several hours in a steady stream of handshakes, hugs, photographs, and autographs.

A day of smiles and thanks, of decorum and pageantry—that's how it must have seemed to the Capitol's visitors. But if all of Washington was on its best behavior that day, collectively pausing to affirm the continuity of our democracy, there remained a certain static in the air, an awareness that the mood would not last. After the family and friends went home, after the receptions ended and the sun slid behind winter's gray shroud, what would linger over the city was the certainty of a single, seemingly inalterable fact: The country was divided, and so Washington was divided, more divided politically than at any time since before World War II.

Both the presidential election and various statistical measures appeared to bear out the conventional wisdom. Across the spectrum of issues, Americans disagreed: on Iraq, taxes, abortion, guns, the Ten Commandments, gay marriage, immigration, trade, education policy, environmental regulation, the size of government, and the role of the courts. Not only did we disagree, but we disagreed vehemently, with partisans on each side of the divide unrestrained in the vitriol they hurled at opponents. We disagreed on the scope of our disagreements, the nature of our disagreements, and the reasons for our disagreements. Everything was contestable, whether it was the cause of climate change or the fact of climate change, the size of the deficit or the culprits to blame for the deficit.

For me, none of this was entirely surprising. From a distance, I had followed the escalating ferocity of Washington's political battles: Iran-Contra and Ollie North, the Bork nomination and Willie Horton, Clarence Thomas and Anita Hill, the Clinton election and the Gingrich Revolution, Whitewater and the Starr investigation, the government shutdown and impeachment, dangling chads and *Bush v. Gore.* With the rest of the public, I had watched campaign culture metastasize throughout the body politic, as an entire industry of insult—both perpetual and somehow profitable—emerged to dominate cable television, talk radio, and the *New York Times* best-seller list.

And for eight years in the Illinois legislature, I had gotten some taste of how the game had come to be played. By the time I arrived in Springfield in 1997, the Illinois Senate's Republican majority had adopted the same rules that Speaker Gingrich was then using to maintain absolute control of the U.S. House of Representatives. Without the capacity to get even the most modest amendment debated, much less passed, Democrats would shout and holler and fulminate, and then stand by helplessly as Republicans passed large corporate tax breaks, stuck it to labor, or slashed social services. Over time, an implacable anger spread through the Democratic Caucus, and my colleagues would carefully record every slight and abuse meted out by the GOP. Six years later, Democrats took control, and Republicans fared no better. Some of the older veterans would wistfully recall the days when Republicans and Democrats met at night for dinner, hashing out a compromise over steaks and cigars. But even among these old bulls, such fond memories rapidly dimmed the first time the other side's political operatives selected them as targets, flooding their districts with mail accusing them of malfeasance, corruption, incompetence, and moral turpitude.

I don't claim to have been a passive bystander in all this. I understood politics as a full-contact sport, and minded neither the sharp elbows nor the occasional blind-side hit. But occupying as I did an ironclad Democratic district, I was spared the worst of Republican invective. Occasionally, I would partner up with even my most conservative colleagues to work on a piece of legislation, and over a poker game or a beer we might conclude that we had more in common than we publicly cared to admit. Which perhaps explains why, throughout my years in Springfield, I had clung to the notion that politics could be different, and that the voters wanted something different; that they were tired of distortion, name-calling, and sound-bite solutions to complicated problems; that if I could reach those voters directly, frame the issues as I felt them, explain the choices in as truthful a fashion as I knew how, then the people's instincts for fair play and common sense would bring them around. If enough of us took that risk, I thought, not only the country's politics but the country's policies would change for the better.

It was with that mind-set that I had entered the 2004 U.S. Senate race. For the duration of the campaign I did my best to say what I thought, keep it clean, and focus on substance. When I won the Democratic primary and then the general election, both by sizable margins, it was tempting to believe that I had proven my point.

There was just one problem: My campaign had gone so well that it looked like a fluke. Political observers would note that in a field of seven Democratic primary candidates, not one of us ran a negative TV ad. The wealthiest candidate of all—a former trader worth at least $300 million—spent $28 million, mostly on a barrage of positive ads, only to flame out in the final weeks due to an unflattering divorce file that the press got unsealed. My Republican opponent, a handsome and wealthy former Goldman Sachs partner turned inner-city teacher, started attacking my record almost from the start, but before his campaign could get off the ground, he was felled by a divorce scandal of his own. For the better part of a month, I traveled Illinois without drawing fire, before being selected to deliver the keynote address at the Democratic National Convention—seventeen minutes of unfiltered, uninterrupted airtime on national television. And finally the Illinois Republican Party inexplicably chose as my opponent former presidential candidate Alan Keyes, a man who had never lived in Illinois and who proved so fierce and unyielding in his positions that even conservative Republicans were scared of him.

Later, some reporters would declare me the luckiest politician in the entire fifty states. Privately, some of my staff bristled at this assessment, feeling that it discounted our hard work and the appeal of our message. Still, there was no point in denying my almost spooky good fortune. I was an outlier, a freak; to political insiders, my victory proved nothing.

No wonder then that upon my arrival in Washington that January, I felt like the rookie who shows up after the game, his uniform spotless, eager to play, even as his mud-splattered teammates tend to their wounds. While I had been busy with interviews and photo shoots, full of high-minded ideas about the need for less partisanship and acrimony, Democrats had been beaten across the board—the presidency, Senate seats, House seats. My new Democratic colleagues could not have been more welcoming toward me; one of our few bright spots, they would call my victory. In the corridors, though, or during a lull in the action on the floor, they'd pull me aside and remind me of what typical Senate campaigns had come to look like.

They told me about their fallen leader, Tom Daschle of South Dakota, who had seen millions of dollars' worth of negative ads rain down on his head—full-page newspaper ads and television spots informing his neighbors day after day that he supported baby-killing and men in wedding gowns, a few even suggesting that he'd treated his first wife badly, despite the fact that she had traveled to South Dakota to help him get reelected. They recalled Max Cleland, the former Georgia incumbent, a triple-amputee war veteran who had lost his seat in the previous cycle after being accused of insufficient patriotism, of aiding and abetting Osama bin Laden.

And then there was the small matter of the Swift Boat Veterans for Truth: the shocking efficiency with which a few well-placed ads and the chants of conservative media could transform a decorated Vietnam war hero into a weak-kneed appeaser.

No doubt there were Republicans who felt similarly abused. And perhaps the newspaper editorials that appeared that first week of session were right; perhaps it was time to put the election behind us, for both parties to store away their animosities and ammunition and, for a year or two at least, get down to governing the country. Maybe that would have been possible had the elections not been so close, or had the war in Iraq not been still raging, or had the advocacy groups, pundits, and all manner of media not stood to gain by stirring the pot. Maybe peace would have broken out with a different kind of White House, one less committed to waging a perpetual campaign—a White House that would see a 51–48 victory as a call to humility and compromise rather than an irrefutable mandate.

But whatever conditions might have been required for such a détente, they did not exist in 2005. There would be no concessions, no gestures of goodwill. Two days after the election, President Bush appeared before cameras and declared that he had political capital to spare and he intended to use it. That same day, conservative activist Grover Norquist, unconstrained by the decorum of public office, observed, in connection with the Democrats' situation, that "any farmer will tell you that certain animals run around and are unpleasant, but when they've been fixed, then they are happy and sedate." Two days after my swearing in, Congresswoman Stephanie Tubbs Jones, out of Cleveland, stood up in the House of Representatives to challenge the certification of Ohio electors, citing the litany of voting irregularities that had taken place in the state on Election Day. Rank-and-file Republicans scowled ("Sore losers," I could hear a few mutter), but Speaker Hastert and Majority Leader DeLay gazed stone-faced from the heights of the dais, placid in the knowledge that they had both the votes and the gavel. Senator Barbara Boxer of California agreed to sign the challenge, and when we returned to the Senate chamber, I found myself casting my first vote, along with seventy-three of the seventy-four others voting that day, to install George W. Bush for a second term as president of the United States.

I would get my first big batch of phone calls and negative mail after this vote. I called back some of my disgruntled Democratic supporters, assuring them that yes, I was familiar with the problems in Ohio, and yes, I thought an investigation was in order, but yes, I still believed George Bush had won the election, and no, as far as I could tell I didn't think I had either sold out or been co-opted after a mere two days on the job. That same week, I happened to run into retiring Senator Zell Miller, the lean, sharp-eyed Georgia Democrat and NRA board member who had gone sour on the Democratic Party, endorsed George Bush, and delivered the blistering keynote address at the Republican National Convention—a no-holds-barred rant against the perfidy of John Kerry and his supposed weakness on national security. Ours was a brief exchange, filled with unspoken irony—the elderly Southerner on his way out, the young black Northerner on his way in, the contrast that the press had noted in our respective convention speeches. Senator Miller was very gracious and wished me luck with my new job. Later, I would happen upon an excerpt from his book, *A Deficit of Decency,* in which he called my speech at the convention one of the best he'd ever heard, before noting—with what I imagined to be a sly smile—that it may not have been the most effective speech in terms of helping to win an election.

In other words: My guy had lost. Zell Miller's guy had won. That was the hard, cold political reality. Everything else was just sentiment.

MY WIFE WILL tell you that by nature I'm not somebody who gets real worked up about things. When I see Ann Coulter or Sean Hannity baying across the television screen, I find it hard to take them seriously; I assume that they must be saying what they do primarily to boost book sales or ratings, although I do wonder who would spend their precious evenings with such sourpusses. When Democrats rush up to me at events and insist that we live in the worst of political times, that a creeping fascism is closing its grip around our throats, I may mention the internment of Japanese Americans under FDR, the Alien and Sedition Acts under John Adams, or a hundred years of lynching under several dozen administrations as having been possibly worse, and suggest we all take a deep breath. When people at dinner parties ask me how I can possibly operate in the current political environment, with all the negative campaigning and personal attacks, I may mention Nelson Mandela, Aleksandr Solzhenitsyn, or some guy in a Chinese or Egyptian prison somewhere. In truth, being called names is not such a bad deal.

Still, I am not immune to distress. And like most Americans, I find it hard to shake the feeling these days that our democracy has gone seriously awry.

It's not simply that a gap exists between our professed ideals as a nation and the reality we witness every day. In one form or another, that gap has existed since America's birth. Wars have been fought, laws passed, systems reformed, unions organized, and protests staged to bring promise and practice into closer alignment.

No, what's troubling is the gap between the magnitude of our challenges and the smallness of our politics—the ease with which we are distracted by the petty and trivial, our chronic avoidance of tough decisions, our seeming inability to build a working consensus to tackle any big problem.

We know that global competition—not to mention any genuine commitment to the values of equal opportunity and upward mobility—requires us to revamp our educational system from top to bottom, replenish our teaching corps, buckle down on math and science instruction, and rescue inner-city kids from illiteracy. And yet our debate on education seems stuck between those who want to dismantle the public school system and those who would defend an indefensible status quo, between those who say money makes no difference in education and those who want more money without any demonstration that it will be put to good use.

We know that our health-care system is broken: wildly expensive, terribly inefficient, and poorly adapted to an economy no longer built on lifetime employment, a system that exposes hardworking Americans to chronic insecurity and possible destitution. But year after year, ideology and political gamesmanship result in inaction, except for 2003, when we got a prescription drug bill that somehow managed to combine the worst aspects of the public and private sectors—price gouging and bureaucratic confusion, gaps in coverage and an eye-popping bill for taxpayers.

We know that the battle against international terrorism is at once an armed struggle and a contest of ideas, that our long-term security depends on both a judicious projection of military power and increased cooperation with other nations, and that addressing the problems of global poverty and failed states is vital to our nation's interests rather than just a matter of charity. But follow most of our foreign policy debates, and you might believe that we have only two choices—belligerence or isolationism.

We think of faith as a source of comfort and understanding but find our expressions of faith sowing division; we believe ourselves to be a tolerant people even as racial, religious, and cultural tensions roil the landscape. And instead of resolving these tensions or mediating these conflicts, our politics fans them, exploits them, and drives us further apart.

Privately, those of us in government will acknowledge this gap between the politics we have and the politics we need. Certainly Democrats aren't happy with the current situation, since for the moment at least they are on the losing side, dominated by Republicans who, thanks to winner-take-all elections, control every branch of government and feel no need to compromise. Thoughtful Republicans shouldn't be too sanguine, though, for if the Democrats have had trouble winning, it appears that the Republicans—having won elections on the basis of pledges that often defy reality (tax cuts without service cuts, privatization of Social Security with no change in benefits, war without sacrifice)—cannot govern.

And yet publicly it's difficult to find much soul-searching or introspection on either side of the divide, or even the slightest admission of responsibility for the gridlock. What we hear instead, not only in campaigns but on editorial pages, on bookstands, or in the ever-expanding blog universe, are deflections of criticism and assignments of blame. Depending on your tastes, our condition is the natural result of radical conservatism or perverse liberalism, Tom DeLay or Nancy Pelosi, big oil or greedy trial lawyers, religious zealots or gay activists, Fox News or the *New York Times*. How well these stories are told, the subtlety of the arguments and the quality of the evidence, will vary by author, and I won't deny my preference for the story the Democrats tell, nor my belief that the arguments of liberals are more often grounded in reason and fact. In distilled form, though, the explanations of both the right and the left have become mirror images of each other. They are stories of conspiracy, of America being hijacked by an evil cabal. Like all good conspiracy theories, both tales contain just enough truth to satisfy those predisposed to believe in them, without admitting any contradictions that might shake up those assumptions. Their purpose is not to persuade the other side but to keep their bases agitated and assured of the rightness of their respective causes—and lure just enough new adherents to beat the other side into submission.

Of course, there is another story to be told, by the millions of Americans who are going about their business every day. They are on the job or looking for work, starting businesses, helping their kids with their homework, and struggling with high gas bills, insufficient health insurance, and a pension that some bankruptcy court somewhere has rendered unenforceable. They are by turns hopeful and frightened about the future. Their lives are full of contradictions and ambiguities. And because politics seems to speak so little to what they are going through—because they understand that politics today is a business and not a mission, and what passes for debate is little more than spectacle—

they turn inward, away from the noise and rage and endless chatter.

A government that truly represents these Americans—that truly serves these Americans—will require a different kind of politics. That politics will need to reflect our lives as they are actually lived. It won't be prepackaged, ready to pull off the shelf. It will have to be constructed from the best of our traditions and will have to account for the darker aspects of our past. We will need to understand just how we got to this place, this land of warring factions and tribal hatreds. And we will need to remind ourselves, despite all our differences, just how much we share: common hopes, common dreams, a bond that will not break.

ONE OF THE first things I noticed upon my arrival in Washington was the relative cordiality among the Senate's older members: the unfailing courtesy that governed every interaction between John Warner and Robert Byrd, or the genuine bond of friendship between Republican Ted Stevens and Democrat Daniel Inouye. It is commonly said that these men represent the last of a dying breed, men who not only love the Senate but who embody a less sharply partisan brand of politics. And in fact it is one of the few things that conservative and liberal commentators agree on, this idea of a time before the fall, a golden age in Washington when, regardless of which party was in power, civility reigned and government worked.

At a reception one evening, I started a conversation with an old Washington hand who had served in and around the Capitol for close to fifty years. I asked him what he thought accounted for the difference in atmosphere between then and now.

"It's generational," he told me without hesitation. "Back then, almost everybody with any power in Washington had served in World War II. We might've fought like cats and dogs on issues. A lot of us came from different backgrounds, different neighborhoods, different political philosophies. But with the war, we all had something in common. That shared experience developed a certain trust and respect. It helped to work through our differences and get things done."

As I listened to the old man reminisce, about Dwight Eisenhower and Sam Rayburn, Dean Acheson and Everett Dirksen, it was hard not to get swept up in the hazy portrait he painted, of a time before twenty-four-hour news cycles and nonstop fundraising, a time of serious men doing serious work. I had to remind myself that his fondness for this bygone era involved a certain selective memory: He had airbrushed out of the picture the images of the Southern Caucus denouncing proposed civil rights legislation from the floor of the Senate; the insidious power of McCarthyism; the numbing poverty that Bobby Kennedy would help highlight before his death; the absence of women and minorities in the halls of power.

I realized, too, that a set of unique circumstances had underwritten the stability of the governing consensus of which he had been a part: not just the shared experiences of the war, but also the near unanimity forged by the Cold War and the Soviet threat, and perhaps more important, the unrivaled dominance of the American economy during the fifties and sixties, as Europe and Japan dug themselves out of the postwar rubble.

Still, there's no denying that American politics in the post–World War II years was far less ideological—and the meaning of party affiliation far more amorphous—than it is today. The Democratic coalition that controlled Congress through most of those years was an amalgam of Northern liberals like Hubert Humphrey, conservative Southern Democrats like James Eastland, and whatever loyalists the big-city machines cared to elevate. What held this coalition together was the economic populism of the New Deal—a vision of fair wages and benefits, patronage and public works, and an ever-rising standard of living. Beyond that, the party cultivated a certain live-and-let-live philosophy:

a philosophy anchored in acquiescence toward or active promotion of racial oppression in the South; a philosophy that depended on a broader culture in which social norms—the nature of sexuality, say, or the role of women—were largely unquestioned; a culture that did not yet possess the vocabulary to force discomfort, much less political dispute, around such issues.

Throughout the fifties and early sixties, the GOP, too, tolerated all sorts of philosophical fissures—between the Western libertarianism of Barry Goldwater and the Eastern paternalism of Nelson Rockefeller; between those who recalled the Republicanism of Abraham Lincoln and Teddy Roosevelt, with its embrace of federal activism, and those who followed the conservatism of Edmund Burke, with its preference of tradition to social experimentation. Accommodating these regional and temperamental differences, on civil rights, federal regulation, or even taxes, was neither neat nor tidy. But as with the Democrats, it was mainly economic interests that bound the GOP together, a philosophy of free markets and fiscal restraint that could appeal to all its constituent parts, from the Main Street storekeeper to the country-club corporate manager. (Republicans may have also embraced a more fervid brand of anticommunism in the fifties, but as John F. Kennedy helped to prove, Democrats were more than willing to call and raise the GOP on that score whenever an election rolled around.)

It was the sixties that upended these political alignments, for reasons and in ways that have been well chronicled. First the civil rights movement arrived, a movement that even in its early, halcyon days fundamentally challenged the existing social structure and forced Americans to choose sides. Ultimately Lyndon Johnson chose the right side of this battle, but as a son of the South, he understood better than most the cost involved with that choice: upon signing the Civil Rights Act of 1964, he would tell aide Bill Moyers that with the stroke of a pen he had just delivered the South to the GOP for the foreseeable future.

Then came the student protests against the Vietnam War and the suggestion that America was not always right, our actions not always justified—that a new generation would not pay any price or bear any burden that its elders might dictate.

And then, with the walls of the status quo breached, every form of "outsider" came streaming through the gates: feminists, Latinos, hippies, Panthers, welfare moms, gays, all asserting their rights, all insisting on recognition, all demanding a seat at the table and a piece of the pie.

It would take several years for the logic of these movements to play itself out. Nixon's Southern strategy, his challenge to court-ordered busing and appeal to the silent majority, paid immediate electoral dividends. But his governing philosophy never congealed into a firm ideology—it was Nixon, after all, who initiated the first federal affirmative action programs and signed the creation of the Environmental Protection Agency and the Occupational Safety and Health Administration into law. Jimmy Carter would prove it possible to combine support for civil rights with a more traditionally conservative Democratic message; and despite defections from their ranks, most Southern Democratic congressmen who chose to stay in the party would retain their seats on the strength of incumbency, helping Democrats maintain control of at least the House of Representatives.

But the country's tectonic plates had shifted. Politics was no longer simply a pocketbook issue but a moral issue as well, subject to moral imperatives and moral absolutes. And politics was decidedly personal, insinuating itself into every interaction—whether between black and white, men and women—and implicating itself in every assertion or rejection of authority.

Accordingly, liberalism and conservatism were now defined in the popular imagination less by class than by attitude—the position you took toward the traditional culture and counterculture. What mattered was not just how you felt about the right to strike or corporate taxation, but also how you felt about sex, drugs, and rock and roll, the Latin Mass or the Western canon. For white ethnic voters in the North, and whites generally in the South, this new liberalism made little sense. The violence in the streets and the excuses for such violence in intellectual circles, blacks moving next door and white kids bused across town, the burning of flags and spitting on vets, all of it seemed to insult and diminish, if not assault, those things—family, faith, flag, neighborhood, and, for some at least, white privilege—that they held most dear. And when, in the midst of this topsy-turvy time, in the wake of assassinations and cities burning and Vietnam's bitter defeat, economic expansion gave way to gas lines and inflation and plant closings, and the best Jimmy Carter could suggest was turning down the thermostat, even as a bunch of Iranian radicals added insult to OPEC's injury—a big chunk of the New Deal coalition began looking for another political home.

I'VE ALWAYS FELT a curious relationship to the sixties. In a sense, I'm a pure product of that era: As the child of a mixed marriage, my life would have been impossible, my opportunities entirely foreclosed, without the social upheavals that were then taking place. But I was too young at the time to fully grasp the nature of those changes, too removed—living as I did in Hawaii and Indonesia—to see the fallout on America's psyche. Much of what I absorbed from the sixties was filtered through my mother, who to the end of her life would proudly proclaim herself an unreconstructed liberal. The civil rights movement, in particular, inspired her reverence; whenever the opportunity presented itself, she would drill into me the values that she saw there: tolerance, equality, standing up for the disadvantaged.

In many ways, though, my mother's understanding of the sixties was limited, both by distance (she had left the mainland of the United States in 1960) and by her incorrigible, sweet-natured romanticism. Intellectually she might have tried to understand

Black Power or SDS or those women friends of hers who had stopped shaving their legs, but the anger, the oppositional spirit, just wasn't in her. Emotionally her liberalism would always remain of a decidedly pre-1967 vintage, her heart a time capsule filled with images of the space program, the Peace Corps and Freedom Rides, Mahalia Jackson and Joan Baez.

It was only as I got older, then, during the seventies, that I came to appreciate the degree to which—for those who had experienced more directly some of the sixties' seminal events—things must have seemed to be spinning out of control. Partly I understood this through the grumblings of my maternal grandparents, longtime Democrats who would admit that they'd voted for Nixon in 1968, an act of betrayal that my mother never let them live down. Mainly my understanding of the sixties came as a result of my own investigations, as my adolescent rebellion sought justification in the political and cultural changes that by then had already begun to ebb. In my teens, I became fascinated with the Dionysian, up-for-grabs quality of the era, and through books, film, and music, I soaked in a vision of the sixties very different from the one my mother talked about: images of Huey Newton, the '68 Democratic National Convention, the Saigon airlift, and the Stones at Altamont. If I had no immediate reasons to pursue revolution, I decided nevertheless that in style and attitude I, too, could be a rebel, unconstrained by the received wisdom of the over-thirty crowd.

Eventually, my rejection of authority spilled into self-indulgence and self-destructiveness, and by the time I enrolled in college, I'd begun to see how any challenge to convention harbored within it the possibility of its own excesses and its own orthodoxy. I started to reexamine my assumptions, and recalled the values my mother and grandparents had taught me. In this slow, fitful process of sorting out what I believed, I began silently registering the point in dorm-room conversations when my college friends and I stopped thinking and slipped into cant: the point at which the denunciations of capitalism or American imperialism came too easily, and the freedom from the constraints of monogamy or religion was proclaimed without fully understanding the value of such constraints, and the role of victim was too readily embraced as a means of shedding responsibility, or asserting entitlement, or claiming moral superiority over those not so victimized.

All of which may explain why, as disturbed as I might have been by Ronald Reagan's election in 1980, as unconvinced as I might have been by his John Wayne, *Father Knows Best* pose, his policy by anecdote, and his gratuitous assaults on the poor, I understood his appeal. It was the same appeal that the military bases back in Hawaii had always held for me as a young boy, with their tidy streets and well-oiled machinery, the crisp uniforms and crisper salutes. It was related to the pleasure I still get from watching a well-played baseball game, or my wife gets from watching reruns of *The Dick Van Dyke Show*. Reagan spoke to America's longing for order, our need to believe that we are not simply subject to blind, impersonal forces but that we can shape our individual and collective destinies, so long as we rediscover the traditional virtues of hard work, patriotism, personal responsibility, optimism, and faith.

That Reagan's message found such a receptive audience spoke not only to his skills as a communicator; it also spoke to the failures of liberal government, during a period of economic stagnation, to give middle-class voters any sense that it was fighting for them. For the fact was that government at every level had become too cavalier about spending taxpayer money. Too often, bureaucracies were oblivious to the cost of their mandates. A lot of liberal rhetoric did seem to value rights and entitlements over duties and responsibilities. Reagan may have exaggerated the sins of the welfare state, and certainly liberals were right to complain that his domestic policies tilted heavily toward economic elites, with corporate raiders making tidy profits throughout the eighties while unions were busted and the income for the average working stiff flatlined.

Nevertheless, by promising to side with those who worked hard, obeyed the law, cared for their families, and loved their country, Reagan offered Americans a sense of a common purpose that liberals seemed no longer able to muster. And the more his critics carped, the more those critics played into the role he'd written for them—a band of out-of-touch, tax-and-spend, blame-America-first, politically correct elites.

WHAT I FIND remarkable is not that the political formula developed by Reagan worked at the time, but just how durable the narrative that he helped promote has proven to be. Despite a forty-year remove, the tumult of the sixties and the subsequent backlash continues to drive our political discourse. Partly it underscores how deeply felt the conflicts of the sixties must have been for the men and women who came of age at that time, and the degree to which the arguments of the era were understood not simply as political disputes but as individual choices that defined personal identity and moral standing.

I suppose it also highlights the fact that the flash-point issues of the sixties were never fully resolved. The fury of the counterculture may have dissipated into consumerism, lifestyle choices, and musical preferences rather than political commitments, but the problems of race, war, poverty, and relations between the sexes did not go away.

And maybe it just has to do with the sheer size of the Baby Boom generation, a demographic force that exerts the same gravitational pull in politics that it exerts on everything else, from the market for Viagra to the number of cup holders automakers put in their cars.

Whatever the explanation, after Reagan the lines between

Republican and Democrat, liberal and conservative, would be drawn in more sharply ideological terms. This was true, of course, for the hot-button issues of affirmative action, crime, welfare, abortion, and school prayer, all of which were extensions of earlier battles. But it was also now true for every other issue, large or small, domestic or foreign, all of which were reduced to a menu of either-or, for-or-against, sound-bite-ready choices. No longer was economic policy a matter of weighing trade-offs between competing goals of productivity and distributional justice, of growing the pie and slicing the pie. You were for either tax cuts or tax hikes, small government or big government. No longer was environmental policy a matter of balancing sound stewardship of our natural resources with the demands of a modern economy; you either supported unchecked development, drilling, strip-mining, and the like, or you supported stifling bureaucracy and red tape that choked off growth. In politics, if not in policy, simplicity was a virtue.

Sometimes I suspect that even the Republican leaders who immediately followed Reagan weren't entirely comfortable with the direction politics had taken. In the mouths of men like George H. W. Bush and Bob Dole, the polarizing rhetoric and the politics of resentment always seemed forced, a way of peeling off voters from the Democratic base and not necessarily a recipe for governing.

But for a younger generation of conservative operatives who would soon rise to power, for Newt Gingrich and Karl Rove and Grover Norquist and Ralph Reed, the fiery rhetoric was more than a matter of campaign strategy. They were true believers who meant what they said, whether it was "No new taxes" or "We are a Christian nation." In fact, with their rigid doctrines, slash-and-burn style, and exaggerated sense of having been aggrieved, this new conservative leadership was eerily reminiscent of some of the New Left's leaders during the sixties. As with their left-wing counterparts, this new vanguard of the right viewed politics as a contest not just between competing policy visions, but between good and evil. Activists in both parties began developing litmus tests, checklists of orthodoxy, leaving a Democrat who questioned abortion increasingly lonely, any Republican who championed gun control effectively marooned. In this Manichean struggle, compromise came to look like weakness, to be punished or purged. You were with us or against us. You had to choose sides.

It was Bill Clinton's singular contribution that he tried to transcend this ideological deadlock, recognizing not only that what had come to be meant by the labels of "conservative" and "liberal" played to Republican advantage, but that the categories were inadequate to address the problems we faced. At times during his first campaign, his gestures toward disaffected Reagan Democrats could seem clumsy and transparent (what ever happened to Sister Souljah?) or frighteningly coldhearted (allowing the execution of a mentally retarded death row inmate to go forward on the eve of an important primary). In the first two years of his presidency, he would be forced to abandon some core elements of his platform—universal health care, aggressive investment in education and training—that might have more decisively reversed the long-term trends that were undermining the position of working families in the new economy.

Still, he instinctively understood the falseness of the choices being presented to the American people. He saw that government spending and regulation could, if properly designed, serve as vital ingredients and not inhibitors to economic growth, and how markets and fiscal discipline could help promote social justice. He recognized that not only societal responsibility but personal responsibility was needed to combat poverty. In his platform—if not always in his day-to-day politics—Clinton's Third Way went beyond splitting the difference. It tapped into the pragmatic, nonideological attitude of the majority of Americans.

Indeed, by the end of his presidency, Clinton's policies—recognizably progressive if modest in their goals—enjoyed broad public support. Politically, he had wrung out of the Democratic Party some of the excesses that had kept it from winning elections. That he failed, despite a booming economy, to translate popular policies into anything resembling a governing coalition said something about the demographic difficulties Democrats were facing (in particular, the shift in population growth to an increasingly solid Republican South) and the structural advantages the Republicans enjoyed in the Senate, where the votes of two Republican senators from Wyoming, population 493,782, equaled the votes of two Democratic senators from California, population 33,871,648.

But that failure also testified to the skill with which Gingrich, Rove, Norquist, and the like were able to consolidate and institutionalize the conservative movement. They tapped the unlimited resources of corporate sponsors and wealthy donors to create a network of think tanks and media outlets. They brought state-of-the-art technology to the task of mobilizing their base, and centralized power in the House of Representatives in order to enhance party discipline.

And they understood the threat Clinton posed to their vision of a long-term conservative majority, which helps explain the vehemence with which they went after him. It also explains why they invested so much time attacking Clinton's morality, for if Clinton's policies were hardly radical, his biography (the draft letter saga, the marijuana puffing, the Ivy League intellectualism, the professional wife who didn't bake cookies, and most of all the sex) proved perfect grist for the conservative base. With enough repetition, a looseness with the facts, and the ultimately undeniable evidence of the President's own personal lapses, Clinton could be made to embody the very traits of sixties liberalism that had helped spur the conservative movement in the first place. Clinton may have fought that movement to a draw, but the movement would come out stronger for it—and in George W. Bush's first term, that movement would take over the United States government.

THIS TELLING OF the story is too neat, I know. It ignores critical strands in the historical narrative—how the decline of manufacturing and Reagan's firing of the air traffic controllers critically wounded America's labor movement; the way that the creation of majority-minority congressional districts in the South simultaneously ensured more black representatives and reduced Democratic seats in that region; the lack of cooperation that Clinton received from congressional Democrats, who had grown fat and complacent and didn't realize the fight they were in. It also doesn't capture the degree to which advances in political gerrymandering polarized the Congress, or how efficiently money and negative television ads have poisoned the atmosphere.

Still, when I think about what that old Washington hand told me that night, when I ponder the work of a George Kennan or a George Marshall, when I read the speeches of a Bobby Kennedy or an Everett Dirksen, I can't help feeling that the politics of today suffers from a case of arrested development. For these men, the issues America faced were never abstract and hence never simple. War might be hell and still the right thing to do. Economies could collapse despite the best-laid plans. People could work hard all their lives and still lose everything.

For the generation of leaders who followed, raised in relative comfort, different experiences yielded a different attitude toward politics. In the back-and-forth between Clinton and Gingrich, and in the elections of 2000 and 2004, I sometimes felt as if I were watching the psychodrama of the Baby Boom generation—a tale rooted in old grudges and revenge plots hatched on a handful of college campuses long ago—played out on the national stage. The victories that the sixties generation brought about—

the admission of minorities and women into full citizenship, the strengthening of individual liberties and the healthy willingness to question authority—have made America a far better place for all its citizens. But what has been lost in the process, and has yet to be replaced, are those shared assumptions—that quality of trust and fellow feeling—that bring us together as Americans.

So where does that leave us? Theoretically the Republican Party might have produced its own Clinton, a center-right leader who built on Clinton's fiscal conservatism while moving more aggressively to revamp a creaky federal bureaucracy and experiment with market- or faith-based solutions to social policy. And in fact such a leader may still emerge. Not all Republican elected officials subscribe to the tenets of today's movement conservatives. In both the House and the Senate, and in state capitals across the country, there are those who cling to more traditional conservative virtues of temperance and restraint—men and women who recognize that piling up debt to finance tax cuts for the wealthy is irresponsible, that deficit reduction can't take place on the backs of the poor, that the separation of church and state protects the church as well as the state, that conservation and conservatism don't have to conflict, and that foreign policy should be based on facts and not wishful thinking.

But these Republicans are not the ones who have driven the debate over the past six years. Instead of the "compassionate conservatism" that George Bush promised in his 2000 campaign, what has characterized the ideological core of today's GOP is absolutism, not conservatism. There is the absolutism of the free market, an ideology of no taxes, no regulation, no safety net— indeed, no government beyond what's required to protect private property and provide for the national defense.

There's the religious absolutism of the Christian right, a movement that gained traction on the undeniably difficult issue of abortion, but which soon flowered into something much broader; a movement that insists not only that Christianity is America's dominant faith, but that a particular, fundamentalist brand of that faith should drive public policy, overriding any alternative source of understanding, whether the writings of liberal theologians, the findings of the National Academy of Sciences, or the words of Thomas Jefferson.

And there is the absolute belief in the authority of majority will, or at least those who claim power in the name of the majority—a disdain for those institutional checks (the courts, the Constitution, the press, the Geneva Conventions, the rules of the Senate, or the traditions governing redistricting) that might slow our inexorable march toward the New Jerusalem.

Of course, there are those within the Democratic Party who tend toward similar zealotry. But those who do have never come close to possessing the power of a Rove or a DeLay, the power to take over the party, fill it with loyalists, and enshrine some of their more radical ideas into law. The prevalence of regional, ethnic, and economic differences within the party, the electoral map and the structure of the Senate, the need to raise money from economic elites to finance elections—all these things tend to prevent those Democrats in office from straying too far from the center. In fact, I know very few elected Democrats who neatly fit the liberal caricature; the last I checked, John Kerry believes in maintaining the superiority of the U.S. military, Hillary Clinton believes in the virtues of capitalism, and just about every member of the Congressional Black Caucus believes Jesus Christ died for his or her sins.

Instead, we Democrats are just, well, confused. There are those who still champion the old-time religion, defending every New Deal and Great Society program from Republican encroachment, achieving ratings of 100 percent from the liberal interest groups. But these efforts seem exhausted, a constant game of defense, bereft of the energy and new ideas needed to address the changing circumstances of globalization or a stubbornly isolated inner city. Others pursue a more "centrist" approach, figuring that so long as they split the difference with the conservative leadership, they must be acting reasonably—and failing to notice that with each passing year they are giving up more and more ground. Individually, Democratic legislators and candidates propose a host of sensible if incremental ideas, on energy and education, health care and homeland security, hoping that it all adds up to something resembling a governing philosophy.

Mainly, though, the Democratic Party has become the party of reaction. In reaction to a war that is ill conceived, we appear suspicious of all military action. In reaction to those who proclaim the market can cure all ills, we resist efforts to use market principles to tackle pressing problems. In reaction to religious overreach, we equate tolerance with secularism, and forfeit the moral language that would help infuse our policies with a larger meaning. We lose elections and hope for the courts to foil Republican plans. We lose the courts and wait for a White House scandal.

And increasingly we feel the need to match the Republican right in stridency and hardball tactics. The accepted wisdom that drives many advocacy groups and Democratic activists these days goes something like this: The Republican Party has been able to consistently win elections not by expanding its base but by vilifying Democrats, driving wedges into the electorate, energizing its right wing, and disciplining those who stray from the party line. If the Democrats ever want to get back into power, then they will have to take up the same approach.

I understand the frustration of these activists. The ability of Republicans to repeatedly win on the basis of polarizing campaigns is indeed impressive. I recognize the dangers of subtlety and nuance in the face of the conservative movement's passionate intensity. And in my mind, at least, there are a host of Bush Administration policies that justify righteous indignation.

Ultimately, though, I believe any attempt by Democrats to pursue a more sharply partisan and ideological strategy misapprehends the moment we're in. I am convinced that whenever we exaggerate or demonize, oversimplify or overstate our case, we lose. Whenever we dumb down the political debate, we lose. For it's precisely the pursuit of ideological purity, the rigid orthodoxy and the sheer predictability of our current political debate, that keeps us from finding new ways to meet the challenges we face as a country. It's what keeps us locked in "either/or" thinking: the notion that we can have only big government or no government; the assumption that we must either tolerate forty-six million without health insurance or embrace "socialized medicine."

It is such doctrinaire thinking and stark partisanship that have turned Americans off of politics. This is not a problem for the right; a polarized electorate—or one that easily dismisses both parties because of the nasty, dishonest tone of the debate—works perfectly well for those who seek to chip away at the very idea of government. After all, a cynical electorate is a self-centered electorate.

But for those of us who believe that government has a role to play in promoting opportunity and prosperity for all Americans, a polarized electorate isn't good enough. Eking out a bare Democratic majority isn't good enough. What's needed is a broad majority of Americans—Democrats, Republicans, and independents of goodwill—who are reengaged in the project of national renewal, and who see their own self-interest as inextricably linked to the interests of others.

I'm under no illusion that the task of building such a working majority will be easy. But it's what we must do, precisely because the task of solving America's problems will be hard. It will require tough choices, and it will require sacrifice. Unless political leaders are open to new ideas and not just new packaging, we won't change enough hearts and minds to initiate a serious energy policy or tame the deficit. We won't have the popular support to craft a foreign policy that meets the challenges of globalization or terrorism without resorting to isolationism or eroding civil liberties. We won't have a mandate to overhaul America's broken health-care system. And we won't have the broad political support or the effective strategies needed to lift large numbers of our fellow citizens out of poverty.

I made this same argument in a letter I sent to the left-leaning blog Daily Kos in September 2005, after a number of advocacy groups and activists had attacked some of my Democratic colleagues for voting to confirm Chief Justice John Roberts. My staff was a little nervous about the idea; since I had voted against Roberts's confirmation, they saw no reason for me to agitate such a vocal part of the Democratic base. But I had come to appreciate the give-and-take that the blogs afforded, and in the days following the posting of my letter, in true democratic fashion, more than six hundred people posted their comments. Some agreed with me. Others thought that I was being too idealistic— that the kind of politics I was suggesting could not work in the face of the Republican PR machine. A sizable contingent thought that I had been "sent" by Washington elites to quell dissent in the ranks, and/or had been in Washington too long and was losing touch with the American people, and/or was—as one blogger later put it—simply an "idiot."

Maybe the critics are right. Maybe there's no escaping our great political divide, an endless clash of armies, and any attempts to alter the rules of engagement are futile. Or maybe the trivialization of politics has reached a point of no return, so that most people see it as just one more diversion, a sport, with politicians our paunch-bellied gladiators and those who bother to pay attention just fans on the sidelines: We paint our faces red or blue and cheer our side and boo their side, and if it takes a late hit or cheap shot to beat the other team, so be it, for winning is all that matters.

But I don't think so. They are out there, I think to myself, those ordinary citizens who have grown up in the midst of all the political and cultural battles, but who have found a way—in their own lives, at least—to make peace with their neighbors, and themselves. I imagine the white Southerner who growing up heard his dad talk about niggers this and niggers that but who has struck up a friendship with the black guys at the office and is trying to teach his own son different, who thinks discrimination is wrong but doesn't see why the son of a black doctor should get admitted into law school ahead of his own son. Or the former Black Panther who decided to go into real estate, bought a few buildings in the neighborhood, and is just as tired of the drug dealers in front of those buildings as he is of the bankers who won't give him a loan to expand his business. There's the middle-aged feminist who still mourns her abortion, and the Christian woman who paid for her teenager's abortion, and the millions of waitresses and temp secretaries and nurse's assistants and Wal-Mart associates who hold their breath every single month in the hope that they'll have enough money to support the children that they did bring into the world.

I imagine they are waiting for a politics with the maturity to balance idealism and realism, to distinguish between what can and cannot be compromised, to admit the possibility that the other side might sometimes have a point. They don't always understand the arguments between right and left, conservative and liberal, but they recognize the difference between dogma and common sense, responsibility and irresponsibility, between those things that last and those that are fleeting.

They are out there, waiting for Republicans and Democrats to catch up with them.

Chapter Two

Values

HE FIRST TIME I saw the White House was in 1984. I had just graduated from college and was working as a community organizer out of the Harlem campus of the City College of New York. President Reagan was proposing a round of student aid cuts at the time, and so I worked with a group of student leaders—most of them black, Puerto Rican, or of Eastern European descent, almost all of them the first in their families to attend college—to round up petitions opposing the cuts and then deliver them to the New York congressional delegation.

It was a brief trip, spent mostly navigating the endless corridors of the Rayburn Building, getting polite but cursory audiences with Hill staffers not much older than I was. But at the end of the day, the students and I took the time to walk down to the Mall and the Washington Monument, and then spent a few minutes gazing at the White House. Standing on Pennsylvania Avenue, a few feet away from the Marine guard station at the main entrance, with pedestrians weaving along the sidewalk and traffic whizzing behind us, I marveled not at the White House's elegant sweep, but rather at the fact that it was so exposed to the hustle and bustle of the city; that we were allowed to stand so close to the gate, and could later circle to the other side of the building to peer at the Rose Garden and the residence beyond. The openness of the White House said something about our confidence as a democracy, I thought. It embodied the notion that our leaders were not so different from us; that they remained subject to laws and our collective consent.

Twenty years later, getting close to the White House wasn't so simple. Checkpoints, armed guards, vans, mirrors, dogs, and retractable barricades now sealed off a two-block perimeter around the White House. Unauthorized cars no longer traveled Pennsylvania Avenue. On a cold January afternoon, the day before my swearing in to the Senate, Lafayette Park was mostly empty, and as my car was waved through the White House gates and up the driveway, I felt a glancing sadness at what had been lost.

The inside of the White House doesn't have the luminous quality that you might expect from TV or film; it seems well kept but worn, a big old house that one imagines might be a bit drafty on cold winter nights. Still, as I stood in the foyer and let my eyes wander down the corridors, it was impossible to forget the history that had been made there—John and Bobby Kennedy huddling over the Cuban missile crisis; FDR making last-minute changes to a radio address; Lincoln alone, pacing the halls and shouldering the weight of a nation. (It wasn't until several months later that I would get to see the Lincoln Bedroom, a modest space with antique furniture, a four-poster bed, an original copy of the Gettysburg Address discreetly displayed under glass—and a big flat-screen TV set atop one of the desks. Who, I wondered, flipped on *SportsCenter* while spending the night in the Lincoln Bedroom?)

I was greeted immediately by a member of the White House's legislative staff and led into the Gold Room, where most of the incoming House and Senate members had already gathered. At sixteen hundred hours on the dot, President Bush was announced and walked to the podium, looking vigorous and fit, with that jaunty, determined walk that suggests he's on a schedule and wants to keep detours to a minimum. For ten or so minutes he spoke to the room, making a few jokes, calling for the country to come together, before inviting us to the other end of the White House for refreshments and a picture with him and the First Lady.

I happened to be starving at that moment, so while most of the other legislators started lining up for their photographs, I headed for the buffet. As I munched on hors d'oeuvres and engaged in small talk with a handful of House members, I recalled my previous two encounters with the President, the first a brief congratulatory call after the election, the second a small White House breakfast with me and the other incoming senators. Both times I had found the President to be a likable man, shrewd and disciplined but with the same straightforward manner that had helped him win two elections; you could easily imagine him owning the local car dealership down the street, coaching Little League, and grilling in his backyard—the kind of guy who would make for good company so long as the conversation revolved around sports and the kids.

There had been a moment during the breakfast meeting, though, after the backslapping and the small talk and when all of us were seated, with Vice President Cheney eating his eggs Benedict impassively and Karl Rove at the far end of the table discreetly checking his BlackBerry, that I witnessed a different side of the man. The President had begun to discuss his second-term agenda, mostly a reiteration of his campaign talking points—the importance of staying the course in Iraq and renewing the Patriot Act, the need to reform Social Security and overhaul the tax system, his determination to get an up-or-down vote on his judicial appointees—when suddenly it felt as if somebody in a back room had flipped a switch. The President's eyes became fixed; his voice took on the agitated, rapid tone of someone neither accustomed to nor welcoming interruption; his easy affability was replaced by an almost messianic certainty. As I watched my mostly Republican Senate colleagues hang on his every word, I was reminded of the dangerous isolation that power can bring, and appreciated the Founders' wisdom in designing a system to keep power in check.

"Senator?"

I looked up, shaken out of my memory, and saw one of the older black men who made up most of the White House wait-staff standing next to me.

"Want me to take that plate for you?"

I nodded, trying to swallow a mouthful of chicken something-or-others, and noticed that the line to greet the President had evaporated. Wanting to thank my hosts, I headed toward the Blue Room. A young Marine at the door politely indicated that the photograph session was over and that the President needed to get to his next appointment. But before I could turn around to go, the President himself appeared in the doorway and waved me in.

"Obama!" the President said, shaking my hand. "Come here and meet Laura. Laura, you remember Obama. We saw him on TV during election night. Beautiful family. And that wife of yours—that's one impressive lady."

"We both got better than we deserve, Mr. President," I said, shaking the First Lady's hand and hoping that I'd wiped any crumbs off my face. The President turned to an aide nearby, who squirted a big dollop of hand sanitizer in the President's hand.

"Want some?" the President asked. "Good stuff. Keeps you from getting colds."

Not wanting to seem unhygienic, I took a squirt.

"Come over here for a second," he said, leading me off to one side of the room. "You know," he said quietly, "I hope you don't mind me giving you a piece of advice."

"Not at all, Mr. President."

He nodded. "You've got a bright future," he said. "Very bright. But I've been in this town awhile and, let me tell you, it can be tough. When you get a lot of attention like you've been getting, people start gunnin' for ya. And it won't necessarily just

be coming from my side, you understand. From yours, too. Everybody'll be waiting for you to slip, know what I mean? So watch
yourself."

"Thanks for the advice, Mr. President."

"All right. I gotta get going. You know, me and you got something in common."

"What's that?"

"We both had to debate Alan Keyes. That guy's a piece of
work, isn't he?"

I laughed, and as we walked to the door I told him a few stories from the campaign. It wasn't until he had left the room that
I realized I had briefly put my arm over his shoulder as we
talked—an unconscious habit of mine, but one that I suspected
might have made many of my friends, not to mention the Secret
Service agents in the room, more than a little uneasy.

SINCE MY ARRIVAL in the Senate, I've been a steady and occasionally fierce critic of Bush Administration policies. I consider
the Bush tax cuts for the wealthy to be both fiscally irresponsible
and morally troubling. I have criticized the Administration for
lacking a meaningful health-care agenda, a serious energy policy,
or a strategy for making America more competitive. Back in 2002,
just before announcing my Senate campaign, I made a speech at
one of the first antiwar rallies in Chicago in which I questioned
the Administration's evidence of weapons of mass destruction
and suggested that an invasion of Iraq would prove to be a costly
error. Nothing in the recent news coming out of Baghdad or the
rest of the Middle East has dispelled these views.

So Democratic audiences are often surprised when I tell them
that I don't consider George Bush a bad man, and that I assume
he and members of his Administration are trying to do what they
think is best for the country.

I say this not because I am seduced by the proximity to power.

I see my invitations to the White House for what they are—exercises in common political courtesy—and am mindful of how quickly the long knives can come out when the Administration's agenda is threatened in any serious way. Moreover, whenever I write a letter to a family who has lost a loved one in Iraq, or read an email from a constituent who has dropped out of college because her student aid has been cut, I'm reminded that the actions of those in power have enormous consequences—a price that they themselves almost never have to pay.

It is to say that after all the trappings of office—the titles, the staff, the security details—are stripped away, I find the President and those who surround him to be pretty much like everybody else, possessed of the same mix of virtues and vices, insecurities and long-buried injuries, as the rest of us. No matter how wrongheaded I might consider their policies to be—and no matter how much I might insist that they be held accountable for the results of such policies—I still find it possible, in talking to these men and women, to understand their motives, and to recognize in them values I share.

This is not an easy posture to maintain in Washington. The stakes involved in Washington policy debates are often so high— whether we send our young men and women to war; whether we allow stem cell research to go forward—that even small differences in perspective are magnified. The demands of party loyalty, the imperative of campaigns, and the amplification of conflict by the media all contribute to an atmosphere of suspicion. Moreover, most people who serve in Washington have been trained either as lawyers or as political operatives—professions that tend to place a premium on winning arguments rather than solving problems. I can see how, after a certain amount of time in the capital, it becomes tempting to assume that those who disagree with you have fundamentally different values—indeed, that they are motivated by bad faith, and perhaps are bad people.

Outside of Washington, though, America feels less deeply divided. Illinois, for example, is no longer considered a bellwether state. For more than a decade now, it's become more and more Democratic, partly because of increased urbanization, partly because the social conservatism of today's GOP doesn't wear well in the Land of Lincoln. But Illinois remains a microcosm of the country, a rough stew of North and South, East and West, urban and rural, black, white, and everything in between. Chicago may possess all the big-city sophistication of L.A. or New York, but geographically and culturally, the southern end of Illinois is closer to Little Rock or Louisville, and large swaths of the state are considered, in modern political parlance, a deep shade of red.

I first traveled through southern Illinois in 1997. It was the summer after my first term in the Illinois legislature, and Michelle and I were not yet parents. With session adjourned, no law school classes to teach, and Michelle busy with work of her own, I convinced my legislative aide, Dan Shomon, to toss a map and some golf clubs in the car and tool around the state for a week. Dan had been both a UPI reporter and a field coordinator for several downstate campaigns, so he knew the territory pretty well. But as the date of our departure approached, it became apparent that he wasn't quite sure how I would be received in the counties we were planning to visit. Four times he reminded me how to pack—just khakis and polo shirts, he said; no fancy linen trousers or silk shirts. I assured him that I didn't own any linens or silks. On the drive down, we stopped at a TGI Friday's and I ordered a cheeseburger. When the waitress brought the food I asked her if she had any Dijon mustard. Dan shook his head.

"He doesn't want Dijon," he insisted, waving the waitress off. "Here"—he shoved a yellow bottle of French's mustard in my direction—"here's some mustard right here."

The waitress looked confused. "We got Dijon if you want it," she said to me.

I smiled. "That would be great, thanks." As the waitress

walked away, I leaned over to Dan and whispered that I didn't think there were any photographers around.

And so we traveled, stopping once a day to play a round of golf in the sweltering heat, driving past miles of cornfields and thick forests of ash trees and oak trees and shimmering lakes lined with stumps and reeds, through big towns like Carbondale and Mount Vernon, replete with strip malls and Wal-Marts, and tiny towns like Sparta and Pinckneyville, many of them with brick courthouses at the center of town, their main streets barely hanging on with every other store closed, the occasional road-side vendors selling fresh peaches or corn, or in the case of one couple I saw, "Good Deals on Guns and Swords."

We stopped in a coffee shop to eat pie and swap jokes with the mayor of Chester. We posed in front of the fifteen-foot-tall statue of Superman at the center of Metropolis. We heard about all the young people who were moving to the big cities because manufacturing and coal-mining jobs were disappearing. We learned about the local high school football teams' prospects for the coming season, and the vast distances veterans had to drive in order to reach the closest VA facility. We met women who had been missionaries in Kenya and greeted me in Swahili, and farm-ers who tracked the financial pages of the *Wall Street Journal* before setting out on their tractors. Several times a day, I pointed out to Dan the number of men we met sporting white linen slacks or silk Hawaiian shirts. In the small dining room of a Democratic party official in Du Quoin, I asked the local state's attorney about crime trends in his largely rural, almost uniformly white county, expecting him to mention joy-riding sprees or folks hunting out of season.

"The Gangster Disciples," he said, munching on a carrot. "We've got an all-white branch down here—kids without jobs, selling dope and speed."

By the end of the week, I was sorry to leave. Not simply be-cause I had made so many new friends, but because in the faces of all the men and women I'd met I had recognized pieces of my-self. In them I saw my grandfather's openness, my grandmother's matter-of-factness, my mother's kindness. The fried chicken, the potato salad, the grape halves in the Jell-O mold—all of it felt familiar.

It's that sense of familiarity that strikes me wherever I travel across Illinois. I feel it when I'm sitting down at a diner on Chicago's West Side. I feel it as I watch Latino men play soccer while their families cheer them on in a park in Pilsen. I feel it when I'm attending an Indian wedding in one of Chicago's north-ern suburbs.

Not so far beneath the surface, I think, we are becoming more, not less, alike.

I don't mean to exaggerate here, to suggest that the pollsters are wrong and that our differences—racial, religious, regional, or economic—are somehow trivial. In Illinois, as is true every-where, abortion vexes. In certain parts of the state, the mention of gun control constitutes sacrilege. Attitudes about everything from the income tax to sex on TV diverge wildly from place to place.

It is to insist that across Illinois, and across America, a con-stant cross-pollination is occurring, a not entirely orderly but generally peaceful collision among people and cultures. Identities are scrambling, and then cohering in new ways. Beliefs keep slip-ping through the noose of predictability. Facile expectations and simple explanations are being constantly upended. Spend time actually talking to Americans, and you discover that most evan-gelicals are more tolerant than the media would have us believe, most secularists more spiritual. Most rich people want the poor to succeed, and most of the poor are both more self-critical and hold higher aspirations than the popular culture allows. Most Republican strongholds are 40 percent Democrat, and vice versa. The political labels of liberal and conservative rarely track people's personal attributes.

All of which raises the question: What are the core values that we, as Americans, hold in common? That's not how we usually frame the issue, of course; our political culture fixates on where our values clash. In the immediate aftermath of the 2004 election, for example, a major national exit poll was published in which voters ranked "moral values" as having determined how they cast their ballot. Commentators fastened on the data to argue that the most controversial social issues in the election—particularly gay marriage—had swung a number of states. Conservatives heralded the numbers, convinced that they proved the Christian right's growing power.

When these polls were later analyzed, it turned out that the pundits and prognosticators had overstated their case a bit. In fact, voters had considered national security as the election's most important issue, and although large numbers of voters did consider "moral values" an important factor in the way they voted, the meaning of the term was so vague as to include everything from abortion to corporate malfeasance. Immediately, some Democrats could be heard breathing a sigh of relief, as if a diminution in the "values factor" served the liberal cause; as if a discussion of values was a dangerous, unnecessary distraction from those material concerns that characterized the Democratic Party platform.

I think Democrats are wrong to run away from a debate about values, as wrong as those conservatives who see values only as a wedge to pry loose working-class voters from the Democratic base. It is the language of values that people use to map their world. It is what can inspire them to take action, and move them beyond their isolation. The postelection polls may have been poorly composed, but the broader question of shared values—the standards and principles that the majority of Americans deem important in their lives, and in the life of the country—should be the heart of our politics, the cornerstone of any meaningful debate about budgets and projects, regulations and policies.

"WE HOLD THESE truths to be self-evident, that all men are created equal, that they are endowed by their Creator with certain unalienable Rights, that among these are Life, Liberty and the pursuit of Happiness."

Those simple words are our starting point as Americans; they describe not only the foundation of our government but the substance of our common creed. Not every American may be able to recite them; few, if asked, could trace the genesis of the Declaration of Independence to its roots in eighteenth-century liberal and republican thought. But the essential idea behind the Declaration—that we are born into this world free, all of us; that each of us arrives with a bundle of rights that can't be taken away by any person or any state without just cause; that through our own agency we can, and must, make of our lives what we will—is one that every American understands. It orients us, sets our course, each and every day.

Indeed, the value of individual freedom is so deeply ingrained in us that we tend to take it for granted. It is easy to forget that at the time of our nation's founding this idea was entirely radical in its implications, as radical as Martin Luther's posting on the church door. It is an idea that some portion of the world still rejects—and for which an even larger portion of humanity finds scant evidence in their daily lives.

In fact, much of my appreciation of our Bill of Rights comes from having spent part of my childhood in Indonesia and from still having family in Kenya, countries where individual rights are almost entirely subject to the self-restraint of army generals or the whims of corrupt bureaucrats. I remember the first time I took Michelle to Kenya, shortly before we were married. As an

African American, Michelle was bursting with excitement about the idea of visiting the continent of her ancestors, and we had a wonderful time, visiting my grandmother up-country, wandering through the streets of Nairobi, camping in the Serengeti, fishing off the island of Lamu.

But during our travels Michelle also heard—as I had heard during my first trip to Africa—the terrible sense on the part of most Kenyans that their fates were not their own. My cousins told her how difficult it was to find a job or start their own businesses without paying bribes. Activists told us about being jailed for expressing their opposition to government policies. Even within my own family, Michelle saw how suffocating the demands of family ties and tribal loyalties could be, with distant cousins constantly asking for favors, uncles and aunts showing up unannounced. On the flight back to Chicago, Michelle admitted she was looking forward to getting home. "I never realized just how American I was," she said. She hadn't realized just how free she was—or how much she cherished that freedom.

At its most elemental level, we understand our liberty in a negative sense. As a general rule we believe in the right to be left alone, and are suspicious of those—whether Big Brother or nosy neighbors—who want to meddle in our business. But we understand our liberty in a more positive sense as well, in the idea of opportunity and the subsidiary values that help realize opportunity—all those homespun virtues that Benjamin Franklin first popularized in *Poor Richard's Almanack* and that have continued to inspire our allegiance through successive generations. The values of self-reliance and self-improvement and risk-taking. The values of drive, discipline, temperance, and hard work. The values of thrift and personal responsibility.

These values are rooted in a basic optimism about life and a faith in free will—a confidence that through pluck and sweat and smarts, each of us can rise above the circumstances of our birth. But these values also express a broader confidence that so long as individual men and women are free to pursue their own interests, society as a whole will prosper. Our system of self-government and our free-market economy depend on the majority of individual Americans adhering to these values. The legitimacy of our government and our economy depend on the degree to which these values are rewarded, which is why the values of equal opportunity and nondiscrimination complement rather than impinge on our liberty.

If we Americans are individualistic at heart, if we instinctively chafe against a past of tribal allegiances, traditions, customs, and castes, it would be a mistake to assume that this is all we are. Our individualism has always been bound by a set of communal values, the glue upon which every healthy society depends. We value the imperatives of family and the cross-generational obligations that family implies. We value community, the neighborliness that expresses itself through raising the barn or coaching the soccer team. We value patriotism and the obligations of citizenship, a sense of duty and sacrifice on behalf of our nation. We value a faith in something bigger than ourselves, whether that something expresses itself in formal religion or ethical precepts. And we value the constellation of behaviors that express our mutual regard for one another: honesty, fairness, humility, kindness, courtesy, and compassion.

In every society (and in every individual), these twin strands—the individualistic and the communal, autonomy and solidarity—are in tension, and it has been one of the blessings of America that the circumstances of our nation's birth allowed us to negotiate these tensions better than most. We did not have to go through any of the violent upheavals that Europe was forced to endure as it shed its feudal past. Our passage from an agricultural to an industrial society was eased by the sheer size of the continent, vast tracts of land and abundant resources that allowed new immigrants to continually remake themselves.

But we cannot avoid these tensions entirely. At times our values collide because in the hands of men each one is subject to distortion and excess. Self-reliance and independence can transform into selfishness and license, ambition into greed and a frantic desire to succeed at any cost. More than once in our history we've seen patriotism slide into jingoism, xenophobia, the stifling of dissent; we've seen faith calcify into self-righteousness, closed-mindedness, and cruelty toward others. Even the impulse toward charity can drift into a stifling paternalism, an unwillingness to acknowledge the ability of others to do for themselves.

When this happens—when liberty is cited in the defense of a company's decision to dump toxins in our rivers, or when our collective interest in building an upscale new mall is used to justify the destruction of somebody's home—we depend on the strength of countervailing values to temper our judgment and hold such excesses in check.

Sometimes finding the right balance is relatively easy. We all agree, for instance, that society has a right to constrain individual freedom when it threatens to do harm to others. The First Amendment doesn't give you the right to yell "fire" in a crowded theater; your right to practice your religion does not encompass human sacrifice. Likewise, we all agree that there must be limits to the state's power to control our behavior, even if it's for our own good. Not many Americans would feel comfortable with the government monitoring what we eat, no matter how many deaths and how much of our medical spending may be due to rising rates of obesity.

More often, though, finding the right balance between our competing values is difficult. Tensions arise not because we have steered a wrong course, but simply because we live in a complex and contradictory world. I firmly believe, for example, that since 9/11, we have played fast and loose with constitutional principles in the fight against terrorism. But I acknowledge that even the wisest president and most prudent Congress would struggle to balance the critical demands of our collective security against the equally compelling need to uphold civil liberties. I believe our economic policies pay too little attention to the displacement of manufacturing workers and the destruction of manufacturing towns. But I cannot wish away the sometimes competing demands of economic security and competitiveness.

Unfortunately, too often in our national debates we don't even get to the point where we weigh these difficult choices. Instead, we either exaggerate the degree to which policies we don't like impinge on our most sacred values, or play dumb when our own preferred policies conflict with important countervailing values. Conservatives, for instance, tend to bristle when it comes to government interference in the marketplace or their right to bear arms. Yet many of these same conservatives show little to no concern when it comes to government wiretapping without a warrant or government attempts to control people's sexual practices. Conversely, it's easy to get most liberals riled up about government encroachments on freedom of the press or a woman's reproductive freedoms. But if you have a conversation with these same liberals about the potential costs of regulation to a small-business owner, you will often draw a blank stare.

In a country as diverse as ours, there will always be passionate arguments about how we draw the line when it comes to government action. That is how our democracy works. But our democracy might work a bit better if we recognized that all of us possess values that are worthy of respect: if liberals at least acknowledged that the recreational hunter feels the same way about his gun as they feel about their library books, and if conservatives recognized that most women feel as protective of their right to reproductive freedom as evangelicals do of their right to worship.

The results of such an exercise can sometimes be surprising. The year that Democrats regained the majority in the Illinois state senate, I sponsored a bill to require the videotaping of interrogations and confessions in capital cases. While the evidence tells me that the death penalty does little to deter crime, I believe there are some crimes—mass murder, the rape and murder of a child—so heinous, so beyond the pale, that the community is justified in expressing the full measure of its outrage by meting out the ultimate punishment. On the other hand, the way capital cases were tried in Illinois at the time was so rife with error, questionable police tactics, racial bias, and shoddy lawyering that thirteen death row inmates had been exonerated and a Republican governor had decided to institute a moratorium on all executions.

Despite what appeared to be a death penalty system ripe for reform, few people gave my bill much chance of passing. The state prosecutors and police organizations were adamantly opposed, believing that videotaping would be expensive and cumbersome, and would hamstring their ability to close cases. Some who favored abolishing the death penalty feared that any efforts at reform would detract from their larger cause. My fellow legislators were skittish about appearing in any way to be soft on crime. And the newly elected Democratic governor had announced his opposition to videotaping of interrogations during the course of his campaign.

It would have been typical of today's politics for each side to draw a line in the sand: for death penalty opponents to harp on racism and police misconduct and for law enforcement to suggest that my bill coddled criminals. Instead, over the course of several weeks, we convened sometimes daily meetings between prosecutors, public defenders, police organizations, and death penalty opponents, keeping our negotiations as much as possible out of the press.

Instead of focusing on the serious disagreements around the table, I talked about the common value that I believed everyone shared, regardless of how each of us might feel about the death penalty: that is, the basic principle that no innocent person should end up on death row, and that no person guilty of a capital offense should go free. When police representatives presented concrete problems with the bill's design that would have impeded their investigations, we modified the bill. When police representatives offered to videotape only confessions, we held firm, pointing out that the whole purpose of the bill was to give the public confidence that confessions were obtained free of coercion. At the end of the process, the bill had the support of all the parties involved. It passed unanimously in the Illinois Senate and was signed into law.

Of course, this approach to policy making doesn't always work. Sometimes, politicians and interest groups welcome conflict in pursuit of a broader ideological goal. Most antiabortion activists, for example, have openly discouraged legislative allies from even pursuing those compromise measures that would have significantly reduced the incidence of the procedure popularly known as partial-birth abortion, because the image the procedure evokes in the mind of the public has helped them win converts to their position.

And sometimes our ideological predispositions are just so fixed that we have trouble seeing the obvious. Once, while still in the Illinois Senate, I listened to a Republican colleague work himself into a lather over a proposed plan to provide school breakfasts to preschoolers. Such a plan, he insisted, would crush their spirit of self-reliance. I had to point out that not too many five-year-olds I knew were self-reliant, but children who spent their formative years too hungry to learn could very well end up being charges of the state.

Despite my best efforts, the bill still went down in defeat; Illinois preschoolers were temporarily saved from the debilitating effects of cereal and milk (a version of the bill would later pass). But my fellow legislator's speech helps underscore one of the differences between ideology and values: Values are faithfully applied to the facts before us, while ideology overrides whatever facts call theory into question.

MUCH OF THE confusion surrounding the values debate arises out of a misperception on the part of both politicians and the public that politics and government are equivalent. To say that a value is important is not to say that it should be subject to regulation or that it merits a new agency. Conversely, just because a value should not or cannot be legislated doesn't mean it isn't a proper topic for public discussion.

I value good manners, for example. Every time I meet a kid who speaks clearly and looks me in the eye, who says "yes, sir" and "thank you" and "please" and "excuse me," I feel more hopeful about the country. I don't think I am alone in this. I can't legislate good manners. But I can encourage good manners whenever I'm addressing a group of young people.

The same goes for competence. Nothing brightens my day more than dealing with somebody, anybody, who takes pride in their work or goes the extra mile—an accountant, a plumber, a three-star general, the person on the other end of the phone who actually seems to want to solve your problem. My encounters with such competence seem more sporadic lately; I seem to spend more time looking for somebody in the store to help me or waiting for the deliveryman to show. Other people must notice this; it makes us all cranky, and those of us in government, no less than in business, ignore such perceptions at their own peril. (I am convinced—although I have no statistical evidence to back it up—that antitax, antigovernment, antiunion sentiments grow anytime people find themselves standing in line at a government office with only one window open and three or four workers chatting among themselves in full view.)

Progressives in particular seem confused on this point, which is why we so often get our clocks cleaned in elections. I recently gave a speech at the Kaiser Family Foundation after they released a study showing that the amount of sex on television has doubled in recent years. Now I enjoy HBO as much as the next guy, and I generally don't care what adults watch in the privacy of their homes. In the case of children, I think it's primarily the duty of parents to monitor what they are watching on television, and in my speech I even suggested that everyone would benefit if parents—heaven forbid—simply turned off the TV and tried to strike up a conversation with their kids.

Having said all that, I indicated that I wasn't too happy with ads for erectile-dysfunction drugs popping up every fifteen minutes whenever I watched a football game with my daughters in the room. I offered the further observation that a popular show targeted at teens, in which young people with no visible means of support spend several months getting drunk and jumping naked into hot tubs with strangers, was not "the real world." I ended by suggesting that the broadcast and cable industries should adopt better standards and technology to help parents control what streamed into their homes.

You would have thought I was Cotton Mather. In response to my speech, one newspaper editorial intoned that the government had no business regulating protected speech, despite the fact that I hadn't called for regulation. Reporters suggested that I was cynically tacking to the center in preparation for a national race. More than a few supporters wrote our office, complaining that they had voted for me to beat back the Bush agenda, not to act as the town scold.

And yet every parent I know, liberal or conservative, complains about the coarsening of the culture, the promotion of easy materialism and instant gratification, the severing of sexuality from intimacy. They may not want government censorship, but they want those concerns recognized, their experiences validated. When, for fear of appearing censorious, progressive political leaders can't even acknowledge the problem, those parents start listening to those leaders who will—leaders who may be less sensitive to constitutional constraints.

Of course, conservatives have their own blind spots when it comes to addressing problems in the culture. Take executive pay.

In 1980, the average CEO made forty-two times what an average hourly worker took home. By 2005, the ratio was 262 to 1. Conservative outlets like the *Wall Street Journal* editorial page try to justify outlandish salaries and stock options as necessary to attract top talent, and suggest that the economy actually performs better when America's corporate leaders are fat and happy. But the explosion in CEO pay has had little to do with improved performance. In fact, some of the country's most highly compensated CEOs over the past decade have presided over huge drops in earnings, losses in shareholder value, massive layoffs, and the underfunding of their workers' pension funds.

What accounts for the change in CEO pay is not any market imperative. It's cultural. At a time when average workers are experiencing little or no income growth, many of America's CEOs have lost any sense of shame about grabbing whatever their pliant, handpicked corporate boards will allow. Americans understand the damage such an ethic of greed has on our collective lives; in a recent survey, they ranked corruption in government and business, and greed and materialism, as two of the three most important moral challenges facing the nation ("raising kids with the right values" ranked first). Conservatives may be right when they argue that the government should not try to determine executive pay packages. But conservatives should at least be willing to speak out against unseemly behavior in corporate boardrooms with the same moral force, the same sense of outrage, that they direct against dirty rap lyrics.

Of course, there are limits to the power of the bully pulpit. Sometimes only the law can fully vindicate our values, particularly when the rights and opportunities of the powerless in our society are at stake. Certainly this has been true in our efforts to end racial discrimination; as important as moral exhortation was in changing hearts and minds of white Americans during the civil rights era, what ultimately broke the back of Jim Crow and ushered in a new era of race relations were the Supreme Court cases culminating in *Brown v. Board of Education,* the Civil Rights Act of 1964, and the Voting Rights Act of 1965. As these laws were being debated, there were those who argued that government should not interject itself into civil society, that no law could force white people to associate with blacks. Upon hearing these arguments, Dr. King replied, "It may be true that the law cannot make a man love me but it can keep him from lynching me and I think that is pretty important, also."

Sometimes we need both cultural transformation and government action—a change in values and a change in policy—to promote the kind of society we want. The state of our inner-city schools is a case in point. All the money in the world won't boost student achievement if parents make no effort to instill in their children the values of hard work and delayed gratification. But when we as a society pretend that poor children will fulfill their potential in dilapidated, unsafe schools with outdated equipment and teachers who aren't trained in the subjects they teach, we are perpetrating a lie on these children, and on ourselves. We are betraying our values.

That is one of the things that makes me a Democrat, I suppose—this idea that our communal values, our sense of mutual responsibility and social solidarity, should express themselves not just in the church or the mosque or the synagogue; not just on the blocks where we live, in the places where we work, or within our own families; but also through our government. Like many conservatives, I believe in the power of culture to determine both individual success and social cohesion, and I believe we ignore cultural factors at our peril. But I also believe that our government can play a role in shaping that culture for the better—or for the worse.

I OFTEN WONDER what makes it so difficult for politicians to talk about values in ways that don't appear calculated or phony.

Partly, I think, it's because those of us in public life have become so scripted, and the gestures that candidates use to signify their values have become so standardized (a stop at a black church, the hunting trip, the visit to a NASCAR track, the reading in the kindergarten classroom) that it becomes harder and harder for the public to distinguish between honest sentiment and political stagecraft.

Then there's the fact that the practice of modern politics itself seems to be value-free. Politics (and political commentary) not only allows but often rewards behavior that we would normally think of as scandalous: fabricating stories, distorting the obvious meaning of what other people say, insulting or generally questioning their motives, poking through their personal affairs in search of damaging information.

During my general election campaign for the U.S. Senate, for example, my Republican opponent assigned a young man to track all my public appearances with a handheld camera. This has become fairly routine operating procedure in many campaigns, but whether because the young man was overzealous or whether he had been instructed to try to provoke me, his tracking came to resemble stalking. From morning to night, he followed me everywhere, usually from a distance of no more than five or ten feet. He would film me riding down elevators. He would film me coming out of the restroom. He would film me on my cell phone, talking to my wife and children.

At first, I tried reasoning with him. I stopped to ask him his name, told him that I understood he had a job to do, and suggested that he keep enough of a distance to allow me to have a conversation without him listening in. In the face of my entreaties, he remained largely mute, other than to say his name was Justin. I suggested that he call his boss and find out whether this was in fact what the campaign intended for him to do. He told me that I was free to call myself and gave me the number. After two or three days of this, I decided I'd had enough. With

Justin fast on my heels, I strolled into the press office of the state capitol building and asked some of the reporters who were having lunch to gather round.

"Hey, guys," I said, "I want to introduce you to Justin. Justin here's been assigned by the Ryan campaign to stalk me wherever I go."

As I explained the situation, Justin stood there, continuing to film. The reporters turned to him and started peppering him with questions.

"You follow him into the bathroom?"

"Are you this close to him all the time?"

Soon several news crews arrived with their cameras to film Justin filming me. Like a prisoner of war, Justin kept repeating his name, his rank, and the telephone number of his candidate's campaign headquarters. By six o'clock, the story of Justin was on most local broadcasts. The story ended up blanketing the state for a week—cartoons, editorials, and sports radio chatter. After several days of defiance, my opponent succumbed to the pressure, asked Justin to back up a few feet, and issued an apology. Still, the damage to his campaign was done. People might not have understood our contrasting views on Medicare or Middle East diplomacy. But they knew that my opponent's campaign had violated a value—civil behavior—that they considered important.

The gap between what we deem appropriate behavior in everyday life and what it takes to win a campaign is just one of the ways in which a politician's values are tested. In few other professions are you required, each and every day, to weigh so many competing claims—between different sets of constituents, between the interests of your state and the interests of the nation, between party loyalty and your own sense of independence, between the value of service and obligations to your family. There is a constant danger, in the cacophony of voices, that a politician loses his moral bearings and finds himself entirely steered by the winds of public opinion.

Perhaps this explains why we long for that most elusive quality in our leaders—the quality of authenticity, of being who you say you are, of possessing a truthfulness that goes beyond words. My friend the late U.S. senator Paul Simon had that quality. For most of his career, he baffled the pundits by garnering support from people who disagreed, sometimes vigorously, with his liberal politics. It helped that he looked so trustworthy, like a small-town doctor, with his glasses and bow tie and basset-hound face. But people also sensed that he lived out his values: that he was honest, and that he stood up for what he believed in, and perhaps most of all that he cared about them and what they were going through.

That last aspect of Paul's character—a sense of empathy—is one that I find myself appreciating more and more as I get older. It is at the heart of my moral code, and it is how I understand the Golden Rule—not simply as a call to sympathy or charity, but as something more demanding, a call to stand in somebody else's shoes and see through their eyes.

Like most of my values, I learned about empathy from my mother. She disdained any kind of cruelty or thoughtlessness or abuse of power, whether it expressed itself in the form of racial prejudice or bullying in the schoolyard or workers being underpaid. Whenever she saw even a hint of such behavior in me she would look me square in the eyes and ask, "How do you think that would make you feel?"

But it was in my relationship with my grandfather that I think I first internalized the full meaning of empathy. Because my mother's work took her overseas, I often lived with my grandparents during my high school years, and without a father present in the house, my grandfather bore the brunt of much of my adolescent rebellion. He himself was not always easy to get along with; he was at once warmhearted and quick to anger, and in part because his career had not been particularly successful, his feelings could also be easily bruised. By the time I was sixteen we were arguing all the time, usually about me failing to abide by what I considered to be an endless series of petty and arbitrary rules—filling up the gas tank whenever I borrowed his car, say, or making sure that I rinsed out the milk carton before I put it in the garbage.

With a certain talent for rhetoric, as well as an absolute certainty about the merits of my own views, I found that I could generally win these arguments, in the narrow sense of leaving my grandfather flustered, angry, and sounding unreasonable. But at some point, perhaps in my senior year, such victories started to feel less satisfying. I started thinking about the struggles and disappointments he had seen in his life. I started to appreciate his need to feel respected in his own home. I realized that abiding by his rules would cost me little, but to him it would mean a lot. I recognized that sometimes he really did have a point, and that in insisting on getting my own way all the time, without regard to his feelings or needs, I was in some way diminishing myself.

There's nothing extraordinary about such an awakening, of course; in one form or another it is what we all must go through if we are to grow up. And yet I find myself returning again and again to my mother's simple principle—"How would that make you feel?"—as a guidepost for my politics.

It's not a question we ask ourselves enough, I think; as a country, we seem to be suffering from an empathy deficit. We wouldn't tolerate schools that don't teach, that are chronically underfunded and understaffed and underinspired, if we thought that the children in them were like our children. It's hard to imagine the CEO of a company giving himself a multimillion-dollar bonus while cutting health-care coverage for his workers if he thought they were in some sense his equals. And it's safe to assume that those in power would think longer and harder about launching a war if they envisioned their own sons and daughters in harm's way.

I believe a stronger sense of empathy would tilt the balance of our current politics in favor of those people who are struggling in this society. After all, if they are like us, then their struggles are our own. If we fail to help, we diminish ourselves.

But that does not mean that those who are struggling—or those of us who claim to speak for those who are struggling—are thereby freed from trying to understand the perspectives of those who are better off. Black leaders need to appreciate the legitimate fears that may cause some whites to resist affirmative action. Union representatives can't afford not to understand the competitive pressures their employers may be under. I am obligated to try to see the world through George Bush's eyes, no matter how much I may disagree with him. That's what empathy does—it calls us all to task, the conservative and the liberal, the powerful and the powerless, the oppressed and the oppressor. We are all shaken out of our complacency. We are all forced beyond our limited vision.

No one is exempt from the call to find common ground.

Of course, in the end a sense of mutual understanding isn't enough. After all, talk is cheap; like any value, empathy must be acted upon. When I was a community organizer back in the eighties, I would often challenge neighborhood leaders by asking them where they put their time, energy, and money. Those are the true tests of what we value, I'd tell them, regardless of what we like to tell ourselves. If we aren't willing to pay a price for our values, if we aren't willing to make some sacrifices in order to realize them, then we should ask ourselves whether we truly believe in them at all.

By these standards at least, it sometimes appears that Americans today value nothing so much as being rich, thin, young, famous, safe, and entertained. We say we value the legacy we leave the next generation and then saddle that generation with mountains of debt. We say we believe in equal opportunity but then stand idle while millions of American children languish in poverty. We insist that we value family, but then structure our economy and organize our lives so as to ensure that our families get less and less of our time.

And yet a part of us knows better. We hang on to our values, even if they seem at times tarnished and worn; even if, as a nation and in our own lives, we have betrayed them more often than we care to remember. What else is there to guide us? Those values are our inheritance, what makes us who we are as a people. And although we recognize that they are subject to challenge, can be poked and prodded and debunked and turned inside out by intellectuals and cultural critics, they have proven to be both surprisingly durable and surprisingly constant across classes, and races, and faiths, and generations. We can make claims on their behalf, so long as we understand that our values must be tested against fact and experience, so long as we recall that they demand deeds and not just words.

To do otherwise would be to relinquish our best selves.

Chapter Three

Our Constitution

THERE'S A SAYING that senators frequently use when asked to describe their first year on Capitol Hill: "It's like drinking from a fire hose."

The description is apt, for during my first few months in the Senate everything seemed to come at me at once. I had to hire staff and set up offices in Washington and Illinois. I had to negotiate committee assignments and get up to speed on the issues pending before the committees. There was the backlog of ten thousand constituent letters that had accumulated since Election Day, and the three hundred speaking invitations that were arriving every week. In half-hour blocks, I was shuttled from the Senate floor to committee rooms to hotel lobbies to radio stations, entirely dependent on an assortment of recently hired staffers in their twenties and thirties to keep me on schedule, hand me the right briefing book, remind me whom I was meeting with, or steer me to the nearest restroom.

Then, at night, there was the adjustment of living alone. Michelle and I had decided to keep the family in Chicago, in part because we liked the idea of raising the girls outside the hothouse environment of Washington, but also because the arrangement gave Michelle a circle of support—from her mother, brother, other family, and friends—that could help her manage the prolonged absences my job would require. So for the three nights a week that I spent in Washington, I rented a small one-bedroom apartment near Georgetown Law School, in a high-rise between Capitol Hill and downtown.

At first, I tried to embrace my newfound solitude, forcing myself to remember the pleasures of bachelorhood—gathering take-out menus from every restaurant in the neighborhood, watching basketball or reading late into the night, hitting the gym for a midnight workout, leaving dishes in the sink and not making my bed. But it was no use; after thirteen years of marriage, I found myself to be fully domesticated, soft and helpless. My first morning in Washington, I realized I'd forgotten to buy a shower curtain and had to scrunch up against the shower wall in order to avoid flooding the bathroom floor. The next night, watching the game and having a beer, I fell asleep at halftime, and woke up on the couch two hours later with a bad crick in my neck. Take-out food didn't taste so good anymore; the silence irked me. I found myself calling home repeatedly, just to listen to my daughters' voices, aching for the warmth of their hugs and the sweet smell of their skin.

"Hey, sweetie!"

"Hey, Daddy."

"What's happening?"

"Since you called before?"

"Yeah."

"Nothing. You wanna talk to Mommy?"

There were a handful of senators who also had young families, and whenever we met we would compare notes on the pros and cons of moving to Washington, as well as the difficulty in protecting family time from overzealous staff. But most of my new colleagues were considerably older—the average age was sixty—and so as I made the rounds to their offices, their advice usually related to the business of the Senate. They explained to me the advantages of various committee assignments and the temperaments of various committee chairmen. They offered suggestions on how to organize staff, whom to talk to for extra office space, and how to manage constituent requests. Most of the advice I found useful; occasionally it was contradictory. But among Democrats at least, my meetings would end with one consistent recommendation: As soon as possible, they said, I should schedule a meeting with Senator Byrd—not only as a matter of senatorial courtesy, but also because Senator Byrd's senior position on the Appropriations Committee and general stature in the Senate gave him considerable clout.

At eighty-seven years old, Senator Robert C. Byrd was not simply the dean of the Senate; he had come to be seen as the very embodiment of the Senate, a living, breathing fragment of history. Raised by his aunt and uncle in the hardscrabble coal-mining towns of West Virginia, he possessed a native talent that allowed him to recite long passages of poetry from memory and play the fiddle with impressive skill. Unable to afford college tuition, he worked as a meat cutter, a produce salesman, and a welder on battleships during World War II. When he returned to West Virginia after the war, he won a seat in the state legislature, and he was elected to Congress in 1952.

In 1958, he made the jump to the Senate, and during the course of forty-seven years he had held just about every office available—including six years as majority leader and six years as minority leader. All the while he maintained the populist impulse that led him to focus on delivering tangible benefits to the men and women back home: black lung benefits and union protections for miners; roads and buildings and electrification projects for desperately poor communities. In ten years of night courses while serving in Congress he had earned his law degree, and his grasp of Senate rules was legendary. Eventually, he had written a four-volume history of the Senate that reflected not just scholarship and discipline but also an unsurpassed love of the institution that had shaped his life's work. Indeed, it was said that Senator Byrd's passion for the Senate was exceeded only by the tenderness he felt toward his ailing wife of sixty-eight years (who has since passed away)—and perhaps by his reverence for the Constitution, a pocket-sized copy of which he carried with him wherever he went and often pulled out to wave in the midst of debate.

I had already left a message with Senator Byrd's office requesting a meeting when I first had an opportunity to see him in person. It was the day of our swearing in, and we had been in the Old Senate Chamber, a dark, ornate place dominated by a large, gargoyle-like eagle that stretched out over the presiding officer's chair from an awning of dark, bloodred velvet. The somber setting matched the occasion, as the Democratic Caucus was meeting to organize itself after the difficult election and the loss of its leader. After the new leadership team was installed, Minority Leader Harry Reid asked Senator Byrd if he would say a few words. Slowly, the senior senator rose from his seat, a slender man with a still-thick snowy mane, watery blue eyes, and a sharp, prominent nose. For a moment he stood in silence, steadying himself with his cane, his head turned upward, eyes fixed on the ceiling. Then he began to speak, in somber, measured tones, a hint of the Appalachians like a knotty grain of wood beneath polished veneer.

I don't recall the specifics of his speech, but I remember the broad themes, cascading out from the well of the Old Senate Chamber in a rising, Shakespearean rhythm—the clockwork design of the Constitution and the Senate as the essence of that charter's promise; the dangerous encroachment, year after year, of the Executive Branch on the Senate's precious independence; the need for every senator to reread our founding documents, so that we might remain steadfast and faithful and true to the meaning of the Republic. As he spoke, his voice grew more forceful; his forefinger stabbed the air; the dark room seemed to close in on him, until he seemed almost a specter, the spirit of Senates past, his almost fifty years in these chambers reaching back to touch the previous fifty years, and the fifty years before that, and the fifty years before that; back to the time when Jefferson, Adams, and Madison roamed through the halls of the Capitol, and the city itself was still wilderness and farmland and swamp.

Back to a time when neither I nor those who looked like me could have sat within these walls.

Listening to Senator Byrd speak, I felt with full force all the essential contradictions of me in this new place, with its marble busts, its arcane traditions, its memories and its ghosts. I pondered the fact that, according to his own autobiography, Senator Byrd had received his first taste of leadership in his early twenties, as a member of the Raleigh County Ku Klux Klan, an association that he had long disavowed, an error he attributed—no doubt correctly—to the time and place in which he'd been raised, but which continued to surface as an issue throughout his career. I thought about how he had joined other giants of the Senate, like J. William Fulbright of Arkansas and Richard Russell of Georgia, in Southern resistance to civil rights legislation. I wondered if this would matter to the liberals who now lionized Senator Byrd for his principled opposition to the Iraq War resolution— the MoveOn.org crowd, the heirs of the political counterculture the senator had spent much of his career disdaining.

I wondered if it should matter. Senator Byrd's life—like most of ours—has been the struggle of warring impulses, a twining of darkness and light. And in that sense I realized that he really was a proper emblem for the Senate, whose rules and design reflect the grand compromise of America's founding: the bargain between Northern states and Southern states, the Senate's role as a guardian against the passions of the moment, a defender of minority rights and state sovereignty, but also a tool to protect the wealthy from the rabble, and assure slaveholders of non-interference with their peculiar institution. Stamped into the very fiber of the Senate, within its genetic code, was the same contest between power and principle that characterized America as a whole, a lasting expression of that great debate among a few brilliant, flawed men that had concluded with the creation of a form of government unique in its genius—yet blind to the whip and the chain.

The speech ended; fellow senators clapped and congratulated Senator Byrd for his magnificent oratory. I went over to introduce myself and he grasped my hand warmly, saying how much he looked forward to sitting down for a visit. Walking back to my office, I decided I would unpack my old constitutional law books that night and reread the document itself. For Senator Byrd was right: To understand what was happening in Washington in 2005, to understand my new job and to understand Senator Byrd, I needed to circle back to the start, to America's earliest debates and founding documents, to trace how they had played out over time, and make judgments in light of subsequent history.

IF YOU ASK my eight-year-old what I do for a living, she might say I make laws. And yet one of the surprising things about Washington is the amount of time spent arguing not about what the law should be, but rather what the law is. The simplest statute—a requirement, say, that companies provide bathroom breaks to their hourly workers—can become the subject of wildly different interpretations, depending on whom you are talking to: the congressman who sponsored the provision, the staffer who drafted it, the department head whose job it is to enforce it, the lawyer whose client finds it inconvenient, or the judge who may be called upon to apply it.

Some of this is by design, a result of the complex machinery of checks and balances. The diffusion of power between the branches, as well as between federal and state governments, means that no law is ever final, no battle truly finished; there is always the opportunity to strengthen or weaken what appears to be done, to water down a regulation or block its implementation, to contract an agency's power with a cut in its budget, or to seize control of an issue where a vacuum has been left.

Partly it's the nature of the law itself. Much of the time, the law is settled and plain. But life turns up new problems, and lawyers, officials, and citizens debate the meaning of terms that seemed clear years or even months before. For in the end laws are just words on a page—words that are sometimes malleable, opaque, as dependent on context and trust as they are in a story or poem or promise to someone, words whose meanings are subject to erosion, sometimes collapsing in the blink of an eye.

The legal controversies that were stirring Washington in 2005 went beyond the standard problems of legal interpretation, however. Instead, they involved the question of whether those in power were bound by any rules of law at all.

When it came to questions of national security in the post–9/11 era, for example, the White House stood fast against any suggestion that it was answerable to Congress or the courts. During the hearings to confirm Condoleezza Rice as secretary of state, arguments flared over everything from the scope of Congress's resolution authorizing the war in Iraq to the willingness of executive branch members to testify under oath. During the debate surrounding the confirmation of Alberto Gonzales, I reviewed memos drafted in the attorney general's office suggesting that techniques like sleep deprivation or repeated suffocation did not constitute torture so long as they did not cause "severe pain" of the sort "accompanying organ failure, impairment of bodily function, or even death"; transcripts that suggested the Geneva Conventions did not apply to "enemy combatants" captured in a war in Afghanistan; opinions that the Fourth Amendment did not apply to U.S. citizens labeled "enemy combatants" and captured on U.S. soil.

This attitude was by no means confined to the White House. I remember heading toward the Senate floor one day in early March and being stopped briefly by a dark-haired young man.

He led me over to his parents, and explained that they had traveled from Florida in a last-ditch effort to save a young woman—Terri Schiavo—who had fallen into a deep coma, and whose husband was now planning to remove her from life support. It was a heartbreaking story, but I told them there was little precedent for Congress intervening in such cases—not realizing at the time that Tom DeLay and Bill Frist made their own precedent.

The scope of presidential power during wartime. The ethics surrounding end-of-life decisions. These weren't easy issues; as much as I disagreed with Republican policies, I believed they were worthy of serious debate. No, what troubled me was the process—or lack of process—by which the White House and its congressional allies disposed of opposing views; the sense that the rules of governing no longer applied, and that there were no fixed meanings or standards to which we could appeal. It was as if those in power had decided that habeas corpus and separation of powers were niceties that only got in the way, that they complicated what was obvious (the need to stop terrorists) or impeded what was right (the sanctity of life) and could therefore be disregarded, or at least bent to strong wills.

The irony, of course, was that such disregard of the rules and the manipulation of language to achieve a particular outcome were precisely what conservatives had long accused liberals of doing. It was one of the rationales behind Newt Gingrich's Contract with America—the notion that the Democratic barons who then controlled the House of Representatives consistently abused the legislative process for their own gain. It was the basis for the impeachment proceedings against Bill Clinton, the scorn heaped on the sad phrase "it depends on what the meaning of the word 'is' is." It was the basis of conservative broadsides against liberal academics, those high priests of political correctness, it was argued, who refused to acknowledge any eternal truths or hierarchies of knowledge and indoctrinated America's youth with dangerous moral relativism.

And it was at the very heart of the conservative assault on the federal courts.

Gaining control of the courts generally and the Supreme Court in particular had become the holy grail for a generation of conservative activists—and not just, they insisted, because they viewed the courts as the last bastion of pro-abortion, pro-affirmative-action, pro-homosexual, pro-criminal, pro-regulation, anti-religious liberal elitism. According to these activists, liberal judges had placed themselves above the law, basing their opinions not on the Constitution but on their own whims and desired results, finding rights to abortion or sodomy that did not exist in the text, subverting the democratic process and perverting the Founding Fathers' original intent. To return the courts to their proper role required the appointment of "strict constructionists" to the federal bench, men and women who understood the difference between interpreting and making law, men and women who would stick to the original meaning of the Founders' words. Men and women who would follow the rules.

Those on the left saw the situation quite differently. With conservative Republicans making gains in the congressional and presidential elections, many liberals viewed the courts as the only thing standing in the way of a radical effort to roll back civil rights, women's rights, civil liberties, environmental regulation, church/state separation, and the entire legacy of the New Deal. During the Bork nomination, advocacy groups and Democratic leaders organized their opposition with a sophistication that had never been seen for a judicial confirmation. When the nomination was defeated, conservatives realized that they would have to build their own grassroots army.

Since then, each side had claimed incremental advances (Scalia and Thomas for conservatives, Ginsburg and Breyer for liberals) and setbacks (for conservatives, the widely perceived drift toward the center by O'Connor, Kennedy, and especially Souter; for liberals, the packing of lower federal courts with Reagan and Bush I appointees). Democrats complained loudly when Republicans used control of the Judiciary Committee to block sixty-one of Clinton's appointments to appellate and district courts, and for the brief time that they held the majority, the Democrats tried the same tactics on George W. Bush's nominees.

But when the Democrats lost their Senate majority in 2002, they had only one arrow left in their quiver, a strategy that could be summed up in one word, the battle cry around which the Democratic faithful now rallied:

Filibuster!

The Constitution makes no mention of the filibuster; it is a Senate rule, one that dates back to the very first Congress. The basic idea is simple: Because all Senate business is conducted by unanimous consent, any senator can bring proceedings to a halt by exercising his right to unlimited debate and refusing to move on to the next order of business. In other words, he can talk. For as long as he wants. He can talk about the substance of a pending bill, or about the motion to call the pending bill. He can choose to read the entire seven-hundred-page defense authorization bill, line by line, into the record, or relate aspects of the bill to the rise and fall of the Roman Empire, the flight of the hummingbird, or the Atlanta phone book. So long as he or like-minded colleagues are willing to stay on the floor and talk, everything else has to wait—which gives each senator an enormous amount of leverage, and a determined minority effective veto power over any piece of legislation.

The only way to break a filibuster is for three-fifths of the Senate to invoke something called cloture—that is, the cessation of debate. Effectively this means that every action pending before the Senate—every bill, resolution, or nomination—needs the support of sixty senators rather than a simple majority. A series of complex rules has evolved, allowing both filibusters and cloture votes to proceed without fanfare: Just the threat of a filibuster will often be enough to get the majority leader's attention, and a cloture vote will then be organized without anybody having to spend their evenings sleeping in armchairs and cots. But throughout the Senate's modern history, the filibuster has remained a preciously guarded prerogative, one of the distinguishing features, it is said—along with six-year terms and the allocation of two senators to each state, regardless of population—that separates the Senate from the House and serves as a firewall against the dangers of majority overreach.

There is another, grimmer history to the filibuster, though, one that carries special relevance for me. For almost a century, the filibuster was the South's weapon of choice in its efforts to protect Jim Crow from federal interference, the legal blockade that effectively gutted the Fourteenth and Fifteenth Amendments. Decade after decade, courtly, erudite men like Senator Richard B. Russell of Georgia (after whom the most elegant suite of Senate offices is named) used the filibuster to choke off any and every piece of civil rights legislation before the Senate, whether voting rights bills, or fair employment bills, or anti-lynching bills. With words, with rules, with procedures and precedents—with law— Southern senators had succeeded in perpetuating black subjugation in ways that mere violence never could. The filibuster hadn't just stopped bills. For many blacks in the South, the filibuster had snuffed out hope.

Democrats used the filibuster sparingly in George Bush's first term: Of the President's two-hundred-plus judicial nominees, only ten were prevented from getting to the floor for an up-or-down vote. Still, all ten were nominees to appellate courts, the courts that counted; all ten were standard-bearers for the conservative cause; and if Democrats maintained their filibuster on these ten fine jurists, conservatives argued, there would be nothing to prevent them from having their way with future Supreme Court nominees.

So it came to pass that President Bush—emboldened by a bigger Republican majority in the Senate and his self-proclaimed mandate—decided in the first few weeks of his second term to renominate seven previously filibustered judges. As a poke in the eye to the Democrats, it produced the desired response. Democratic Leader Harry Reid called it "a big wet kiss to the far right" and renewed the threat of a filibuster. Advocacy groups on the left and the right rushed to their posts and sent out all-points alerts, dispatching emails and direct mail that implored donors to fund the air wars to come. Republicans, sensing that this was the time to go in for the kill, announced that if Democrats continued in their obstructionist ways, they would have no choice but to invoke the dreaded "nuclear option," a novel procedural maneuver that would involve the Senate's presiding officer (perhaps Vice President Cheney himself) ignoring the opinion of the Senate parliamentarian, breaking two hundred years of Senate precedent, and deciding, with a simple bang of the gavel, that the use of filibusters was no longer permissible under the Senate rules—at least when it came to judicial nominations.

To me, the threat to eliminate the filibuster on judicial nominations was just one more example of Republicans changing the rules in the middle of the game. Moreover, a good argument could be made that a vote on judicial nominations was precisely the situation where the filibuster's supermajority requirement made sense: Because federal judges receive lifetime appointments and often serve through the terms of multiple presidents, it behooves a president—and benefits our democracy—to find moderate nominees who can garner some measure of bipartisan support. Few of the Bush nominees in question fell into the "moderate" category; rather, they showed a pattern of hostility toward civil rights, privacy, and checks on executive power that put them to the right of even most Republican judges (one particularly troubling nominee had derisively called Social Security and other New Deal programs "the triumph of our own socialist revolution").

Still, I remember muffling a laugh the first time I heard the term "nuclear option." It seemed to perfectly capture the loss of perspective that had come to characterize judicial confirmations, part of the spin-fest that permitted groups on the left to run ads featuring scenes of Jimmy Stewart's *Mr. Smith Goes to Washington* without any mention that Strom Thurmond and Jim Eastland had played Mr. Smith in real life; the shameless mythologizing that allowed Southern Republicans to rise on the Senate floor and somberly intone about the impropriety of filibusters, without even a peep of acknowledgment that it was the politicians from their states—their direct political forebears—who had perfected the art for a malicious cause.

Not many of my fellow Democrats appreciated the irony. As the judicial confirmation process began heating up, I had a conversation with a friend in which I admitted concern with some of the strategies we were using to discredit and block nominees. I had no doubt of the damage that some of Bush's judicial nominees might do; I would support the filibuster of some of these judges, if only to signal to the White House the need to moderate its next selections. But elections ultimately meant something, I told my friend. Instead of relying on Senate procedures, there was one way to ensure that judges on the bench reflected our values, and that was to win at the polls.

My friend shook her head vehemently. "Do you really think that if the situations were reversed, Republicans would have any qualms about using the filibuster?" she asked.

I didn't. And yet I doubted that our use of the filibuster would dispel the image of Democrats always being on the defensive—a perception that we used the courts and lawyers and procedural tricks to avoid having to win over popular opinion. The perception wasn't entirely fair: Republicans no less than Democrats often asked the courts to overturn democratic decisions (like campaign finance laws) that they didn't like. Still, I wondered if, in our reliance on the courts to vindicate not only our rights but also our values, progressives had lost too much faith in democracy.

Just as conservatives appeared to have lost any sense that democracy must be more than what the majority insists upon. I thought back to an afternoon several years earlier, when as a member of the Illinois legislature I had argued for an amendment to include a mother's health exception in a Republican bill to ban partial-birth abortion. The amendment failed on a party line vote, and afterward, I stepped out into the hallway with one of my Republican colleagues. Without the amendment, I said, the law would be struck down by the courts as unconstitutional. He turned to me and said it didn't matter what amendment was attached—judges would do whatever they wanted to do anyway.

"It's all politics," he had said, turning to leave. "And right now we've got the votes."

Do any of these fights matter? For many of us, arguments over Senate procedure, separation of powers, judicial nominations, and rules of constitutional interpretation seem pretty esoteric, distant from our everyday concerns—just one more example of partisan jousting.

In fact, they do matter. Not only because the procedural rules of our government help define the results—on everything from whether the government can regulate polluters to whether government can tap your phone—but because they define our democracy just as much as elections do. Our system of self-governance is an intricate affair; it is through that system, and by respecting that system, that we give shape to our values and shared commitments.

Of course, I'm biased. For ten years before coming to Washington, I taught constitutional law at the University of Chicago. I loved the law school classroom: the stripped-down nature of it, the high-wire act of standing in front of a room at the beginning of each class with just blackboard and chalk, the students taking measure of me, some intent or apprehensive, others demonstrative in their boredom, the tension broken by my first question—

"What's this case about?"—and the hands tentatively rising, the initial responses and me pushing back against whatever arguments surfaced, until slowly the bare words were peeled back and what had appeared dry and lifeless just a few minutes before suddenly came alive, and my students' eyes stirred, the text becoming for them a part not just of the past but of their present and their future.

Sometimes I imagined my work to be not so different from the work of the theology professors who taught across campus—for, as I suspect was true for those teaching Scripture, I found that my students often felt they knew the Constitution without having really read it. They were accustomed to plucking out phrases that they'd heard and using them to bolster their immediate arguments, or ignoring passages that seemed to contradict their views.

But what I appreciated most about teaching constitutional law, what I wanted my students to appreciate, was just how accessible the relevant documents remain after two centuries. My students may have used me as a guide, but they needed no intermediary, for unlike the books of Timothy or Luke, the founding documents—the Declaration of Independence, the Federalist Papers, and the Constitution—present themselves as the product of men. We have a record of the Founders' intentions, I would tell my students, their arguments and their palace intrigues. If we can't always divine what was in their hearts, we can at least cut through the mist of time and have some sense of the core ideals that motivated their work.

So how should we understand our Constitution, and what does it say about the current controversies surrounding the courts? To begin with, a careful reading of our founding documents reminds us just how much all of our attitudes have been shaped by them. Take the idea of inalienable rights. More than two hundred years after the Declaration of Independence was written and the Bill of Rights was ratified, we continue to argue about the meaning of a

"reasonable" search, or whether the Second Amendment prohibits all gun regulation, or whether the desecration of the flag
should be considered speech. We debate whether such basic
common-law rights as the right to marry or the right to maintain
our bodily integrity are implicitly, if not explicitly, recognized by
the Constitution, and whether these rights encompass personal
decisions involving abortion, or end-of-life care, or homosexual
partnerships.

And yet for all our disagreements we would be hard pressed
to find a conservative or liberal in America today, whether Republican or Democrat, academic or layman, who doesn't subscribe to the basic set of individual liberties identified by the
Founders and enshrined in our Constitution and our common
law: the right to speak our minds; the right to worship how and
if we wish; the right to peaceably assemble to petition our government; the right to own, buy, and sell property and not have it
taken without fair compensation; the right to be free from unreasonable searches and seizures; the right not to be detained by
the state without due process; the right to a fair and speedy trial;
and the right to make our own determinations, with minimal re-
striction, regarding family life and the way we raise our children.

We consider these rights to be universal, a codification of liberty's meaning, constraining all levels of government and ap-
plicable to all people within the boundaries of our political
community. Moreover, we recognize that the very idea of these
universal rights presupposes the equal worth of every individual.
In that sense, wherever we lie on the political spectrum, we all
subscribe to the Founders' teachings.

We also understand that a declaration is not a government;
a creed is not enough. The Founders recognized that there were
seeds of anarchy in the idea of individual freedom, an intoxicat-
ing danger in the idea of equality, for if everybody is truly free,
without the constraints of birth or rank or an inherited social
order—if my notion of faith is no better or worse than yours,

and my notions of truth and goodness and beauty are as true and good and beautiful as yours—then how can we ever hope to form a society that coheres? Enlightenment thinkers like Hobbes and Locke suggested that free men would form governments as a bargain to ensure that one man's freedom did not become another man's tyranny; that they would sacrifice individual license to better preserve their liberty. And building on this concept, political theorists writing before the American Revolution concluded that only a democracy could fulfill the need for both freedom and order—a form of government in which those who are governed grant their consent, and the laws constraining liberty are uniform, predictable, and transparent, applying equally to the rulers and the ruled.

The Founders were steeped in these theories, and yet they were faced with a discouraging fact: In the history of the world to that point, there were scant examples of functioning democracies, and none that were larger than the city-states of ancient Greece. With thirteen far-flung states and a diverse population of three or four million, an Athenian model of democracy was out of the question, the direct democracy of the New England town meeting unmanageable. A republican form of government, in which the people elected representatives, seemed more promising, but even the most optimistic republicans had assumed that such a system could work only for a geographically compact and homogeneous political community—a community in which a common culture, a common faith, and a well-developed set of civic virtues on the part of each and every citizen limited contention and strife.

The solution that the Founders arrived at, after contentious debate and multiple drafts, proved to be their novel contribution to the world. The outlines of Madison's constitutional architecture are so familiar that even schoolchildren can recite them: not only rule of law and representative government, not just a bill of rights, but also the separation of the national government into three coequal branches, a bicameral Congress, and a concept of federalism that preserved authority in state governments, all of it designed to diffuse power, check factions, balance interests, and prevent tyranny by either the few or the many. Moreover, our history has vindicated one of the Founders' central insights: that republican self-government could actually work better in a large and diverse society, where, in Hamilton's words, the "jarring of parties" and differences of opinion could "promote deliberation and circumspection." As with our understanding of the Declaration, we debate the details of constitutional construction; we may object to Congress's abuse of expanded commerce clause powers to the detriment of the states, or to the erosion of Congress's power to declare war. But we are confident in the fundamental soundness of the Founders' blueprints and the democratic house that resulted. Conservative or liberal, we are all constitutionalists.

So if we all believe in individual liberty and we all believe in these rules of democracy, what is the modern argument between conservatives and liberals really about? If we're honest with ourselves, we'll admit that much of the time we are arguing about results—the actual decisions that the courts and the legislature make about the profound and difficult issues that help shape our lives. Should we let teachers lead our children in prayer and leave open the possibility that the minority faiths of some children are diminished? Or do we forbid such prayer and force parents of faith to hand over their children to a secular world eight hours a day? Is a university being fair by taking the history of racial discrimination and exclusion into account when filling a limited number of slots in its medical school? Or does fairness demand that universities treat every applicant in a color-blind fashion? More often than not, if a particular procedural rule—the right to filibuster, say, or the Supreme Court's approach to constitutional interpretation—helps us win the argument and yields the outcome we want, then for that moment at least we think it's a pretty good rule. If it doesn't help us win, then we tend not to like it so much.

In that sense, my colleague in the Illinois legislature was right when he said that today's constitutional arguments can't be separated from politics. But there's more than just outcomes at stake in our current debates about the Constitution and the proper role of the courts. We're also arguing about how to argue—the means, in a big, crowded, noisy democracy, of settling our disputes peacefully. We want to get our way, but most of us also recognize the need for consistency, predictability, and coherence. We want the rules governing our democracy to be fair.

And so, when we get in a tussle about abortion or flag burning, we appeal to a higher authority—the Founding Fathers and the Constitution's ratifiers—to give us more direction. Some, like Justice Scalia, conclude that the original understanding must be followed and that if we strictly obey this rule, then democracy is respected.

Others, like Justice Breyer, don't dispute that the original meaning of constitutional provisions matters. But they insist that sometimes the original understanding can take you only so far— that on the truly hard cases, the truly big arguments, we have to take context, history, and the practical outcomes of a decision into account. According to this view, the Founding Fathers and original ratifiers have told us *how* to think but are no longer around to tell us *what* to think. We are on our own, and have only our own reason and our judgment to rely on.

Who's right? I'm not unsympathetic to Justice Scalia's position; after all, in many cases the language of the Constitution is perfectly clear and can be strictly applied. We don't have to interpret how often elections are held, for example, or how old a president must be, and whenever possible judges should hew as closely as possible to the clear meaning of the text.

Moreover, I understand the strict constructionists' reverence for the Founders; indeed, I've often wondered whether the Founders themselves recognized at the time the scope of their accomplishment. They didn't simply design the Constitution in the wake of revolution; they wrote the Federalist Papers to support it, shepherded the document through ratification, and amended it with the Bill of Rights—all in the span of a few short years. As we read these documents, they seem so incredibly right that it's easy to believe they are the result of natural law if not divine inspiration. So I appreciate the temptation on the part of Justice Scalia and others to assume our democracy should be treated as fixed and unwavering; the fundamentalist faith that if the original understanding of the Constitution is followed without question or deviation, and if we remain true to the rules that the Founders set forth, as they intended, then we will be rewarded and all good will flow.

Ultimately, though, I have to side with Justice Breyer's view of the Constitution—that it is not a static but rather a living document, and must be read in the context of an ever-changing world.

How could it be otherwise? The constitutional text provides us with the general principle that we aren't subject to unreasonable searches by the government. It can't tell us the Founders' specific views on the reasonableness of an NSA computer data-mining operation. The constitutional text tells us that freedom of speech must be protected, but it doesn't tell us what such freedom means in the context of the Internet.

Moreover, while much of the Constitution's language is clear and can be strictly applied, our understanding of many of its most important provisions—like the due process clause and the equal protection clause—has evolved greatly over time. The original understanding of the Fourteenth Amendment, for example, would certainly allow sex discrimination and might even allow racial segregation—an understanding of equality to which few of us would want to return.

Finally, anyone looking to resolve our modern constitutional dispute through strict construction has one more problem: The Founders and ratifiers themselves disagreed profoundly, vehe-

mently, on the meaning of their masterpiece. Before the ink on
the constitutional parchment was dry, arguments had erupted,
not just about minor provisions but about first principles, not
just between peripheral figures but within the Revolution's very
core. They argued about how much power the national government should have—to regulate the economy, to supersede state
laws, to form a standing army, or to assume debt. They argued
about the president's role in establishing treaties with foreign
powers, and about the Supreme Court's role in determining the
law. They argued about the meaning of such basic rights as freedom of speech and freedom of assembly, and on several occa-
sions, when the fragile state seemed threatened, they were not
averse to ignoring those rights altogether. Given what we know
of this scrum, with all its shifting alliances and occasionally
underhanded tactics, it is unrealistic to believe that a judge, two
hundred years later, can somehow discern the original intent of
the Founders or ratifiers.

Some historians and legal theorists take the argument against
strict construction one step further. They conclude that the Constitution itself was largely a happy accident, a document cobbled
together not as the result of principle but as the result of power
and passion; that we can never hope to discern the Founders'
"original intentions" since the intentions of Jefferson were never
those of Hamilton, and those of Hamilton differed greatly from
those of Adams; that because the "rules" of the Constitution
were contingent on time and place and the ambitions of the men
who drafted them, our interpretation of the rules will necessarily
reflect the same contingency, the same raw competition, the same
imperatives—cloaked in high-minded phrasing—of those factions that ultimately prevail. And just as I recognize the comfort
offered by the strict constructionist, so I see a certain appeal to
this shattering of myth, to the temptation to believe that the constitutional text doesn't constrain us much at all, so that we are
free to assert our own values unencumbered by fidelity to the

stodgy traditions of a distant past. It's the freedom of the relativist, the rule breaker, the teenager who has discovered his parents are imperfect and has learned to play one off of the other—the freedom of the apostate.

And yet, ultimately, such apostasy leaves me unsatisfied as well. Maybe I am too steeped in the myth of the founding to reject it entirely. Maybe like those who reject Darwin in favor of intelligent design, I prefer to assume that someone's at the wheel. In the end, the question I keep asking myself is why, if the Constitution is only about power and not about principle, if all we are doing is just making it up as we go along, has our own republic not only survived but served as the rough model for so many of the successful societies on earth?

The answer I settle on—which is by no means original to me—requires a shift in metaphors, one that sees our democracy not as a house to be built, but as a conversation to be had. According to this conception, the genius of Madison's design is not that it provides us a fixed blueprint for action, the way a draftsman plots a building's construction. It provides us with a framework and with rules, but fidelity to these rules will not guarantee a just society or assure agreement on what's right. It won't tell us whether abortion is good or bad, a decision for a woman to make or a decision for a legislature. Nor will it tell us whether school prayer is better than no prayer at all.

What the framework of our Constitution can do is organize the way by which we argue about our future. All of its elaborate machinery—its separation of powers and checks and balances and federalist principles and Bill of Rights—are designed to force us into a conversation, a "deliberative democracy" in which all citizens are required to engage in a process of testing their ideas against an external reality, persuading others of their point of view, and building shifting alliances of consent. Because power in our government is so diffuse, the process of making law in America compels us to entertain the possibility that we are not always right and to sometimes change our minds; it challenges us to examine our motives and our interests constantly, and suggests that both our individual and collective judgments are at once legitimate and highly fallible.

The historical record supports such a view. After all, if there was one impulse shared by all the Founders, it was a rejection of all forms of absolute authority, whether the king, the theocrat, the general, the oligarch, the dictator, the majority, or anyone else who claims to make choices for us. George Washington declined Caesar's crown because of this impulse, and stepped down after two terms. Hamilton's plans for leading a New Army foundered and Adams's reputation after the Alien and Sedition Acts suffered for failing to abide by this impulse. It was Jefferson, not some liberal judge in the sixties, who called for a wall between church and state—and if we have declined to heed Jefferson's advice to engage in a revolution every two or three generations, it's only because the Constitution itself proved a sufficient defense against tyranny.

It's not just absolute power that the Founders sought to prevent. Implicit in its structure, in the very idea of ordered liberty, was a rejection of absolute truth, the infallibility of any idea or ideology or theology or "ism," any tyrannical consistency that might lock future generations into a single, unalterable course, or drive both majorities and minorities into the cruelties of the Inquisition, the pogrom, the gulag, or the jihad. The Founders may have trusted in God, but true to the Enlightenment spirit, they also trusted in the minds and senses that God had given them. They were suspicious of abstraction and liked asking questions, which is why at every turn in our early history theory yielded to fact and necessity. Jefferson helped consolidate the power of the national government even as he claimed to deplore and reject such power. Adams's ideal of a politics grounded solely in the public interest—a politics without politics—was proven obsolete the moment Washington stepped down from office. It may be the vision of the Founders that inspires us, but it was their realism, their practicality and flexibility and curiosity, that ensured the Union's survival.

I confess that there is a fundamental humility to this reading of the Constitution and our democratic process. It seems to champion compromise, modesty, and muddling through; to justify logrolling, deal-making, self-interest, pork barrels, paralysis, and inefficiency—all the sausage-making that no one wants to see and that editorialists throughout our history have often labeled as corrupt. And yet I think we make a mistake in assuming that democratic deliberation requires abandonment of our highest ideals, or of a commitment to the common good. After all, the Constitution ensures our free speech not just so that we can shout at one another as loud as we please, deaf to what others might have to say (although we have that right). It also offers us the possibility of a genuine marketplace of ideas, one in which the "jarring of parties" works on behalf of "deliberation and circumspection"; a marketplace in which, through debate and competition, we can expand our perspective, change our minds, and eventually arrive not merely at agreements but at sound and fair agreements.

The Constitution's system of checks and balances, separation of powers, and federalism may often lead to groups with fixed interests angling and sparring for narrow advantage, but it doesn't have to. Such diffusion of power may also force groups to take other interests into account and, indeed, may even alter over time how those groups think and feel about their own interests.

The rejection of absolutism implicit in our constitutional structure may sometimes make our politics seem unprincipled. But for most of our history it has encouraged the very process of information gathering, analysis, and argument that allows us to make better, if not perfect, choices, not only about the means to our ends but also about the ends themselves. Whether we are for or against affirmative action, for or against prayer in schools, we must test out our ideals, vision, and values against the realities of a common life, so that over time they may be refined, discarded, or replaced by new ideals, sharper visions, deeper values. Indeed, it is that process, according to Madison, that brought about the Constitution itself, through a convention in which "no man felt himself obliged to retain his opinions any longer than he was satisfied of their propriety and truth, and was open to the force of argument."

IN SUM, the Constitution envisions a road map by which we marry passion to reason, the ideal of individual freedom to the demands of community. And the amazing thing is that it's worked. Through the early days of the Union, through depressions and world wars, through the multiple transformations of the economy and Western expansion and the arrival of millions of immigrants to our shores, our democracy has not only survived but has thrived. It has been tested, of course, during times of war and fear, and it will no doubt be tested again in the future.

But only once has the conversation broken down completely, and that was over the one subject the Founders refused to talk about.

The Declaration of Independence may have been, in the words of historian Joseph Ellis, "a transformative moment in world history, when all laws and human relationships dependent on coercion would be swept away forever." But that spirit of liberty didn't extend, in the minds of the Founders, to the slaves who worked their fields, made their beds, and nursed their children.

The Constitution's exquisite machinery would secure the rights of citizens, those deemed members of America's political community. But it provided no protection to those outside the constitutional circle—the Native American whose treaties proved worthless before the court of the conqueror, or the black man Dred Scott, who would walk into the Supreme Court a free man and leave a slave.

Democratic deliberation might have been sufficient to expand the franchise to white men without property and eventually women; reason, argument, and American pragmatism might have eased the economic growing pains of a great nation and helped lessen religious and class tensions that would plague other nations. But deliberation alone could not provide the slave his freedom or cleanse America of its original sin. In the end, it was the sword that would sever his chains.

What does this say about our democracy? There's a school of thought that sees the Founding Fathers only as hypocrites and the Constitution only as a betrayal of the grand ideals set forth by the Declaration of Independence; that agrees with early abolitionists that the Great Compromise between North and South was a pact with the Devil. Others, representing the safer, more conventional wisdom, will insist that all the constitutional compromise on slavery—the omission of abolitionist sentiments from the original draft of the Declaration, the Three-fifths Clause and the Fugitive Slave Clause and the Importation Clause, the self-imposed gag rule that the Twenty-fourth Congress would place on all debate regarding the issue of slavery, the very structure of federalism and the Senate—was a necessary, if unfortunate, requirement for the formation of the Union; that in their silence, the Founders only sought to postpone what they were certain would be slavery's ultimate demise; that this single lapse cannot detract from the genius of the Constitution, which permitted the space for abolitionists to rally and the debate to proceed, and provided the framework by which, after the Civil War had been fought, the Thirteenth, Fourteenth, and Fifteenth Amendments could be passed, and the Union finally perfected.

How can I, an American with the blood of Africa coursing through my veins, choose sides in such a dispute? I can't. I love America too much, am too invested in what this country has become, too committed to its institutions, its beauty, and even its ugliness, to focus entirely on the circumstances of its birth. But neither can I brush aside the magnitude of the injustice done, or erase the ghosts of generations past, or ignore the open wound, the aching spirit, that ails this country still.

The best I can do in the face of our history is remind myself that it has not always been the pragmatist, the voice of reason, or the force of compromise, that has created the conditions for liberty. The hard, cold facts remind me that it was unbending idealists like William Lloyd Garrison who first sounded the clarion call for justice; that it was slaves and former slaves, men like Denmark Vesey and Frederick Douglass and women like Harriet Tubman, who recognized power would concede nothing without a fight. It was the wild-eyed prophecies of John Brown, his willingness to spill blood and not just words on behalf of his visions, that helped force the issue of a nation half slave and half free. I'm reminded that deliberation and the constitutional order may sometimes be the luxury of the powerful, and that it has sometimes been the cranks, the zealots, the prophets, the agitators, and the unreasonable—in other words, the absolutists—that have fought for a new order. Knowing this, I can't summarily dismiss those possessed of similar certainty today—the antiabortion activist who pickets my town hall meeting, or the animal rights activist who raids a laboratory—no matter how deeply I disagree with their views. I am robbed even of the certainty of uncertainty— for sometimes absolute truths may well be absolute.

I'M LEFT THEN with Lincoln, who like no man before or since understood both the deliberative function of our democracy and the limits of such deliberation. We remember him for the firmness and depth of his convictions—his unyielding opposition to slavery and his determination that a house divided could not stand. But his presidency was guided by a practicality that would distress us today, a practicality that led him to test various bargains with the South in order to maintain the Union without war; to appoint and discard general after general, strategy after strategy, once war broke out; to stretch the Constitution to the breaking point in order to see the war through to a successful conclusion. I like to believe that for Lincoln, it was never a matter of abandoning conviction for the sake of expediency. Rather, it was a matter of maintaining within himself the balance between two contradictory ideas—that we must talk and reach for common understandings, precisely because all of us are imperfect and can never act with the certainty that God is on our side; and yet at times we must act nonetheless, as if we are certain, protected from error only by providence.

That self-awareness, that humility, led Lincoln to advance his principles through the framework of our democracy, through speeches and debate, through the reasoned arguments that might appeal to the better angels of our nature. It was this same humility that allowed him, once the conversation between North and South broke down and war became inevitable, to resist the temptation to demonize the fathers and sons who did battle on the other side, or to diminish the horror of war, no matter how just it might be. The blood of slaves reminds us that our pragmatism can sometimes be moral cowardice. Lincoln, and those buried at Gettysburg, remind us that we should pursue our own absolute truths only if we acknowledge that there may be a terrible price to pay.

SUCH LATE-NIGHT meditations proved unnecessary in my immediate decision about George W. Bush's nominees to the federal court of appeals. In the end, the crisis in the Senate was averted, or at least postponed: Seven Democratic senators agreed not to filibuster three of Bush's five controversial nominees, and pledged that in the future they would reserve the filibuster for more "extraordinary circumstances." In exchange, seven Republicans agreed to vote against a "nuclear option" that would permanently eliminate the filibuster—again, with the caveat that they could change their minds in the event of "extraordinary circumstances." What constituted "extraordinary circumstances" no one could say, and both Democratic and Republican activists, itching for a fight, complained bitterly at what they perceived to be their side's capitulation.

I declined to be a part of what would be called the Gang of Fourteen; given the profiles of some of the judges involved, it was hard to see what judicial nominee might be so much worse as to constitute an "extraordinary circumstance" worthy of filibuster. Still, I could not fault my colleagues for their efforts. The Democrats involved had made a practical decision—without the deal, the "nuclear option" would have likely gone through.

No one was more ecstatic with this turn of events than Senator Byrd. The day the deal was announced, he walked triumphantly down the halls of the Capitol with Republican John Warner of Virginia, the younger members of the Gang trailing behind the old lions. "We have kept the Republic!" Senator Byrd announced to a pack of reporters, and I smiled to myself, thinking back to the visit that the two of us had finally been able to arrange a few months earlier.

It was in Senator Byrd's hideaway on the first floor of the Capitol, tucked alongside a series of small, beautifully painted rooms where Senate committees once regularly met. His secretary had led me into his private office, which was filled with books and what looked to be aging manuscripts, the walls lined with old photographs and campaign memorabilia. Senator Byrd asked me if it would be all right if we took a few photographs together, and we shook hands and smiled for the photographer who was present. After the secretary and the photographer had left, we sat down in a pair of well-worn chairs. I inquired after his wife, who I had heard had taken a turn for the worse, and asked about some of the figures in the photos. Eventually I asked him what advice he would give me as a new member of the Senate.

"Learn the rules," he said. "Not just the rules, but the precedents as well." He pointed to a series of thick binders behind him, each one affixed with a handwritten label. "Not many people bother to learn them these days. Everything is so rushed, so many demands on a senator's time. But these rules unlock the power of the Senate. They're the keys to the kingdom."

We spoke about the Senate's past, the presidents he had known, the bills he had managed. He told me I would do well in the Senate but that I shouldn't be in too much of a rush—so many senators today became fixated on the White House, not understanding that in the constitutional design it was the Senate that was supreme, the heart and soul of the Republic.

"So few people read the Constitution today," Senator Byrd said, pulling out his copy from his breast pocket. "I've always said, this document and the Holy Bible, they've been all the guidance I need."

Before I left, he insisted that his secretary bring in a set of his Senate histories for me to have. As he slowly set the beautifully bound books on the table and searched for a pen, I told him how remarkable it was that he had found the time to write.

"Oh, I have been very fortunate," he said, nodding to himself. "Much to be thankful for. There's not much I wouldn't do over." Suddenly he paused and looked squarely into my eyes. "I only have one regret, you know. The foolishness of youth . . ."

We sat there for a moment, considering the gap of years and experience between us.

"We all have regrets, Senator," I said finally. "We just ask that in the end, God's grace shines upon us."

He studied my face for a moment, then nodded with the slightest of smiles and flipped open the cover of one of the books. "God's grace. Yes indeed. Let me sign these for you then," he said, and taking one hand to steady the other, he slowly scratched his name on the gift.

Chapter Four

Politics

ONE OF MY favorite tasks of being a senator is hosting town hall meetings. I held thirty-nine of them my first year in the Senate, all across Illinois, in tiny rural towns like Anna and prosperous suburbs like Naperville, in black churches on the South Side and a college in Rock Island. There's not a lot of fanfare involved. My staff will call up the local high school, library, or community college to see if they're willing to host the event. A week or so in advance, we advertise in the town newspaper, in church bulletins, and on the local radio station. On the day of the meeting I'll show up a half hour early to chat with town leaders and we'll discuss local issues, perhaps a road in need of repaving or plans for a new senior center. After taking a few photographs, we enter the hall where the crowd is waiting. I shake hands on my way to the stage, which is usually bare except for a podium, a microphone, a bottle of water, and an American flag posted in its stand. And then, for the next hour or so, I answer to the people who sent me to Washington.

Attendance varies at these meetings: We've had as few as fifty people turn out, as many as two thousand. But however many people show up, I am grateful to see them. They are a cross-section of the counties we visit: Republican and Democrat, old and young, fat and skinny, truck drivers, college professors, stay-at-home moms, veterans, schoolteachers, insurance agents, CPAs, secretaries, doctors, and social workers. They are generally polite and attentive, even when they disagree with me (or one another). They ask me about prescription drugs, the deficit, human rights in Myanmar, ethanol, bird flu, school funding, and the space program. Often they will surprise me: A young flaxen-haired woman in the middle of farm country will deliver a passionate plea for intervention in Darfur, or an elderly black gentleman in an inner-city neighborhood will quiz me on soil conservation.

And as I look out over the crowd, I somehow feel encouraged. In their bearing I see hard work. In the way they handle their children I see hope. My time with them is like a dip in a cool stream. I feel cleansed afterward, glad for the work I have chosen.

At the end of the meeting, people will usually come up to shake hands, take pictures, or nudge their child forward to ask for an autograph. They slip things into my hand—articles, business cards, handwritten notes, armed-services medallions, small religious objects, good-luck charms. And sometimes someone will grab my hand and tell me that they have great hopes for me, but that they are worried that Washington is going to change me and I will end up just like all the rest of the people in power.

Please stay who you are, they will say to me.

Please don't disappoint us.

It is an American tradition to attribute the problem with our politics to the quality of our politicians. At times this is expressed in very specific terms: The president is a moron, or Congressman So-and-So is a bum. Sometimes a broader indictment is issued, as in "They're all in the pockets of the special interests." Most voters conclude that everyone in Washington is "just playing politics," meaning that votes or positions are taken contrary to conscience, that they are based on campaign contributions or the polls or loyalty to party rather than on trying to do what is right. Often, the fiercest criticism is reserved for the politician from one's own ranks, the Democrat who "doesn't stand for anything" or the "Republican in Name Only." All of which leads to the conclusion that if we want anything to change in Washington, we'll need to throw the rascals out.

And yet year after year we keep the rascals right where they are, with the reelection rate for House members hovering at around 96 percent.

Political scientists can give you a number of reasons for this phenomenon. In today's interconnected world, it's difficult to penetrate the consciousness of a busy and distracted electorate. As a result, winning in politics mainly comes down to a simple matter of name recognition, which is why most incumbents spend inordinate amounts of their time between elections making sure their names are repeated over and over again, whether at ribbon cuttings or Fourth of July parades or on the Sunday morning talk show circuit. There's the well-known fund-raising advantage that incumbents enjoy, for interest groups—whether on the left or the right—tend to go with the odds when it comes to political contributions. And there's the role of political gerrymandering in insulating House members from significant challenge: These days, almost every congressional district is drawn by the ruling party with computer-driven precision to ensure that a clear majority of Democrats or Republicans reside within its borders. Indeed, it's not a stretch to say that most voters no longer choose their representatives; instead, representatives choose their voters.

Another factor comes into play, though, one that is rarely mentioned but that helps explain why polls consistently show voters hating Congress but liking their congressman. Hard as it may be to believe, most politicians are pretty likable folks.

Certainly I found this to be true of my Senate colleagues. One-on-one they made for wonderful company—I would be

hard-pressed to name better storytellers than Ted Kennedy or
Trent Lott, or sharper wits than Kent Conrad or Richard Shelby,
or warmer individuals than Debbie Stabenow or Mel Martinez.
As a rule they proved to be intelligent, thoughtful, and hardworking people, willing to devote long hours and attention to
the issues affecting their states. Yes, there were those who lived
up to the stereotype, those who talked interminably or bullied
their staffs; and the more time I spent on the Senate floor, the
more frequently I could identify in each senator the flaws that we
all suffer from to varying degrees—a bad temper here, a deep
stubbornness or unquenchable vanity there. For the most part,
though, the quotient of such attributes in the Senate seemed no
higher than would be found in any random slice of the general
population. Even when talking to those colleagues with whom I
most deeply disagreed, I was usually struck by their basic sincerity—their desire to get things right and leave the country better
and stronger; their desire to represent their constituents and their
values as faithfully as circumstances would allow.

So what happened to make these men and women appear as
the grim, uncompromising, insincere, and occasionally mean
characters that populate our nightly news? What was it about
the process that prevented reasonable, conscientious people from
doing the nation's business? The longer I served in Washington,
the more I saw friends studying my face for signs of a change,
probing me for a newfound pomposity, searching for hints of
argumentativeness or guardedness. I began examining myself in
the same way; I began to see certain characteristics that I held in
common with my new colleagues, and I wondered what might
prevent my own transformation into the stock politician of bad
TV movies.

ONE PLACE TO start my inquiry was to understand the nature of
ambition, for in this regard at least, senators are different. Few

people end up being United States senators by accident; at a minimum, it requires a certain megalomania, a belief that of all the gifted people in your state, you are somehow uniquely qualified to speak on their behalf; a belief sufficiently strong that you are willing to endure the sometimes uplifting, occasionally harrowing, but always slightly ridiculous process we call campaigns.

Moreover, ambition alone is not enough. Whatever the tangle of motives, both sacred and profane, that push us toward the goal of becoming a senator, those who succeed must exhibit an almost fanatical single-mindedness, often disregarding their health, relationships, mental balance, and dignity. After my primary campaign was over, I remember looking at my calendar and realizing that over a span of a year and a half, I had taken exactly seven days off. The rest of the time I had typically worked twelve to sixteen hours a day. This was not something I was particularly proud of. As Michelle pointed out to me several times a week during the campaign, it just wasn't normal.

Neither ambition nor single-mindedness fully accounts for the behavior of politicians, however. There is a companion emotion, perhaps more pervasive and certainly more destructive, an emotion that, after the giddiness of your official announcement as a candidate, rapidly locks you in its grip and doesn't release you until after Election Day. That emotion is fear. Not just fear of losing—although that is bad enough—but fear of total, complete humiliation.

I still burn, for example, with the thought of my one loss in politics, a drubbing in 2000 at the hands of incumbent Democratic Congressman Bobby Rush. It was a race in which everything that could go wrong did go wrong, in which my own mistakes were compounded by tragedy and farce. Two weeks after announcing my candidacy, with a few thousand dollars raised, I commissioned my first poll and discovered that Mr. Rush's name recognition stood at about 90 percent, while mine stood at 11 percent. His approval rating hovered around 70 percent—mine at 8.

In that way I learned one of the cardinal rules of modern politics: Do the poll before you announce.

Things went downhill from there. In October, on my way to a meeting to secure an endorsement from one of the few party officials who had not already committed to my opponent, I heard a news flash on the radio that Congressman Rush's adult son had been shot and killed by a pair of drug dealers outside his house. I was shocked and saddened for the congressman, and effectively suspended my campaign for a month.

Then, during the Christmas holidays, after having traveled to Hawaii for an abbreviated five-day trip to visit my grandmother and reacquaint myself with Michelle and then-eighteen-month-old Malia, the state legislature was called back into special session to vote on a piece of gun control legislation. With Malia sick and unable to fly, I missed the vote, and the bill failed. Two days later, I got off the red-eye at O'Hare Airport, a wailing baby in tow, Michelle not speaking to me, and was greeted by a front-page story in the *Chicago Tribune* indicating that the gun bill had fallen a few votes short, and that state senator and congressional candidate Obama "had decided to remain on vacation" in Hawaii. My campaign manager called, mentioning the potential ad the congressman might be running soon—palm trees, a man in a beach chair and straw hat sipping a mai tai, a slack key guitar being strummed softly in the background, the voice-over explaining, "While Chicago suffered the highest murder rate in its history, Barack Obama . . ."

I stopped him there, having gotten the idea.

And so, less than halfway into the campaign, I knew in my bones that I was going to lose. Each morning from that point forward I awoke with a vague sense of dread, realizing that I would have to spend the day smiling and shaking hands and pretending that everything was going according to plan. In the few weeks before the primary, my campaign recovered a bit: I did well in the sparsely covered debates, received some positive coverage for proposals on health care and education, and even received the *Tribune* endorsement. But it was too little too late. I arrived at my victory party to discover that the race had already been called and that I had lost by thirty-one points.

I'm not suggesting that politicians are unique in suffering such disappointments. It's that unlike most people, who have the luxury of licking their wounds privately, the politician's loss is on public display. There's the cheerful concession speech you have to make to a half-empty ballroom, the brave face you put on as you comfort staff and supporters, the thank-you calls to those who helped, and the awkward requests for further help in retiring debt. You perform these tasks as best you can, and yet no matter how much you tell yourself differently—no matter how convincingly you attribute the loss to bad timing or bad luck or lack of money—it's impossible not to feel at some level as if you have been personally repudiated by the entire community, that you don't quite have what it takes, and that everywhere you go the word "loser" is flashing through people's minds. They're the sorts of feelings that most people haven't experienced since high school, when the girl you'd been pining over dismissed you with a joke in front of her friends, or you missed a pair of free throws with the big game on the line—the kinds of feelings that most adults wisely organize their lives to avoid.

Imagine then the impact of these same emotions on the average big-time politician, who (unlike me) has rarely failed at anything in his life—who was the high school quarterback or the class valedictorian and whose father was a senator or admiral and who has been told since he was a child that he was destined for great things. I remember talking once to a corporate executive who had been a big supporter of Vice President Al Gore during the 2000 presidential race. We were in his suitably plush office, overlooking all of midtown Manhattan, and he began describing to me a meeting that had taken place six months or so after the election, when Gore was seeking investors for his then-fledgling television venture.

"It was strange," the executive told me. "Here he was, a former vice president, a man who just a few months earlier had been on the verge of being the most powerful man on the planet. During the campaign, I would take his calls any time of day, would rearrange my schedule whenever he wanted to meet. But suddenly, after the election, when he walked in, I couldn't help feeling that the meeting was a chore. I hate to admit it, because I really like the guy. But at some level he wasn't Al Gore, former vice president. He was just one of the hundred guys a day who are coming to me looking for money. It made me realize what a big steep cliff you guys are on."

A big steep cliff, the precipitous fall. Over the past five years, Al Gore has shown the satisfaction and influence that a life after politics can bring, and I suspect the executive is eagerly taking the former vice president's calls once again. Still, in the aftermath of his 2000 loss, I imagine Gore would have sensed the change in his friend. Sitting there, pitching his television idea, trying to make the best of a bad situation, he might have thought how ridiculous were the circumstances in which he found himself; how after a lifetime of work he could have lost it all because of a butterfly ballot that didn't align, while his friend the executive, sitting across from him with the condescending smile, could afford to come in second in his business year after year, maybe see his company's stock tumble or make an ill-considered investment, and yet still be considered successful, still enjoy the pride of accomplishment, the lavish compensation, the exercise of power. It wasn't fair, but that wouldn't change the facts for the former vice president. Like most men and women who followed the path of public life, Gore knew what he was getting himself into the moment he decided to run. In politics, there may be second acts, but there is no second place.

MOST OF THE other sins of politics are derivative of this larger sin—the need to win, but also the need not to lose. Certainly that's what the money chase is all about. There was a time, before campaign finance laws and snooping reporters, when money shaped politics through outright bribery; when a politician could treat his campaign fund as his personal bank account and accept fancy junkets; when big honoraria from those who sought influence were commonplace, and the shape of legislation went to the highest bidder. If recent news reports are accurate, these ranker forms of corruption have not gone away entirely; apparently there are still those in Washington who view politics as a means of getting rich, and who, while generally not dumb enough to accept bags of small bills, are perfectly prepared to take care of contributors and properly feather their beds until the time is finally ripe to jump into the lucrative practice of lobbying on behalf of those they once regulated.

More often, though, that's not the way money influences politics. Few lobbyists proffer an explicit quid pro quo to elected officials. They don't have to. Their influence comes simply from having more access to those officials than the average voter, having better information than the average voter, and having more staying power when it comes to promoting an obscure provision in the tax code that means billions for their clients and that nobody else cares about.

As for most politicians, money isn't about getting rich. In the Senate, at least, most members are already rich. It's about maintaining status and power; it's about scaring off challengers and fighting off the fear. Money can't guarantee victory—it can't buy passion, charisma, or the ability to tell a story. But without money, and the television ads that consume all the money, you are pretty much guaranteed to lose.

The amounts of money involved are breathtaking, particularly in big state races with multiple media markets. While in the state legislature, I never needed to spend more than $100,000 on a race; in fact, I developed a reputation for being something of a stick-in-the-mud when it came to fund-raising, coauthoring the first campaign finance legislation to pass in twenty-five years, refusing meals from lobbyists, rejecting checks from gaming and tobacco interests. When I decided to run for the U.S. Senate, my media consultant, David Axelrod, had to sit me down to explain the facts of life. Our campaign plan called for a bare-bones budget, a heavy reliance on grassroots support and "earned media"— that is, an ability to make our own news. Still, David informed me that one week of television advertising in the Chicago media market would cost approximately half a million dollars. Covering the rest of the state for a week would run about $250,000. Figuring four weeks of TV, and all the overhead and staff for a statewide campaign, the final budget for the primary would be around $5 million. Assuming I won the primary, I would then need to raise another $10 or $15 million for the general election.

I went home that night and in neat columns proceeded to write down all the people I knew who might give me a contribution. Next to their names, I wrote down the maximum amounts that I would feel comfortable asking them for.

My grand total came to $500,000.

Absent great personal wealth, there is basically one way of raising the kind of money involved in a U.S. Senate race. You have to ask rich people for it. In the first three months of my campaign, I would shut myself in a room with my fund-raising assistant and cold-call previous Democratic donors. It was not fun. Sometimes people would hang up on me. More often their secretary would take a message and I wouldn't get a return call, and I would call back two or three times until either I gave up or the person I was calling finally answered and gave me the courtesy of a person-to-person rejection. I started engaging in elaborate games of avoidance during call time—frequent bathroom breaks, extended coffee runs, suggestions to my policy staff that we fine-tune that education speech for the third or fourth time. At times during these sessions I thought of my grandfather, who in middle age had sold life insurance but wasn't very good at it. I recalled his anguish whenever he tried to schedule appointments with people who would rather have had a root canal than talk to an insurance agent, as well as the disapproving glances he received from my grandmother, who for most of their marriage made more money than he did.

More than ever, I understood how my grandfather must have felt.

At the end of three months, our campaign had raised just $250,000—well below the threshold of what it would take to be credible. To make matters worse, my race featured what many politicians consider their worst nightmare: a self-financing candidate with bottomless pockets. His name was Blair Hull, and he had sold his financial trading business to Goldman Sachs a few years earlier for $531 million. Undoubtedly he had a genuine, if undefined, desire to serve, and by all accounts he was a brilliant man. But on the campaign trail he was almost painfully shy, with the quirky, inward manner of someone who'd spent most of his life alone in front of a computer screen. I suspect that like many people, he figured that being a politician—unlike being a doctor or airline pilot or plumber—required no special expertise in anything useful, and that a businessman like himself could perform at least as well, and probably better, than any of the professional pols he saw on TV. In fact, Mr. Hull viewed his facility with numbers as an invaluable asset: At one point in the campaign, he divulged to a reporter a mathematical formula that he'd developed for winning campaigns, an algorithm that began

$$\text{Probability} = 1/(1 + \exp(-1 \times (-3.9659056 + (\text{General Election Weight} \times 1.92380219) \ldots$$

and ended several indecipherable factors later.

All of which made it easy to write off Mr. Hull as an opponent—until one morning in April or May, when I pulled out of
the circular driveway of my condo complex on the way to the office and was greeted by row upon row of large red, white, and
blue lawn signs marching up and down the block. BLAIR HULL
FOR U.S. SENATE, the signs read, and for the next five miles I
saw them on every street and along every major thoroughfare, in
every direction and in every nook and cranny, in barbershop
windows and posted on abandoned buildings, in front of bus
stops and behind grocery store counters—Hull signs everywhere,
dotting the landscape like daisies in spring.

There is a saying in Illinois politics that "signs don't vote,"
meaning that you can't judge a race by how many signs a candidate has. But nobody in Illinois had ever seen during the course
of an entire campaign the number of signs and billboards that
Mr. Hull had put up in a single day, or the frightening efficiency
with which his crews of paid workers could yank up everybody
else's yard signs and replace them with Hull signs in the span of
a single evening. We began to read about certain neighborhood
leaders in the black community who had suddenly decided that
Mr. Hull was a champion of the inner city, certain downstate
leaders who extolled Mr. Hull's support of the family farm. And
then the television ads hit, six months out and ubiquitous until
Election Day, on every station around the state around the
clock—Blair Hull with seniors, Blair Hull with children, Blair
Hull ready to take back Washington from the special interests.
By January 2004, Mr. Hull had moved into first place in the polls
and my supporters began swamping me with calls, insisting that
I had to do something, telling me I had to get on TV immediately
or all would be lost.

What could I do? I explained that unlike Mr. Hull I practically had a negative net worth. Assuming the best-case scenario,
our campaign would have enough money for exactly four weeks
of television ads, and given this fact it probably didn't make

sense for us to blow the entire campaign budget in August. Everybody just needed to be patient, I would tell supporters. Stay confident. Don't panic. Then I'd hang up the phone, look out the window, and happen to catch sight of the RV in which Hull tooled around the state, big as an ocean liner and reputedly just as well appointed, and I would wonder to myself if perhaps it was time to panic after all.

In many ways, I was luckier than most candidates in such circumstances. For whatever reason, at some point my campaign began to generate that mysterious, elusive quality of momentum, of buzz; it became fashionable among wealthy donors to promote my cause, and small donors around the state began sending checks through the Internet at a pace we had never anticipated. Ironically, my dark-horse status protected me from some of the more dangerous pitfalls of fund-raising: Most of the corporate PACs avoided me, and so I owed them nothing; the handful of PACs that did give, like the League of Conservation Voters, typically represented causes I believed in and had long fought for. Mr. Hull still ended up outspending me by a factor of six to one. But to his credit (although perhaps to his regret) he never ran a negative TV ad against me. My poll numbers stayed within shouting distance of his, and in the final weeks of the campaign, just as my own TV spots started running and my numbers began to surge, his campaign imploded when allegations surfaced that he'd had some ugly run-ins with an ex-wife.

So for me, at least, the lack of wealth or significant corporate support wasn't a barrier to victory. Still, I can't assume that the money chase didn't alter me in some ways. Certainly it eliminated any sense of shame I once had in asking strangers for large sums of money. By the end of the campaign, the banter and small talk that had once accompanied my solicitation calls were eliminated. I cut to the chase and tried not to take no for an answer.

But I worry that there was also another change at work. Increasingly I found myself spending time with people of means—

law firm partners and investment bankers, hedge fund managers and venture capitalists. As a rule, they were smart, interesting people, knowledgeable about public policy, liberal in their politics, expecting nothing more than a hearing of their opinions in exchange for their checks. But they reflected, almost uniformly, the perspectives of their class: the top 1 percent or so of the income scale that can afford to write a $2,000 check to a political candidate. They believed in the free market and an educational meritocracy; they found it hard to imagine that there might be any social ill that could not be cured by a high SAT score. They had no patience with protectionism, found unions troublesome, and were not particularly sympathetic to those whose lives were upended by the movements of global capital. Most were adamantly prochoice and antigun and were vaguely suspicious of deep religious sentiment.

And although my own worldview and theirs corresponded in many ways—I had gone to the same schools, after all, had read the same books, and worried about my kids in many of the same ways—I found myself avoiding certain topics during conversations with them, papering over possible differences, anticipating their expectations. On core issues I was candid; I had no problem telling well-heeled supporters that the tax cuts they'd received from George Bush should be reversed. Whenever I could, I would try to share with them some of the perspectives I was hearing from other portions of the electorate: the legitimate role of faith in politics, say, or the deep cultural meaning of guns in rural parts of the state.

Still, I know that as a consequence of my fund-raising I became more like the wealthy donors I met, in the very particular sense that I spent more and more of my time above the fray, outside the world of immediate hunger, disappointment, fear, irrationality, and frequent hardship of the other 99 percent of the population—that is, the people that I'd entered public life to serve. And in one fashion or another, I suspect this is true for every senator: The longer you are a senator, the narrower the scope of your interactions. You may fight it, with town hall meetings and listening tours and stops by the old neighborhood. But your schedule dictates that you move in a different orbit from most of the people you represent.

And perhaps as the next race approaches, a voice within tells you that you don't want to have to go through all the misery of raising all that money in small increments all over again. You realize that you no longer have the cachet you did as the upstart, the fresh face; you haven't changed Washington, and you've made a lot of people unhappy with difficult votes. The path of least resistance—of fund-raisers organized by the special interests, the corporate PACs, and the top lobbying shops—starts to look awfully tempting, and if the opinions of these insiders don't quite jibe with those you once held, you learn to rationalize the changes as a matter of realism, of compromise, of learning the ropes. The problems of ordinary people, the voices of the Rust Belt town or the dwindling heartland, become a distant echo rather than a palpable reality, abstractions to be managed rather than battles to be fought.

THERE ARE OTHER forces at work on a senator. As important as money is in campaigns, it's not just fund-raising that puts a candidate over the top. If you want to win in politics—if you don't want to lose—then organized people can be just as important as cash, particularly in the low-turnout primaries that, in the world of the gerrymandered political map and divided electorates, are often the most significant race a candidate faces. Few people these days have the time or inclination to volunteer on a political campaign, particularly since the day-to-day tasks of working on a campaign generally involve licking envelopes and knocking on doors, not drafting speeches and thinking big thoughts. And so, if you are a candidate in need of political workers or voter lists, you go where people are already organized. For Democrats, this means the unions, the environmental groups, and the prochoice groups. For Republicans, it means the religious right, local chambers of commerce, the NRA, and the antitax organizations.

I've never been entirely comfortable with the term "special interests," which lumps together ExxonMobil and bricklayers, the pharmaceutical lobby and the parents of special-ed kids. Most political scientists would probably disagree with me, but to my mind, there's a difference between a corporate lobby whose clout is based on money alone, and a group of like-minded individuals—whether they be textile workers, gun aficionados, veterans, or family farmers—coming together to promote their interests; between those who use their economic power to magnify their political influence far beyond what their numbers might justify, and those who are simply seeking to pool their votes to sway their representatives. The former subvert the very idea of democracy. The latter are its essence.

Still, the impact of interest groups on candidates for office is not always pretty. To maintain an active membership, keep the donations coming in, and be heard above the din, the groups that have an impact on politics aren't fashioned to promote the public interest. They aren't searching for the most thoughtful, well-qualified, or broad-minded candidate to support. Instead, they are focused on a narrow set of concerns—their pensions, their crop supports, their cause. Simply put, they have an ax to grind. And they want you, the elected official, to help them grind it.

During my own primary campaign, for example, I must have filled out at least fifty questionnaires. None of them were subtle. Typically they would contain a list of ten or twelve questions, phrased along the following lines: "If elected, will you solemnly pledge to repeal the Scrooge Law, which has resulted in widows and orphans being kicked to the curb?"

Time dictated that I fill out only those questionnaires sent by organizations that might actually endorse me (given my voting record, the NRA and National Right to Life, for example, did not make the cut), so I could usually answer "yes" to most questions without any major discomfort. But every so often I would come across a question that gave me pause. I might agree with a union on the need to enforce labor and environmental standards in our trade laws, but did I believe that NAFTA should be repealed? I might agree that universal health care should be one of the nation's top priorities, but did it follow that a constitutional amendment was the best way to achieve that goal? I found myself hedging on such questions, writing in the margins, explaining the difficult policy choices involved. My staff would shake their heads. Get one answer wrong, they explained, and the endorsement, the workers, and the mailing list would all go to the other guy. Get them all right, I thought, and you have just locked yourself into the pattern of reflexive, partisan jousting that you have promised to help end.

Say one thing during the campaign and do another thing once in office, and you're a typical, two-faced politician.

I lost some endorsements by not giving the right answer. A couple of times, a group surprised us and gave me their endorsement despite a wrong answer.

And then sometimes it didn't matter how you filled out your questionnaire. In addition to Mr. Hull, my most formidable opponent in the Democratic primary for U.S. Senate was the Illinois state comptroller, Dan Hynes, a fine man and able public servant whose father, Tom Hynes, happened to be a former state senate president, Cook County assessor, ward committeeman, Democratic National Committee member, and one of the most well-connected political figures in the state. Before even entering the race, Dan had already sewn up the support of 85 of the 102 Democratic county chairmen in the state, the majority of my colleagues in the state legislature, and Mike Madigan, who served as both Speaker of the House and chairman of the Illinois Democratic Party. Scrolling down the list of endorsements on

Dan's website was like watching the credits at the end of a movie—you left before it was finished.

Despite all this, I held out hope for a few endorsements of my own, particularly those of organized labor. For seven years I had been their ally in the state legislature, sponsoring many of their bills and making their case on the floor. I knew that traditionally the AFL-CIO endorsed those who had a strong record of voting on their behalf. But as the campaign got rolling, odd things began to happen. The Teamsters held their endorsement session in Chicago on a day when I had to be in Springfield for a vote; they refused to reschedule, and Mr. Hynes got their endorsement without them ever talking to me. Visiting a labor reception during the Illinois State Fair, we were told that no campaign signs would be allowed; when my staff and I arrived, we discovered the room plastered with Hynes posters. On the evening of the AFL-CIO endorsement session, I noticed a number of my labor friends averting their eyes as I walked through the room. An older guy who headed up one of the state's bigger locals walked up and patted me on the back.

"It's nothing personal, Barack," he said with a rueful smile. "You know, Tom Hynes and me go back fifty years. Grew up in the same neighborhood. Belonged to the same parish. Hell, I watched Danny grow up."

I told him I understood.

"Maybe you could run for Danny's spot once he goes to the Senate. Whaddya think? You'd make a heck of a comptroller."

I went over to my staff to tell them we would not be getting the AFL-CIO endorsement.

Again things worked out. The leaders of several of the largest service workers unions—the Illinois Federation of Teachers, SEIU, AFSCME, and UNITE HERE, representing textile, hotel, and foodservice workers—broke ranks and chose to endorse me over Hynes, support that proved critical in giving my campaign some semblance of weight. It was a risky move on their part; had I lost, those unions might have paid a price in access, in support, in credibility with their members.

So I owe those unions. When their leaders call, I do my best to call them back right away. I don't consider this corrupting in any way; I don't mind feeling obligated toward home health-care workers who clean bedpans every day for little more than the minimum wage, or toward teachers in some of the toughest schools in the country, many of whom have to dip into their own pockets at the beginning of every school year to buy crayons and books for their students. I got into politics to fight for these folks, and I'm glad a union is around to remind me of their struggles.

But I also understand that there will be times when these obligations collide with other obligations—the obligation to inner-city children who are unable to read, say, or the obligation to children not yet born whom we are saddling with debt. Already there have been some strains—I've proposed experimenting with merit pay for teachers, for example, and have called for raising fuel-efficiency standards despite opposition from my friends at the United Auto Workers. I like to tell myself that I will continue to weigh the issues on the merits—just as I hope my Republican counterpart will weigh the no-new-tax pledge or opposition to stem cell research that he made before the election in light of what's best for the country as a whole, regardless of what his supporters demand. I hope that I can always go to my union friends and explain why my position makes sense, how it's consistent with both my values and their long-term interests.

But I suspect that the union leaders won't always see it that way. There may be times when they will see it as betrayal. They may alert their members that I have sold them out. I may get angry mail and angry phone calls. They may not endorse me the next time around.

And perhaps, if that happens to you enough times, and you almost lose a race because a critical constituency is mad at you, or you find yourself fending off a primary challenger who's call-

ing you a traitor, you start to lose your stomach for confrontation. You ask yourself, just what does good conscience dictate
exactly: that you avoid capture by "special interests" or that you
avoid dumping on your friends? The answer is not obvious. So
you start voting as you would answer a questionnaire. You don't
ponder your positions too deeply. You check the yes box up and
down the line.

POLITICIANS HELD CAPTIVE by their big-money contributors
or succumbing to interest-group pressure—this is a staple of
modern political reporting, the story line that weaves its way
into just about every analysis of what's wrong with our democracy. But for the politician who is worried about keeping his seat,
there is a third force that pushes and pulls at him, that shapes the
nature of political debate and defines the scope of what he feels
he can and can't do, the positions he can and can't take. Forty
or fifty years ago, that force would have been the party appara-
tus: the big-city bosses, the political fixers, the power brokers in
Washington who could make or break a career with a phone
call. Today, that force is the media.

A disclaimer here: For a three-year span, from the time that I
announced my candidacy for the Senate to the end of my first
year as a senator, I was the beneficiary of unusually—and at
times undeservedly—positive press coverage. No doubt some of
this had to do with my status as an underdog in my Senate primary, as well as my novelty as a black candidate with an exotic
background. Maybe it also had something to do with my style of
communicating, which can be rambling, hesitant, and overly ver-
bose (both my staff and Michelle often remind me of this), but
which perhaps finds sympathy in the literary class.

Moreover, even when I've been at the receiving end of negative stories, the political reporters I've dealt with have generally
been straight shooters. They've taped our conversations, tried to

provide the context for my statements, and called me to get a response whenever I've been criticized.

So personally, at least, I have no cause for complaint. That doesn't mean, though, that I can afford to ignore the press. Precisely because I've watched the press cast me in a light that can be hard to live up to, I am mindful of how rapidly that process can work in reverse.

Simple math tells the tale. In the thirty-nine town hall meetings I held during my first year in office, turnout at each meeting averaged four to five hundred people, which means that I was able to meet with maybe fifteen to twenty thousand people. Should I sustain this pace for the remainder of my term, I will have had direct, personal contact with maybe ninety-five to one hundred thousand of my constituents by the time Election Day rolls around.

In contrast, a three-minute story on the lowest-rated local news broadcast in the Chicago media market may reach two hundred thousand people. In other words, I—like every politician at the federal level—am almost entirely dependent on the media to reach my constituents. It is the filter through which my votes are interpreted, my statements analyzed, my beliefs examined. For the broad public at least, I am who the media says I am. I say what they say I say. I become who they say I've become.

The media's influence on our politics comes in many forms. What gets the most attention these days is the growth of an unabashedly partisan press: talk radio, Fox News, newspaper editorialists, the cable talk-show circuit, and most recently the bloggers, all of them trading insults, accusations, gossip, and innuendo twenty-four hours a day, seven days a week. As others have noted, this style of opinion journalism isn't really new; in some ways, it marks a return to the dominant tradition of American journalism, an approach to the news that was nurtured by publishers like William Randolph Hearst and Colonel McCormick before a more antiseptic notion of objective journalism emerged after World War II.

Still, it's hard to deny that all the sound and fury, magnified through television and the Internet, coarsens the political culture. It makes tempers flare, helps breed distrust. And whether we politicians like to admit it or not, the constant vitriol can wear on the spirit. Oddly enough, the cruder broadsides you don't worry about too much; if Rush Limbaugh's listeners enjoy hearing him call me "Osama Obama," my attitude is, let them have their fun. It's the more sophisticated practitioners who can sting you, in part because they have more credibility with the general public, in part because of the skill with which they can pounce on your words and make you seem like a jerk.

In April 2005, for example, I appeared on the program to dedicate the new Lincoln Presidential Library in Springfield. It was a five-minute speech in which I suggested that Abraham Lincoln's humanity, his imperfections, were the qualities that made him so compelling. "In [Lincoln's] rise from poverty," I said in one part of my remarks, "his self-study and ultimate mastery of language and of law, in his capacity to overcome personal loss and remain determined in the face of repeated defeat—in all of this, we see a fundamental element of the American character, a belief that we can constantly remake ourselves to fit our larger dreams."

A few months later, *Time* magazine asked if I would be interested in writing an essay for a special issue on Lincoln. I didn't have time to write something new, so I asked the magazine's editors if my speech would be acceptable. They said it was, but asked if I could personalize it a bit more—say something about Lincoln's impact on my life. In between meetings I dashed off a few changes. One of those changes was to the passage quoted above, which now read, "In Lincoln's rise from poverty, his ultimate mastery of language and law, his capacity to overcome personal loss and remain determined in the face of repeated defeat—in all this, he reminded me not just of my own struggles."

No sooner had the essay appeared than Peggy Noonan, former Reagan speechwriter and columnist for the *Wall Street Journal,* weighed in. Under the title "Conceit of Government," she wrote: "This week comes the previously careful Sen. Barack Obama, flapping his wings in Time Magazine and explaining that he's a lot like Abraham Lincoln, only sort of better." She went on to say, "There is nothing wrong with Barack Obama's resume, but it is a log-cabin-free zone. So far it is also a greatness-free zone. If he keeps talking about himself like this it always will be."

Ouch!

It's hard to tell, of course, whether Ms. Noonan seriously thought I was comparing myself to Lincoln, or whether she just took pleasure in filleting me so elegantly. As potshots from the press go, it was very mild—and not entirely undeserved.

Still, I was reminded of what my veteran colleagues already knew—that every statement I made would be subject to scrutiny, dissected by every manner of pundit, interpreted in ways over which I had no control, and combed through for a potential error, misstatement, omission, or contradiction that might be filed away by the opposition party and appear in an unpleasant TV ad somewhere down the road. In an environment in which a single ill-considered remark can generate more bad publicity than years of ill-considered policies, it should have come as no surprise to me that on Capitol Hill jokes got screened, irony became suspect, spontaneity was frowned upon, and passion was considered downright dangerous. I started to wonder how long it took for a politician to internalize all this; how long before the committee of scribes and editors and censors took residence in your head; how long before even the "candid" moments became scripted, so that you choked up or expressed outrage only on cue.

How long before you started sounding like a politician?

There was another lesson to be learned: As soon as Ms. Noonan's column hit, it went racing across the Internet, appearing on every right-wing website as proof of what an arrogant, shallow boob I was (just the quote Ms. Noonan selected, and not the essay itself, generally made an appearance on these sites). In that sense, the episode hinted at a more subtle and corrosive aspect of modern media—how a particular narrative, repeated over and over again and hurled through cyberspace at the speed of light, eventually becomes a hard particle of reality; how political caricatures and nuggets of conventional wisdom lodge themselves in our brain without us ever taking the time to examine them.

For example, it's hard to find any mention of Democrats these days that doesn't suggest we are "weak" and "don't stand for anything." Republicans, on the other hand, are "strong" (if a little mean), and Bush is "decisive" no matter how often he changes his mind. A vote or speech by Hillary Clinton that runs against type is immediately labeled calculating; the same move by John McCain burnishes his maverick credentials. "By law," according to one caustic observer, my name in any article must be preceded by the words "rising star"—although Noonan's piece lays the groundwork for a different if equally familiar story line: the cautionary tale of a young man who comes to Washington, loses his head with all the publicity, and ultimately becomes either calculating or partisan (unless he can somehow manage to move decisively into the maverick camp).

Of course, the PR machinery of politicians and their parties helps feed these narratives, and over the last few election cycles, at least, Republicans have been far better at such "messaging" than the Democrats have been (a cliché that, unfortunately for us Democrats, really is true). The spin works, though, precisely because the media itself are hospitable to spin. Every reporter in Washington is working under pressures imposed by editors and producers, who in turn are answering to publishers or network executives, who in turn are poring over last week's ratings or last

year's circulation figures and trying to survive the growing preference for PlayStation and reality TV. To make the deadline, to
maintain market share and feed the cable news beast, reporters
start to move in packs, working off the same news releases, the
same set pieces, the same stock figures. Meanwhile, for busy and
therefore casual news consumers, a well-worn narrative is not
entirely unwelcome. It makes few demands on our thought or
time; it's quick and easy to digest. Accepting spin is easier on
everybody.

This element of convenience also helps explain why, even
among the most scrupulous reporters, objectivity often means
publishing the talking points of different sides of a debate without any perspective on which side might actually be right. A typical story might begin: "The White House today reported that
despite the latest round of tax cuts, the deficit is projected to be
cut in half by the year 2010." This lead will then be followed by
a quote from a liberal analyst attacking the White House numbers
and a conservative analyst defending the White House numbers. Is
one analyst more credible than the other? Is there an independent
analyst somewhere who might walk us through the numbers?
Who knows? Rarely does the reporter have time for such details;
the story is not really about the merits of the tax cut or the dangers
of the deficit but rather about the dispute between the parties.
After a few paragraphs, the reader can conclude that Republicans and Democrats are just bickering again and turn to the
sports page, where the story line is less predictable and the box
score tells you who won.

Indeed, part of what makes the juxtaposition of competing
press releases so alluring to reporters is that it feeds that old jour-
nalistic standby—personal conflict. It's hard to deny that political civility has declined in the past decade, and that the parties
differ sharply on major policy issues. But at least some of the decline in civility arises from the fact that, from the press's perspective, civility is boring. Your quote doesn't run if you say, "I see

the other guy's point of view" or "The issue's really complicated." Go on the attack, though, and you can barely fight off the cameras. Often, reporters will go out of their way to stir up the pot, asking questions in such a way as to provoke an inflammatory response. One TV reporter I know back in Chicago was so notorious for feeding you the quote he wanted that his interviews felt like a Laurel and Hardy routine.

"Do you feel betrayed by the Governor's decision yesterday?" he would ask me.

"No. I've talked to the Governor, and I'm sure we can work out our differences before the end of session."

"Sure . . . but do you feel betrayed by the Governor?"

"I wouldn't use that word. His view is that . . ."

"But isn't this really a betrayal on the Governor's part?"

The spin, the amplification of conflict, the indiscriminate search for scandal and miscues—the cumulative impact of all this is to erode any agreed-upon standards for judging the truth. There's a wonderful, perhaps apocryphal story that people tell about Daniel Patrick Moynihan, the brilliant, prickly, and iconoclastic late senator from New York. Apparently, Moynihan was in a heated argument with one of his colleagues over an issue, and the other senator, sensing he was on the losing side of the argument, blurted out: "Well, you may disagree with me, Pat, but I'm entitled to my own opinion." To which Moynihan frostily replied, "You are entitled to your own opinion, but you are not entitled to your own facts."

Moynihan's assertion no longer holds. We have no authoritative figure, no Walter Cronkite or Edward R. Murrow whom we all listen to and trust to sort out contradictory claims. Instead, the media is splintered into a thousand fragments, each with its own version of reality, each claiming the loyalty of a splintered nation. Depending on your viewing preferences, global climate change is or is not dangerously accelerating; the budget deficit is going down or going up.

Nor is the phenomenon restricted to reporting on complicated issues. In early 2005, *Newsweek* published allegations that U.S. guards and interrogators at the Guantanamo Bay detention center had goaded and abused prisoners by, among other things, flushing a Koran down the toilet. The White House insisted there was absolutely no truth to the story. Without hard documentation and in the wake of violent protests in Pakistan regarding the article, *Newsweek* was forced to publish a self-immolating retraction. Several months later, the Pentagon released a report indicating that some U.S. personnel at Guantanamo had in fact engaged in multiple instances of inappropriate activity—including instances in which U.S. female personnel pretended to smear menstrual blood on detainees during questioning, and at least one instance of a guard splashing a Koran and a prisoner with urine. The Fox News crawl that afternoon: "Pentagon finds no evidence of Koran being flushed down the toilet."

I understand that facts alone can't always settle our political disputes. Our views on abortion aren't determined by the science of fetal development, and our judgment on whether and when to pull troops out of Iraq must necessarily be based on probabilities. But sometimes there are more accurate and less accurate answers; sometimes there are facts that cannot be spun, just as an argument about whether it's raining can usually be settled by stepping outside. The absence of even rough agreement on the facts puts every opinion on equal footing and therefore eliminates the basis for thoughtful compromise. It rewards not those who are right, but those—like the White House press office— who can make their arguments most loudly, most frequently, most obstinately, and with the best backdrop.

Today's politician understands this. He may not lie, but he understands that there is no great reward in store for those who speak the truth, particularly when the truth may be complicated. The truth may cause consternation; the truth will be attacked; the media won't have the patience to sort out all the facts and so the public may not know the difference between truth and falsehood. What comes to matter then is positioning—the statement on an issue that will avoid controversy or generate needed publicity, the stance that will fit both the image his press folks have constructed for him and one of the narrative boxes the media has created for politics in general. The politician may still, as a matter of personal integrity, insist on telling the truth as he sees it. But he does so knowing that whether he believes in his positions matters less than whether he looks like he believes; that straight talk counts less than whether it sounds straight on TV.

From what I've observed, there are countless politicians who have crossed these hurdles and kept their integrity intact, men and women who raise campaign contributions without being corrupted, garner support without being held captive by special interests, and manage the media without losing their sense of self. But there is one final hurdle that, once you've settled in Washington, you cannot entirely avoid, one that is certain to make at least a sizable portion of your constituency think ill of you—and that is the thoroughly unsatisfactory nature of the legislative process.

I don't know a single legislator who doesn't anguish on a regular basis over the votes he or she has to take. There are times when one feels a piece of legislation to be so obviously right that it merits little internal debate (John McCain's amendment prohibiting torture by the U.S. government comes to mind). At other times, a bill appears on the floor that's so blatantly one-sided or poorly designed that one wonders how the sponsor can maintain a straight face during debate.

But most of the time, legislation is a murky brew, the product of one hundred compromises large and small, a blend of legitimate policy aims, political grandstanding, jerry-rigged regulatory schemes, and old-fashioned pork barrels. Often, as I read through the bills coming to the floor my first few months in the Senate, I was confronted with the fact that the principled thing was less clear than I had originally thought; that either an aye vote or a nay vote would leave me with some trace of remorse. Should I vote for an energy bill that includes my provision to boost alternative fuel production and improves the status quo, but that's wholly inadequate to the task of lessening America's dependence on foreign oil? Should I vote against a change in the Clean Air Act that will weaken regulations in some areas but strengthen regulation in others, and create a more predictable system for corporate compliance? What if the bill increases pollution but funds clean coal technology that may bring jobs to an impoverished part of Illinois?

Again and again I find myself poring over the evidence, pro and con, as best I can in the limited time available. My staff will inform me that the mail and phone calls are evenly divided and that interest groups on both sides are keeping score. As the hour approaches to cast my vote, I am frequently reminded of something John F. Kennedy wrote fifty years ago in his book *Profiles in Courage*:

> Few, if any, face the same dread finality of decision that confronts a Senator facing an important call of the roll. He may want more time for his decision—he may believe there is something to be said for both sides—he may feel that a slight amendment could remove all difficulties—but when that roll is called he cannot hide, he cannot equivocate, he cannot delay—and he senses that his constituency, like the Raven in Poe's poem, is perched there on his Senate desk, croaking "Nevermore" as he casts the vote that stakes his political future.

That may be a little dramatic. Still, no legislator, state or federal, is immune from such difficult moments—and they are always far worse for the party out of power. As a member of the majority, you will have some input in any bill that's important to you before it hits the floor. You can ask the committee chairman to include language that helps your constituents or eliminate language that hurts them. You can even ask the majority leader or the chief sponsor to hold the bill until a compromise more to your liking is reached.

If you're in the minority party, you have no such protection. You must vote yes or no on whatever bill comes up, with the knowledge that it's unlikely to be a compromise that either you or your supporters consider fair or just. In an era of indiscriminate logrolling and massive omnibus spending bills, you can also rest assured that no matter how many bad provisions there are in the bill, there will be something—funding for body armor for our troops, say, or some modest increase in veterans' benefits— that makes the bill painful to oppose.

In its first term, at least, the Bush White House was a master of such legislative gamesmanship. There's an instructive story about the negotiations surrounding the first round of Bush tax cuts, when Karl Rove invited a Democratic senator over to the White House to discuss the senator's potential support for the President's package. Bush had won the senator's state handily in the previous election—in part on a platform of tax cuts—and the senator was generally supportive of lower marginal rates. Still, he was troubled by the degree to which the proposed tax cuts were skewed toward the wealthy and suggested a few changes that would moderate the package's impact.

"Make these changes," the senator told Rove, "and not only will I vote for the bill, but I guarantee you'll get seventy votes out of the Senate."

"We don't want seventy votes," Rove reportedly replied. "We want fifty-one."

Rove may or may not have thought the White House bill was good policy, but he knew a political winner when he saw one. Either the senator voted aye and helped pass the President's program, or he voted no and became a plump target during the next election.

In the end, the senator—like several red state Democrats—voted aye, which no doubt reflected the prevailing sentiment about tax cuts in his home state. Still, stories like this illustrate some of the difficulties that any minority party faces in being "bipartisan." Everybody likes the idea of bipartisanship. The media, in particular, is enamored with the term, since it contrasts neatly with the "partisan bickering" that is the dominant story line of reporting on Capitol Hill.

Genuine bipartisanship, though, assumes an honest process of give-and-take, and that the quality of the compromise is measured by how well it serves some agreed-upon goal, whether better schools or lower deficits. This in turn assumes that the majority will be constrained—by an exacting press corps and ultimately an informed electorate—to negotiate in good faith. If these conditions do not hold—if nobody outside Washington is really paying attention to the substance of the bill, if the true costs of the tax cut are buried in phony accounting and understated by a trillion dollars or so—the majority party can begin every negotiation by asking for 100 percent of what it wants, go on to concede 10 percent, and then accuse any member of the minority party who fails to support this "compromise" of being "obstructionist." For the minority party in such circumstances, "bipartisanship" comes to mean getting chronically steamrolled, although individual senators may enjoy certain political rewards by consistently going along with the majority and hence gaining a reputation for being "moderate" or "centrist."

Not surprisingly, there are activists who insist that Democratic senators stand fast against any Republican initiative these days—even those initiatives that have some merit—as a matter of principle. It's fair to say that none of these individuals has ever run for high public office as a Democrat in a predominantly Republican state, nor has any been a target of several million dollars' worth of negative TV ads. What every senator understands is that while it's easy to make a vote on a complicated piece of legislation look evil and depraved in a thirty-second television commercial, it's very hard to explain the wisdom of that same vote in less than twenty minutes. What every senator also knows is that during the course of a single term, he or she will have cast several thousand votes. That's a whole lot of potential explaining to do come election time.

Perhaps my greatest bit of good fortune during my own Senate campaign was that no candidate ran a negative TV ad about me. This had to do entirely with the odd circumstances of my Senate race, and not an absence of material with which to work. After all, I had been in the state legislature for seven years when I ran, had been in the minority for six of those years, and had cast thousands of sometimes difficult votes. As is standard practice these days, the National Republican Senatorial Committee had prepared a fat binder of opposition research on me before I was even nominated, and my own research team spent many hours combing through my record in an effort to anticipate what negative ads the Republicans might have up their sleeves.

They didn't find a lot, but they found enough to do the trick—a dozen or so votes that, if described without context, could be made to sound pretty scary. When my media consultant, David Axelrod, tested them in a poll, my approval rating immediately dropped ten points. There was the criminal law bill that purported to crack down on drug dealing in schools but had been so poorly drafted that I concluded it was both ineffective and unconstitutional—"Obama voted to weaken penalties on gang-bangers who deal drugs in schools," is how the poll described it. There was a bill sponsored by antiabortion activists that on its face sounded reasonable enough—it mandated lifesaving measures for premature babies (the bill didn't mention that such measures were already the law)—but also extended "personhood" to previable fetuses, thereby effectively overturning *Roe v. Wade;* in the poll, I was said to have "voted to deny lifesaving treatment to babies born alive." Running down the list, I came across a claim that while in the state legislature I had voted against a bill to "protect our children from sex offenders."

"Wait a minute," I said, snatching the sheet from David's hands. "I accidentally pressed the wrong button on that bill. I meant to vote aye, and had it immediately corrected in the official record."

David smiled. "Somehow I don't think that portion of the official record will make it into a Republican ad." He gently retrieved the poll from my hands. "Anyway, cheer up," he added, clapping me on the back. "I'm sure this will help you with the sex offender vote."

I WONDER SOMETIMES how things might have turned out had those ads actually run. Not so much whether I would have won or lost—by the time the primaries were over, I had a twenty-point lead over my Republican opponent—but rather how the voters would have perceived me, how, entering into the Senate, I would have had a much smaller cushion of goodwill. For that is how most of my colleagues, Republican and Democrat, enter the Senate, their mistakes trumpeted, their words distorted, and their motives questioned. They are baptized in that fire; it haunts them each and every time they cast a vote, each and every time they issue a press release or make a statement, the fear of losing not just a political race, but of losing favor in the eyes of those who sent them to Washington—all those people who have said to them at one time or another: "We have great hopes for you. Please don't disappoint us."

Of course, there are technical fixes to our democracy that might relieve some of this pressure on politicians, structural changes that would strengthen the link between voters and their representatives. Nonpartisan districting, same-day registration, and weekend elections would all increase the competitiveness of races and might spur more participation from the electorate—and the more the electorate is paying attention, the more integrity is rewarded. Public financing of campaigns or free television and radio time could drastically reduce the constant scrounging for money and the influence of special interests. Changes in the rules in the House and the Senate might empower legislators in the minority, increase transparency in the process, and encourage more probing reporting.

But none of these changes can happen of their own accord. Each would require a change in attitude among those in power. Each would demand that individual politicians challenge the existing order; loosen their hold on incumbency; fight with their friends as well as their enemies on behalf of abstract ideas in which the public appears to have little interest. Each would require from men and women a willingness to risk what they already have.

In the end, then, it still comes back to that quality that JFK sought to define early in his career as he lay convalescing from surgery, mindful of his heroism in war but perhaps pondering the more ambiguous challenges ahead—the quality of courage. In some ways, the longer you are in politics, the easier it should be to muster such courage, for there is a certain liberation that comes from realizing that no matter what you do, someone will be angry at you, that political attacks will come no matter how cautiously you vote, that judgment may be taken as cowardice and courage itself may be seen as calculation. I find comfort in the fact that the longer I'm in politics the less nourishing popularity becomes, that a striving for power and rank and fame seems to betray a poverty of ambition, and that I am answerable mainly to the steady gaze of my own conscience.

And my constituents. After one town hall meeting in Godfrey, an older gentleman came up and expressed outrage that despite my having opposed the Iraq War, I had not yet called for a full withdrawal of troops. We had a brief and pleasant argument, in which I explained my concern that too precipitous a withdrawal would lead to all-out civil war in the country and the potential for widening conflict throughout the Middle East. At the end of our conversation he shook my hand.

"I still think you're wrong," he said, "but at least it seems like you've thought about it. Hell, you'd probably disappoint me if you agreed with me all the time."

"Thanks," I said. As he walked away, I was reminded of something Justice Louis Brandeis once said: that in a democracy, the most important office is the office of citizen.

Chapter Five

Opportunity

ONE THING ABOUT being a U.S. senator—you fly a lot. There are the flights back and forth from Washington at least once a week. There are the trips to other states to deliver a speech, raise money, or campaign for your colleagues. If you represent a big state like Illinois, there are flights upstate or downstate, to attend town meetings or ribbon cuttings and to make sure that the folks don't think you've forgotten them.

Most of the time I fly commercial and sit in coach, hoping for an aisle or window seat and crossing my fingers that the guy in front of me doesn't want to recline.

But there are times when—because I'm making multiple stops on a West Coast swing, say, or need to get to another city after the last commercial flight has left—I fly on a private jet. I hadn't been aware of this option at first, assuming the cost would be prohibitive. But during the campaign, my staff explained that under Senate rules, a senator or candidate could travel on someone else's jet and just pay the equivalent of a first-class airfare. After looking at my campaign schedule and thinking about all the time I would save, I decided to give private jets a try.

It turns out that the flying experience is a good deal different on a private jet. Private jets depart from privately owned and managed terminals, with lounges that feature big soft couches

and big-screen TVs and old aviation photographs on the walls.
The restrooms are generally empty and spotless, and have those
mechanical shoe-shine machines and mouthwash and mints in a
bowl. There's no sense of hurriedness at these terminals; the
plane is waiting for you if you're late, ready for you if you're
early. A lot of times you can bypass the lounge altogether and
drive your car straight onto the tarmac. Otherwise the pilots will
greet you in the terminal, take your bags, and walk you out to
the plane.

And the planes, well, they're nice. The first time I took such a
flight, I was on a Citation X, a sleek, compact, shiny machine
with wood paneling and leather seats that you could pull together to make a bed anytime you decided you wanted a nap. A
shrimp salad and cheese plate occupied the seat behind me; up
front, the minibar was fully stocked. The pilots hung up my coat,
offered me my choice of newspapers, and asked me if I was comfortable. I was.

Then the plane took off, its Rolls-Royce engines gripping the
air the way a well-made sports car grips the road. Shooting
through the clouds, I turned on the small TV monitor in front of
my seat. A map of the United States appeared, with the image of
our plane tracking west, along with our speed, our altitude, our
time to destination, and the temperature outside. At forty thousand feet, the plane leveled off, and I looked down at the curving
horizon and the scattered clouds, the geography of the earth laid
out before me—first the flat, checkerboard fields of western Illinois, then the python curves of the Mississippi, then more farmland and ranch land and eventually the jagged Rockies, still
snow-peaked, until the sun went down and the orange sky narrowed to a thin red line that was finally consumed by night and
stars and moon.

I could see how people might get used to this.

The purpose of that particular trip was fund-raising, mostly—
in preparation for my general election campaign, several friends

and supporters had organized events for me in L.A., San Diego, and San Francisco. But the most memorable part of the trip was a visit that I paid to the town of Mountain View, California, a few miles south of Stanford University and Palo Alto, in the heart of Silicon Valley, where the search engine company Google maintains its corporate headquarters.

Google had already achieved iconic status by mid-2004, a symbol not just of the growing power of the Internet but of the global economy's rapid transformation. On the drive down from San Francisco, I reviewed the company's history: how two Stanford Ph.D. candidates in computer science, Larry Page and Sergey Brin, had collaborated in a dorm room to develop a better way to search the web; how in 1998, with a million dollars raised from various contacts, they had formed Google, with three employees operating out of a garage; how Google figured out an advertising model—based on text ads that were nonintrusive and relevant to the user's search—that made the company profitable even as the dot-com boom went bust; and how, six years after the company's founding, Google was about to go public at stock prices that would make Mr. Page and Mr. Brin two of the richest people on earth.

Mountain View looked like a typical suburban California community—quiet streets, sparkling new office parks, unassuming homes that, because of the unique purchasing power of Silicon Valley residents, probably ran a cool million or more. We pulled in front of a set of modern, modular buildings and were met by Google's general counsel, David Drummond, an African American around my age who'd made the arrangements for my visit.

"When Larry and Sergey came to me looking to incorporate, I figured they were just a couple of really smart guys with another start-up idea," David said. "I can't say I expected all this."

He took me on a tour of the main building, which felt more like a college student center than an office—a café on the ground floor, where the former chef of the Grateful Dead supervised the preparation of gourmet meals for the entire staff; video games and a Ping-Pong table and a fully equipped gym. ("People spend a lot of time here, so we want to keep them happy.") On the second floor, we passed clusters of men and women in jeans and T-shirts, all of them in their twenties, working intently in front of their computer screens, or sprawled on couches and big rubber exercise balls, engaged in animated conversation.

Eventually we found Larry Page, talking to an engineer about a software problem. He was dressed like his employees and, except for a few traces of early gray in his hair, didn't look any older. We spoke about Google's mission—to organize all of the world's information into a universally accessible, unfiltered, and usable form—and the Google site index, which already included more than six billion web pages. Recently the company had launched a new web-based email system with a built-in search function; they were working on technology that would allow you to initiate a voice search over the telephone, and had already started the Book Project, the goal of which was to scan every book ever published into a web-accessible format, creating a virtual library that would store the entirety of human knowledge.

Toward the end of the tour, Larry led me to a room where a three-dimensional image of the earth rotated on a large flat-panel monitor. Larry asked the young Indian American engineer who was working nearby to explain what we were looking at.

"These lights represent all the searches that are going on right now," the engineer said. "Each color is a different language. If you move the toggle this way"—he caused the screen to alter—"you can see the traffic patterns of the entire Internet system."

The image was mesmerizing, more organic than mechanical, as if I were glimpsing the early stages of some accelerating evolutionary process, in which all the boundaries between men—nationality, race, religion, wealth—were rendered invisible and irrelevant, so that the physicist in Cambridge, the bond trader in

Tokyo, the student in a remote Indian village, and the manager of a Mexico City department store were drawn into a single, constant, thrumming conversation, time and space giving way to a world spun entirely of light. Then I noticed the broad swaths of darkness as the globe spun on its axis—most of Africa, chunks of South Asia, even some portions of the United States, where the thick cords of light dissolved into a few discrete strands.

My reverie was broken by the appearance of Sergey, a compact man perhaps a few years younger than Larry. He suggested that I go with them to their TGIF assembly, a tradition that they had maintained since the beginning of the company, when all of Google's employees got together over beer and food and discussed whatever they had on their minds. As we entered a large hall, throngs of young people were already seated, some drinking and laughing, others still typing into PDAs or laptops, a buzz of excitement in the air. A group of fifty or so seemed more attentive than the rest, and David explained that these were the new hires, fresh from graduate school; today was their induction into the Google team. One by one, the new employees were introduced, their faces flashing on a big screen alongside information about their degrees, hobbies, and interests. At least half of the group looked Asian; a large percentage of the whites had Eastern European names. As far as I could tell, not one was black or Latino. Later, walking back to my car, I mentioned this to David and he nodded.

"We know it's a problem," he said, and mentioned efforts Google was making to provide scholarships to expand the pool of minority and female math and science students. In the meantime, Google needed to stay competitive, which meant hiring the top graduates of the top math, engineering, and computer science programs in the country—MIT, Caltech, Stanford, Berkeley. You could count on two hands, David told me, the number of black and Latino kids in those programs.

In fact, according to David, just finding American-born

engineers, whatever their race, was getting harder—which was why every company in Silicon Valley had come to rely heavily on foreign students. Lately, high-tech employers had a new set of worries: Since 9/11 a lot of foreign students were having second thoughts about studying in the States due to the difficulties in obtaining visas. Top-notch engineers or software designers didn't need to come to Silicon Valley anymore to find work or get financing for a start-up. High-tech firms were setting up operations in India and China at a rapid pace, and venture funds were now global; they would just as readily invest in Mumbai or Shanghai as in California. And over the long term, David explained, that could spell trouble for the U.S. economy.

"We'll be able to keep attracting talent," he said, "because we're so well branded. But for the start-ups, some of the less established companies, the next Google, who knows? I just hope somebody in Washington understands how competitive things have become. Our dominance isn't inevitable."

AROUND THE SAME time that I visited Google, I took another trip that made me think about what was happening with the economy. This one was by car, not jet, along miles of empty highway, to a town called Galesburg, forty-five minutes or so from the Iowa border in western Illinois.

Founded in 1836, Galesburg had begun as a college town when a group of Presbyterian and Congregational ministers in New York decided to bring their blend of social reform and practical education to the Western frontier. The resulting school, Knox College, became a hotbed of abolitionist activity before the Civil War—a branch of the Underground Railroad had run through Galesburg, and Hiram Revels, the nation's first black U.S. senator, attended the college's prep school before moving back to Mississippi. In 1854, the Chicago, Burlington & Quincy railroad line was completed through Galesburg, causing a boom in the region's commerce. And four years later, some ten thousand people gathered to hear the fifth of the Lincoln-Douglas debates, during which Lincoln first framed his opposition to slavery as a moral issue.

It wasn't this rich history, though, that had taken me to Galesburg. Instead, I'd gone to meet with a group of union leaders from the Maytag plant, for the company had announced plans to lay off 1,600 employees and shift operations to Mexico. Like towns all across central and western Illinois, Galesburg had been pounded by the shift of manufacturing overseas. In the previous few years, the town had lost industrial parts makers and a rubber-hose manufacturer; it was now in the process of seeing Butler Manufacturing, a steelmaker recently bought by Australians, shutter its doors. Already, Galesburg's unemployment rate hovered near 8 percent. With the Maytag plant's closing, the town stood to lose another 5 to 10 percent of its entire employment base.

Inside the machinists' union hall, seven or eight men and two or three women had gathered on metal folding chairs, talking in muted voices, a few smoking cigarettes, most of them in their late forties or early fifties, all of them dressed in jeans or khakis, T-shirts or plaid work shirts. The union president, Dave Bevard, was a big, barrel-chested man in his mid-fifties, with a dark beard, tinted glasses, and a fedora that made him look like a member of the band ZZ Top. He explained that the union had tried every possible tactic to get Maytag to change its mind— talking to the press, contacting shareholders, soliciting support from local and state officials. The Maytag management had been unmoved.

"It ain't like these guys aren't making a profit," Dave told me. "And if you ask 'em, they'll tell you we're one of the most productive plants in the company. Quality workmanship. Low error rates. We've taken cuts in pay, cuts in benefits, layoffs. The state and the city have given Maytag at least $10 million in tax breaks over the last eight years, based on their promise to stay. But it's never enough. Some CEO who's already making millions of dollars decides he needs to boost the company stock price so he can cash in his options, and the easiest way to do that is to send the work to Mexico and pay the workers there a sixth of what we make."

I asked them what steps state or federal agencies had taken to retrain workers, and almost in unison the room laughed derisively. "Retraining is a joke," the union vice president, Doug Dennison, said. "What are you going to retrain for when there aren't any jobs out there?" He talked about how an employment counselor had suggested that he try becoming a nursing aide, with wages not much higher than what Wal-Mart paid their floor clerks. One of the younger men in the group told me a particularly cruel story: He had made up his mind to retrain as a computer technician, but a week into his courses, Maytag called him back. The Maytag work was temporary, but according to the rules, if this man refused to accept Maytag's offer, he'd no longer be eligible for retraining money. If, on the other hand, he did go back to Maytag and dropped out of the courses he was already taking, then the federal agency would consider him to have used up his one-time training opportunity and wouldn't pay for any retraining in the future.

I told the group that I'd tell their story during the campaign and offered a few proposals that my staff had developed— amending the tax code to eliminate tax breaks for companies who shifted operations offshore; revamping and better funding federal retraining programs. As I was getting ready to go, a big, sturdy man in a baseball cap spoke up. He said his name was Tim Wheeler, and he'd been the head of the union at the nearby Butler steel plant. Workers had already received their pink slips there, and Tim was collecting unemployment insurance, trying to figure out what to do next. His big worry now was health-care coverage.

"My son Mark needs a liver transplant," he said grimly. "We're on the waiting list for a donor, but with my health-care benefits used up, we're trying to figure out if Medicaid will cover the costs. Nobody can give me a clear answer, and you know, I'll sell everything I got for Mark, go into debt, but I still . . ." Tim's voice cracked; his wife, sitting beside him, buried her head in her hands. I tried to assure them that we would find out exactly what Medicaid would cover. Tim nodded, putting his arm around his wife's shoulder.

On the drive back to Chicago, I tried to imagine Tim's desperation: no job, an ailing son, his savings running out.

Those were the stories you missed on a private jet at forty thousand feet.

You'll get little argument these days, from either the left or the right, with the notion that we're going through a fundamental economic transformation. Advances in digital technology, fiber optics, the Internet, satellites, and transportation have effectively leveled the economic barriers between countries and continents. Pools of capital scour the earth in search of the best returns, with trillions of dollars moving across borders with only a few keystrokes. The collapse of the Soviet Union, the institution of market-based reforms in India and China, the lowering of trade barriers, and the advent of big-box retailers like Wal-Mart have brought several billion people into direct competition with American companies and American workers. Whether or not the world is already flat, as columnist and author Thomas Friedman says, it is certainly getting flatter every day.

There's no doubt that globalization has brought significant benefits to American consumers. It's lowered prices on goods once considered luxuries, from big-screen TVs to peaches in winter, and increased the purchasing power of low-income Americans. It's helped keep inflation in check, boosted returns for the

millions of Americans now invested in the stock market, provided new markets for U.S. goods and services, and allowed
countries like China and India to dramatically reduce poverty,
which over the long term makes for a more stable world.

But there's also no denying that globalization has greatly increased economic instability for millions of ordinary Americans.
To stay competitive and keep investors happy in the global marketplace, U.S.-based companies have automated, downsized,
outsourced, and offshored. They've held the line on wage increases, and replaced defined-benefit health and retirement plans
with 401(k)s and Health Savings Accounts that shift more cost
and risk onto workers.

The result has been the emergence of what some call a "winner-
take-all" economy, in which a rising tide doesn't necessarily lift
all boats. Over the past decade, we've seen strong economic
growth but anemic job growth; big leaps in productivity but
flatlining wages; hefty corporate profits, but a shrinking share of
those profits going to workers. For those like Larry Page and
Sergey Brin, for those with unique skills and talents and for the
knowledge workers—the engineers, lawyers, consultants, and
marketers—who facilitate their work, the potential rewards of a
global marketplace have never been greater. But for those like
the workers at Maytag, whose skills can be automated or digi-
tized or shifted to countries with cheaper wages, the effects can
be dire—a future in the ever-growing pool of low-wage service
work, with few benefits, the risk of financial ruin in the event
of an illness, and the inability to save for either retirement or a
child's college education.

The question is what we should do about all this. Since the
early nineties, when these trends first began to appear, one wing
of the Democratic Party—led by Bill Clinton—has embraced the
new economy, promoting free trade, fiscal discipline, and reforms in education and training that will help workers to compete for the high-value, high-wage jobs of the future. But a

sizable chunk of the Democratic base—particularly blue-collar union workers like Dave Bevard—has resisted this agenda. As far as they're concerned, free trade has served the interests of Wall Street but has done little to stop the hemorrhaging of good-paying American jobs.

The Republican Party isn't immune from these tensions. With the recent uproar around illegal immigration, for example, Pat Buchanan's brand of "America first" conservatism may see a resurgence within the GOP, and present a challenge to the Bush Administration's free trade policies. And in his 2000 campaign and early in his first term, George W. Bush suggested a legitimate role for government, a "compassionate conservatism" that, the White House argues, has expressed itself in the Medicare prescription drug plan and the educational reform effort known as No Child Left Behind—and that has given small-government conservatives heartburn.

For the most part, though, the Republican economic agenda under President Bush has been devoted to tax cuts, reduced regulation, the privatization of government services—and more tax cuts. Administration officials call this the Ownership Society, but most of its central tenets have been staples of laissez-faire economics since at least the 1930s: a belief that a sharp reduction— or in some cases, elimination—of taxes on incomes, large estates, capital gains, and dividends will encourage capital formation, higher savings rates, more business investment, and greater economic growth; a belief that government regulation inhibits and distorts the efficient working of the market; and a belief that government entitlement programs are inherently inefficient, breed dependency, and reduce individual responsibility, initiative, and choice.

Or, as Ronald Reagan succinctly put it: "Government is not the solution to our problem; government is the problem."

So far, the Bush Administration has only achieved one-half of its equation; the Republican-controlled Congress has pushed through successive rounds of tax cuts, but has refused to make tough choices to control spending—special interest appropriations, also known as earmarks, are up 64 percent since Bush took office. Meanwhile, Democratic lawmakers (and the public) have resisted drastic cuts in vital investments—and outright rejected the Administration's proposal to privatize Social Security. Whether the Administration actually believes that the resulting federal budget deficits and ballooning national debt don't matter is unclear. What is clear is that the sea of red ink has made it more difficult for future administrations to initiate any new investments to address the economic challenges of globalization or to strengthen America's social safety net.

I don't want to exaggerate the consequences of this stalemate. A strategy of doing nothing and letting globalization run its course won't result in the imminent collapse of the U.S. economy. America's GDP remains larger than China's and India's combined. For now, at least, U.S.-based companies continue to hold an edge in such knowledge-based sectors as software design and pharmaceutical research, and our network of universities and colleges remains the envy of the world.

But over the long term, doing nothing probably means an America very different from the one most of us grew up in. It will mean a nation even more stratified economically and socially than it currently is: one in which an increasingly prosperous knowledge class, living in exclusive enclaves, will be able to purchase whatever they want on the marketplace—private schools, private health care, private security, and private jets—while a growing number of their fellow citizens are consigned to low-paying service jobs, vulnerable to dislocation, pressed to work longer hours, dependent on an underfunded, overburdened, and underperforming public sector for their health care, their retirement, and their children's educations.

It will mean an America in which we continue to mortgage our assets to foreign lenders and expose ourselves to the whims of oil producers; an America in which we underinvest in the basic scientific research and workforce training that will determine our long-term economic prospects and neglect potential environmental crises. It will mean an America that's more politically polarized and more politically unstable, as economic frustration boils over and leads people to turn on each other.

Worst of all, it will mean fewer opportunities for younger Americans, a decline in the upward mobility that's been at the heart of this country's promise since its founding.

That's not the America we want for ourselves or our children. And I'm confident that we have the talent and the resources to create a better future, a future in which the economy grows and prosperity is shared. What's preventing us from shaping that future isn't the absence of good ideas. It's the absence of a national commitment to take the tough steps necessary to make America more competitive—and the absence of a new consensus around the appropriate role of government in the marketplace.

To BUILD THAT consensus, we need to take a look at how our market system has evolved over time. Calvin Coolidge once said that "the chief business of the American people is business," and indeed, it would be hard to find a country on earth that's been more consistently hospitable to the logic of the marketplace. Our Constitution places the ownership of private property at the very heart of our system of liberty. Our religious traditions celebrate the value of hard work and express the conviction that a virtuous life will result in material reward. Rather than vilify the rich, we hold them up as role models, and our mythology is steeped in stories of men on the make—the immigrant who comes to this country with nothing and strikes it big, the young man who heads West in search of his fortune. As Ted Turner famously said, in America money is how we keep score.

The result of this business culture has been a prosperity that's unmatched in human history. It takes a trip overseas to fully appreciate just how good Americans have it; even our poor take for granted goods and services—electricity, clean water, indoor plumbing, telephones, televisions, and household appliances—that are still unattainable for most of the world. America may have been blessed with some of the planet's best real estate, but clearly it's not just our natural resources that account for our economic success. Our greatest asset has been our system of social organization, a system that for generations has encouraged constant innovation, individual initiative, and the efficient allocation of resources.

It should come as no surprise, then, that we have a tendency to take our free-market system as a given, to assume that it flows naturally from the laws of supply and demand and Adam Smith's invisible hand. And from this assumption, it's not much of a leap to assume that any government intrusion into the magical workings of the market—whether through taxation, regulation, lawsuits, tariffs, labor protections, or spending on entitlements—necessarily undermines private enterprise and inhibits economic growth. The bankruptcy of communism and socialism as alternative means of economic organization has only reinforced this assumption. In our standard economics textbooks and in our modern political debates, laissez-faire is the default rule; anyone who would challenge it swims against the prevailing tide.

It's useful to remind ourselves, then, that our free-market system is the result neither of natural law nor of divine providence. Rather, it emerged through a painful process of trial and error, a series of difficult choices between efficiency and fairness, stability and change. And although the benefits of our free-market system have mostly derived from the individual efforts of generations of men and women pursuing their own vision of happiness, in each and every period of great economic upheaval and transition we've depended on government action to open up opportunity, encourage competition, and make the market work better.

In broad outline, government action has taken three forms. First, government has been called upon throughout our history to build the infrastructure, train the workforce, and otherwise lay the foundations necessary for economic growth. All the Founding Fathers recognized the connection between private property and liberty, but it was Alexander Hamilton who also recognized the vast potential of a national economy—one based not on America's agrarian past but on a commercial and industrial future. To realize this potential, Hamilton argued, America needed a strong and active national government, and as America's first Treasury secretary he set about putting his ideas to work. He nationalized the Revolutionary War debt, which not only stitched together the economies of the individual states but helped spur a national system of credit and fluid capital markets. He promoted policies—from strong patent laws to high tariffs—to encourage American manufacturing, and proposed investment in roads and bridges needed to move products to market.

Hamilton encountered fierce resistance from Thomas Jefferson, who feared that a strong national government tied to wealthy commercial interests would undermine his vision of an egalitarian democracy tied to the land. But Hamilton understood that only through the liberation of capital from local landed interests could America tap into its most powerful resource—namely the energy and enterprise of the American people. This idea of social mobility constituted one of the great early bargains of American capitalism; industrial and commercial capitalism might lead to greater instability, but it would be a dynamic system in which anyone with enough energy and talent could rise to the top. And on this point, at least, Jefferson agreed—it was based on his belief in a meritocracy, rather than a hereditary aristocracy, that Jefferson would champion the creation of a national, government-financed university that could educate and train talent across the new nation, and that he considered the founding of the University of Virginia to be one of his greatest achievements.

This tradition, of government investment in America's physical infrastructure and in its people, was thoroughly embraced by Abraham Lincoln and the early Republican Party. For Lincoln, the essence of America was opportunity, the ability of "free labor" to advance in life. Lincoln considered capitalism the best means of creating such opportunity, but he also saw how the transition from an agricultural to an industrial society was disrupting lives and destroying communities.

So in the midst of civil war, Lincoln embarked on a series of policies that not only laid the groundwork for a fully integrated national economy but extended the ladders of opportunity downward to reach more and more people. He pushed for the construction of the first transcontinental railroad. He incorporated the National Academy of Sciences, to spur basic research and scientific discovery that could lead to new technology and commercial applications. He passed the landmark Homestead Act of 1862, which turned over vast amounts of public land across the western United States to settlers from the East and immigrants from around the world, so that they, too, could claim a stake in the nation's growing economy. And then, rather than leave these homesteaders to fend for themselves, he created a system of land grant colleges to instruct farmers on the latest agricultural techniques, and to provide them the liberal education that would allow them to dream beyond the confines of life on the farm.

Hamilton's and Lincoln's basic insight—that the resources and power of the national government can facilitate, rather than supplant, a vibrant free market—has continued to be one of the cornerstones of both Republican and Democratic policies at every stage of America's development. The Hoover Dam, the Tennessee Valley Authority, the interstate highway system, the Internet, the Human Genome Project—time and again, government investment has helped pave the way for an explosion of private economic activity. And through the creation of a system of public schools and institutions of higher education, as well as programs like the GI Bill that made a college education available to millions, government has helped provide individuals the tools to adapt and innovate in a climate of constant technological change.

Aside from making needed investments that private enterprise can't or won't make on its own, an active national government has also been indispensable in dealing with market failures—those recurring snags in any capitalist system that either inhibit the efficient workings of the market or result in harm to the public. Teddy Roosevelt recognized that monopoly power could restrict competition, and made "trust busting" a centerpiece of his administration. Woodrow Wilson instituted the Federal Reserve Bank, to manage the money supply and curb periodic panics in the financial markets. Federal and state governments established the first consumer laws—the Pure Food and Drug Act, the Meat Inspection Act—to protect Americans from harmful products.

But it was during the stock market crash of 1929 and the subsequent Depression that the government's vital role in regulating the marketplace became fully apparent. With investor confidence shattered, bank runs threatening the collapse of the financial system, and a downward spiral in consumer demand and business investment, FDR engineered a series of government interventions that arrested further economic contraction. For the next eight years, the New Deal administration experimented with policies to restart the economy, and although not all of these interventions produced their intended results, they did leave behind a regulatory structure that helps limit the risk of economic crisis: a Securities and Exchange Commission to ensure transparency in the financial markets and protect smaller investors from fraud and insider manipulation; FDIC insurance to provide confidence to bank depositors; and countercyclical fiscal and monetary policies, whether in the form of tax cuts, increased liquidity, or direct government spending, to stimulate demand when business and consumers have pulled back from the market.

Finally—and most controversially—government has helped
structure the social compact between business and the American
worker. During America's first 150 years, as capital became more
concentrated in trusts and limited liability corporations, workers
were prevented by law and by violence from forming unions that
would increase their own leverage. Workers had almost no protections from unsafe or inhumane working conditions, whether
in sweatshops or meatpacking plants. Nor did American culture
have much sympathy for workers left impoverished by capitalism's periodic gales of "creative destruction"—the recipe for
individual success was greater toil, not pampering from the state.
What safety net did exist came from the uneven and meager resources of private charity.

Again, it took the shock of the Great Depression, with a third
of all people finding themselves out of work, ill housed, ill clothed,
and ill fed, for government to correct this imbalance. Two years
into office, FDR was able to push through Congress the Social
Security Act of 1935, the centerpiece of the new welfare state,
a safety net that would lift almost half of all senior citizens out
of poverty, provide unemployment insurance for those who had
lost their jobs, and provide modest welfare payments to the disabled and the elderly poor. FDR also initiated laws that fundamentally changed the relationship between capital and labor: the
forty-hour workweek, child labor laws, and minimum wage laws;
and the National Labor Relations Act, which made it possible to
organize broad-based industrial unions and forced employers to
bargain in good faith.

Part of FDR's rationale in passing these laws came straight
out of Keynesian economics: One cure for economic depression
was putting more disposable income in the pockets of American
workers. But FDR also understood that capitalism in a democracy
required the consent of the people, and that by giving workers a
larger share of the economic pie, his reforms would undercut the
potential appeal of government-managed, command-and-control

systems—whether fascist, socialist, or communist—that were gaining support all across Europe. As he would explain in 1944, "People who are hungry, people who are out of a job are the stuff of which dictatorships are made."

For a while this seemed to be where the story would end—with FDR saving capitalism from itself through an activist federal government that invests in its people and infrastructure, regulates the marketplace, and protects labor from chronic deprivation. And in fact, for the next twenty-five years, through Republican and Democratic administrations, this model of the American welfare state enjoyed a broad consensus. There were those on the right who complained of creeping socialism, and those on the left who believed FDR had not gone far enough. But the enormous growth of America's mass production economy, and the enormous gap in productive capacity between the United States and the war-torn economies of Europe and Asia, muted most ideological battles. Without any serious rivals, U.S. companies could routinely pass on higher labor and regulatory costs to their customers. Full employment allowed unionized factory workers to move into the middle class, support a family on a single income, and enjoy the stability of health and retirement security. And in such an environment of steady corporate profits and rising wages, policy makers found only modest political resistance to higher taxes and more regulation to tackle pressing social problems—hence the creation of the Great Society programs, including Medicare, Medicaid, and welfare, under Johnson; and the creation of the Environmental Protection Agency and Occupational Health and Safety Administration under Nixon.

There was only one problem with this liberal triumph—capitalism would not stand still. By the seventies, U.S. productivity growth, the engine of the postwar economy, began to lag. The increased assertiveness of OPEC allowed foreign oil producers to lop off a much bigger share of the global economy, exposing America's vulnerability to disruptions in energy supplies. U.S.

companies began to experience competition from low-cost producers in Asia, and by the eighties a flood of cheap imports—in textiles, shoes, electronics, and even automobiles—had started grabbing big chunks of the domestic market. Meanwhile, U.S.-based multinational corporations began locating some of their production facilities overseas—partly to access these foreign markets, but also to take advantage of cheap labor.

In this more competitive global environment, the old corporate formula of steady profits and stodgy management no longer worked. With less ability to pass on higher costs or shoddy products to consumers, corporate profits and market share shrank, and corporate shareholders began demanding more value. Some corporations found ways to improve productivity through innovation and automation. Others relied primarily on brutal layoffs, resistance to unionization, and a further shift of production overseas. Those corporate managers who didn't adapt were vulnerable to corporate raiders and leveraged buyout artists, who would make the changes for them, without any regard for the employees whose lives might be upended or the communities that might be torn apart. One way or another, American companies became leaner and meaner—with old-line manufacturing workers and towns like Galesburg bearing the brunt of this transformation.

It wasn't just the private sector that had to adapt to this new environment. As Ronald Reagan's election made clear, the people wanted the government to change as well.

In his rhetoric, Reagan tended to exaggerate the degree to which the welfare state had grown over the previous twenty-five years. At its peak, the federal budget as a total share of the U.S. economy remained far below the comparable figures in Western Europe, even when you factored in the enormous U.S. defense budget. Still, the conservative revolution that Reagan helped usher in gained traction because Reagan's central insight—that the liberal welfare state had grown complacent and overly bureaucratic, with Democratic policy makers more obsessed with slicing the economic pie than with growing the pie—contained a good deal of truth. Just as too many corporate managers, shielded from competition, had stopped delivering value, too many government bureaucracies had stopped asking whether their shareholders (the American taxpayer) and their consumers (the users of government services) were getting their money's worth.

Not every government program worked the way it was advertised. Some functions could be better carried out by the private sector, just as in some cases market-based incentives could achieve the same results as command-and-control-style regulations, at a lower cost and with greater flexibility. The high marginal tax rates that existed when Reagan took office may not have curbed incentives to work or invest, but they did distort investment decisions—and did lead to a wasteful industry of setting up tax shelters. And while welfare certainly provided relief for many impoverished Americans, it did create some perverse incentives when it came to the work ethic and family stability.

Forced to compromise with a Democrat-controlled Congress, Reagan would never achieve many of his most ambitious plans for reducing government. But he fundamentally changed the terms of the political debate. The middle-class tax revolt became a permanent fixture in national politics and placed a ceiling on how much government could expand. For many Republicans, noninterference with the marketplace became an article of faith.

Of course, many voters continued to look to the government during economic downturns, and Bill Clinton's call for more aggressive government action on the economy helped lift him to the White House. After the politically disastrous defeat of his health-care plan and the election of a Republican Congress in 1994, Clinton had to trim his ambitions but was able to put a progressive slant on some of Reagan's goals. Declaring the era of big government over, Clinton signed welfare reform into law, pushed tax cuts for the middle class and working poor, and worked to reduce bureaucracy and red tape. And it was Clinton who would accomplish what Reagan never did, putting the nation's fiscal house in order even while lessening poverty and making modest new investments in education and job training. By the time Clinton left office, it appeared as if some equilibrium had been achieved—a smaller government, but one that retained the social safety net FDR had first put into place.

Except capitalism is still not standing still. The policies of Reagan and Clinton may have trimmed some of the fat of the liberal welfare state, but they couldn't change the underlying realities of global competition and technological revolution. Jobs are still moving overseas—not just manufacturing work, but increasingly work in the service sector that can be digitally transmitted, like basic computer programming. Businesses continue to struggle with high health-care costs. America continues to import far more than it exports, to borrow far more than it lends.

Without any clear governing philosophy, the Bush Administration and its congressional allies have responded by pushing the conservative revolution to its logical conclusion—even lower taxes, even fewer regulations, and an even smaller safety net. But in taking this approach, Republicans are fighting the last war, the war they waged and won in the eighties, while Democrats are forced to fight a rearguard action, defending the New Deal programs of the thirties.

Neither strategy will work anymore. America can't compete with China and India simply by cutting costs and shrinking government—unless we're willing to tolerate a drastic decline in American living standards, with smog-choked cities and beggars lining the streets. Nor can America compete simply by erecting trade barriers and raising the minimum wage—unless we're willing to confiscate all the world's computers.

But our history should give us confidence that we don't have to choose between an oppressive, government-run economy and a chaotic and unforgiving capitalism. It tells us that we can emerge from great economic upheavals stronger, not weaker. Like those who came before us, we should be asking ourselves what mix of policies will lead to a dynamic free market and widespread economic security, entrepreneurial innovation and upward mobility. And we can be guided throughout by Lincoln's simple maxim: that we will do collectively, through our government, only those things that we cannot do as well or at all individually and privately.

In other words, we should be guided by what works.

WHAT MIGHT SUCH a new economic consensus look like? I won't pretend to have all the answers, and a detailed discussion of U.S. economic policy would fill up several volumes. But I can offer a few examples of where we can break free of our current political stalemate; places where, in the tradition of Hamilton and Lincoln, we can invest in our infrastructure and our people; ways that we can begin to modernize and rebuild the social contract that FDR first stitched together in the middle of the last century.

Let's start with those investments that can make America more competitive in the global economy: investments in education, science and technology, and energy independence.

Throughout our history, education has been at the heart of a bargain this nation makes with its citizens: If you work hard and take responsibility, you'll have a chance for a better life. And in a world where knowledge determines value in the job market, where a child in Los Angeles has to compete not just with a child in Boston but also with millions of children in Bangalore and Beijing, too many of America's schools are not holding up their end of the bargain.

In 2005 I paid a visit to Thornton Township High School, a predominantly black high school in Chicago's southern suburbs. My staff had worked with teachers there to organize a youth town hall meeting—representatives of each class spent weeks conducting surveys to find out what issues their fellow students were concerned about and then presented the results in a series of questions to me. At the meeting they talked about violence in the neighborhoods and a shortage of computers in their classrooms. But their number one issue was this: Because the school district couldn't afford to keep teachers for a full school day, Thornton let out every day at 1:30 in the afternoon. With the abbreviated schedule, there was no time for students to take science lab or foreign language classes.

How come we're getting shortchanged? they asked me. Seems like nobody even expects us to go to college, they said.

They wanted more school.

We've become accustomed to such stories, of poor black and Latino children languishing in schools that can't prepare them for the old industrial economy, much less the information age. But the problems with our educational system aren't restricted to the inner city. America now has one of the highest high school dropout rates in the industrialized world. By their senior year, American high school students score lower on math and science tests than most of their foreign peers. Half of all teenagers can't understand basic fractions, half of all nine-year-olds can't perform basic multiplication or division, and although more American students than ever are taking college entrance exams, only 22 percent are prepared to take college-level classes in English, math, and science.

I don't believe government alone can turn these statistics around. Parents have the primary responsibility for instilling an ethic of hard work and educational achievement in their children. But parents rightly expect their government, through the public schools, to serve as full partners in the educational process—just as it has for earlier generations of Americans.

Unfortunately, instead of innovation and bold reform of our schools—the reforms that would allow the kids at Thornton to compete for the jobs at Google—what we've seen from government for close to two decades has been tinkering around the edges and a tolerance for mediocrity. Partly this is a result of ideological battles that are as outdated as they are predictable. Many conservatives argue that money doesn't matter in raising educational achievement; that the problems in public schools are caused by hapless bureaucracies and intransigent teachers' unions; and that the only solution is to break up the government's education monopoly by handing out vouchers. Meanwhile, those on the left often find themselves defending an indefensible status quo, insisting that more spending alone will improve educational outcomes.

Both assumptions are wrong. Money does matter in education—otherwise why would parents pay so much to live in well-funded suburban school districts?—and many urban and rural schools still suffer from overcrowded classrooms, outdated books, inadequate equipment, and teachers who are forced to pay out of pocket for basic supplies. But there's no denying that the way many public schools are managed poses at least as big a problem as how well they're funded.

Our task, then, is to identify those reforms that have the highest impact on student achievement, fund them adequately, and eliminate those programs that don't produce results. And in fact we already have hard evidence of reforms that work: a more challenging and rigorous curriculum with emphasis on math, science, and literacy skills; longer hours and more days to give children the time and sustained attention they need to learn; early childhood education for every child, so they're not already behind on their first day of school; meaningful, performance-based assessments that can provide a fuller picture of how a student is doing; and the recruitment and training of transformative principals and more effective teachers.

This last point—the need for good teachers—deserves emphasis. Recent studies show that the single most important factor in determining a student's achievement isn't the color of his skin or where he comes from, but who the child's teacher is. Unfortunately, too many of our schools depend on inexperienced teachers with little training in the subjects they're teaching, and too often those teachers are concentrated in already struggling schools. Moreover, the situation is getting worse, not better: Each year, school districts are hemorrhaging experienced teachers as the Baby Boomers reach retirement, and two million teachers must be recruited in the next decade just to meet the needs of rising enrollment.

The problem isn't that there's no interest in teaching; I constantly meet young people who've graduated from top colleges and have signed up, through programs like Teach for America, for two-year stints in some of the country's toughest public schools. They find the work extraordinarily rewarding; the kids they teach benefit from their creativity and enthusiasm. But by the end of two years, most have either changed careers or moved to suburban schools—a consequence of low pay, a lack of support from the educational bureaucracy, and a pervasive feeling of isolation.

If we're serious about building a twenty-first-century school system, we're going to have to take the teaching profession seriously. This means changing the certification process to allow a chemistry major who wants to teach to avoid expensive additional course work; pairing up new recruits with master teachers to break their isolation; and giving proven teachers more control over what goes on in their classrooms.

It also means paying teachers what they're worth. There's no reason why an experienced, highly qualified, and effective teacher shouldn't earn $100,000 annually at the peak of his or her career. Highly skilled teachers in such critical fields as math and science—as well as those willing to teach in the toughest urban schools—should be paid even more.

There's just one catch. In exchange for more money, teachers need to become more accountable for their performance—and school districts need to have greater ability to get rid of ineffective teachers.

So far, teacher's unions have resisted the idea of pay for performance, in part because it could be disbursed at the whim of a principal. The unions also argue—rightly, I think—that most school districts rely solely on test scores to measure teacher performance, and that test scores may be highly dependent on factors beyond any teacher's control, like the number of low-income or special-needs students in their classroom.

But these aren't insoluble problems. Working with teacher's unions, states and school districts can develop better measures of performance, ones that combine test data with a system of peer review (most teachers can tell you with amazing consistency which teachers in their schools are really good, and which are really bad). And we can make sure that nonperforming teachers no longer handicap children who want to learn.

Indeed, if we're to make the investments required to revamp our schools, then we will need to rediscover our faith that every child *can* learn. Recently, I had the chance to visit Dodge Elementary School, on the West Side of Chicago, a school that had once been near the bottom on every measure but that is in the midst of a turnaround. While I was talking to some of the teachers about the challenges they faced, one young teacher mentioned what she called the "These Kids Syndrome"—the willingness of society to find a million excuses for why "these kids" can't learn; how "these kids come from tough backgrounds" or "these kids are too far behind."

"When I hear that term, it drives me nuts," the teacher told me. "They're not 'these kids.' They're our kids."

How America's economy performs in the years to come may depend largely on how well we take such wisdom to heart.

OUR INVESTMENT IN education can't end with an improved elementary and secondary school system. In a knowledge-based economy where eight of the nine fastest-growing occupations this decade require scientific or technological skills, most work-ers are going to need some form of higher education to fill the jobs of the future. And just as our government instituted free and mandatory public high schools at the dawn of the twentieth cen-tury to provide workers the skills needed for the industrial age, our government has to help today's workforce adjust to twenty-first-century realities.

In many ways, our task should be easier than it was for pol-icy makers a hundred years ago. For one thing, our network of universities and community colleges already exists and is well equipped to take on more students. And Americans certainly don't need to be convinced of the value of a higher education—the percentage of young adults getting bachelor's degrees has risen steadily each decade, from around 16 percent in 1980 to almost 33 percent today.

Where Americans do need help, immediately, is in managing the rising cost of college—something with which Michelle and I are all too familiar (for the first ten years of our marriage, our com-bined monthly payments on our undergraduate and law school debt exceeded our mortgage by a healthy margin). Over the last five years, the average tuition and fees at four-year public colleges, adjusted for inflation, have risen 40 percent. To absorb these costs, students have been taking on ever-increasing debt levels, which discourages many undergraduates from pursuing careers in less lucrative fields like teaching. And an estimated two hundred thou-sand college-qualified students each year choose to forgo college altogether because they can't figure out how to pay the bills.

There are a number of steps we can take to control costs and improve access to higher education. States can limit annual tuition increases at public universities. For many nontraditional students, technical schools and online courses may provide a cost-effective option for retooling in a constantly changing economy. And stu-dents can insist that their institutions focus their fund-raising efforts more on improving the quality of instruction than on building new football stadiums.

But no matter how well we do in controlling the spiraling cost of education, we will still need to provide many students and parents with more direct help in meeting college expenses, whether through grants, low-interest loans, tax-free educational savings accounts, or full tax deductibility of tuition and fees. So far, Congress has been moving in the opposite direction, by raising interest rates on federally guaranteed student loans and failing to increase the size of grants for low-income students to keep pace with inflation. There's no justification for such policies—not if we want to maintain opportunity and upward mobility as the hallmark of the U.S. economy.

There's one other aspect of our educational system that merits attention—one that speaks to the heart of America's competitiveness. Since Lincoln signed the Morrill Act and created the system of land grant colleges, institutions of higher learning have served as the nation's primary research and development laboratories. It's through these institutions that we've trained the innovators of the future, with the federal government providing critical support for the infrastructure—everything from chemistry labs to particle accelerators—and the dollars for research that may not have an immediate commercial application but that can ultimately lead to major scientific breakthroughs.

Here, too, our policies have been moving in the wrong direction. At the 2006 Northwestern University commencement, I fell into a conversation with Dr. Robert Langer, an Institute Professor of chemical engineering at MIT and one of the nation's foremost scientists. Langer isn't just an ivory tower academic—he holds more than five hundred patents, and his research has led to everything from the development of the nicotine patch to brain cancer treatments. As we waited for the procession to begin, I asked him about his current work, and he mentioned his research in tissue engineering, research that promised new, more effective methods of delivering drugs to the body. Remembering the recent controversies surrounding stem cell research, I asked him whether the Bush Administration's limitation on the number of stem cell lines was the biggest impediment to advances in his field. He shook his head.

"Having more stem cell lines would definitely be useful," Langer told me, "but the real problem we're seeing is significant cutbacks in federal grants." He explained that fifteen years ago, 20 to 30 percent of all research proposals received significant federal support. That level is now closer to 10 percent. For scientists and researchers, this means more time spent raising money and less time spent on research. It also means that each year, more and more promising avenues of research are cut off— especially the high-risk research that may ultimately yield the biggest rewards.

Dr. Langer's observation isn't unique. Each month, it seems, scientists and engineers visit my office to discuss the federal government's diminished commitment to funding basic scientific research. Over the last three decades federal funding for the physical, mathematical, and engineering sciences has declined as a percentage of GDP—just at the time when other countries are substantially increasing their own R & D budgets. And as Dr. Langer points out, our declining support for basic research has a direct impact on the number of young people going into math, science, and engineering—which helps explain why China is graduating eight times as many engineers as the United States every year.

If we want an innovation economy, one that generates more Googles each year, then we have to invest in our future innovators—by doubling federal funding of basic research over the next five years, training one hundred thousand more engineers and scientists over the next four years, or providing new research grants to the most outstanding early-career researchers in the country. The total price tag for maintaining our scientific and technological edge comes out to approximately $42 billion over five years—real money, to be sure, but just 15 percent of the most recent federal highway bill.

In other words, we can afford to do what needs to be done. What's missing is not money, but a national sense of urgency.

THE LAST CRITICAL investment we need to make America more competitive is in an energy infrastructure that can move us toward energy independence. In the past, war or a direct threat to national security has shaken America out of its complacency and led to bigger investments in education and science, all with an eye toward minimizing our vulnerabilities. That's what happened at the height of the Cold War, when the launching of the satellite Sputnik led to fears that the Soviets were slipping ahead of us technologically. In response, President Eisenhower doubled federal aid to education and provided an entire generation of scientists and engineers the training they needed to lead revolutionary advances. That same year, the Defense Advanced Research Projects Agency, or DARPA, was formed, providing billions of dollars to basic research that would eventually help create the Internet, bar codes, and computer-aided design. And in 1961, President Kennedy would launch the Apollo space program, further inspiring young people across the country to enter the New Frontier of science.

Our current situation demands that we take the same approach with energy. It's hard to overstate the degree to which our addiction to oil undermines our future. According to the National Commission on Energy Policy, without any changes to our energy policy U.S. demand for oil will jump 40 percent over the next twenty years. Over the same period, worldwide demand is expected to jump at least 30 percent, as rapidly developing countries like China and India expand industrial capacity and add 140 million cars to their roads.

Our dependence on oil doesn't just affect our economy. It undermines our national security. A large portion of the $800 million we spend on foreign oil every day goes to some of the world's most volatile regimes—Saudi Arabia, Nigeria, Venezuela, and, indirectly at least, Iran. It doesn't matter whether they are despotic regimes with nuclear intentions or havens for madrassas that plant the seeds of terror in young minds—they get our money because we need their oil.

What's worse, the potential for supply disruption is severe. In the Persian Gulf, Al Qaeda has been attempting attacks on poorly defended oil refineries for years; a successful attack on just one of the Saudis' major oil complexes could send the U.S. economy into a tailspin. Osama bin Laden himself advises his followers to "focus your operations on [oil], especially in Iraq and the Gulf area, since this will cause them to die off."

And then there are the environmental consequences of our fossil fuel–based economy. Just about every scientist outside the White House believes climate change is real, is serious, and is accelerated by the continued release of carbon dioxide. If the prospect of melting ice caps, rising sea levels, changing weather patterns, more frequent hurricanes, more violent tornadoes, endless dust storms, decaying forests, dying coral reefs, and increases in respiratory illness and insect-borne diseases—if all that doesn't constitute a serious threat, I don't know what does.

So far, the Bush Administration's energy policy has been focused on subsidies to big oil companies and expanded drilling—coupled with token investments in the development of alternative fuels. This approach might make economic sense if America harbored plentiful and untapped oil supplies that could meet its needs (and if oil companies weren't experiencing record profits). But such supplies don't exist. The United States has 3 percent of the world's oil reserves. We use 25 percent of the world's oil. We can't drill our way out of the problem.

What we can do is create renewable, cleaner energy sources for the twenty-first century. Instead of subsidizing the oil industry, we should end every single tax break the industry currently receives and demand that 1 percent of the revenues from oil companies with over $1 billion in quarterly profits go toward financing alternative energy research and the necessary infrastructure. Not only would such a project pay huge economic, foreign policy, and environmental dividends—it could be the vehicle by which we train an entire new generation of American scientists and engineers and a source of new export industries and high-wage jobs.

Countries like Brazil have already done this. Over the last thirty years, Brazil has used a mix of regulation and direct government investment to develop a highly efficient biofuel industry; 70 percent of its new vehicles now run on sugar-based ethanol instead of gasoline. Without the same governmental attention, the U.S. ethanol industry is just now catching up. Free-market proponents argue that the heavy-handed approach of the Brazilian government has no place in the more market-oriented U.S. economy. But regulation, if applied with flexibility and sensitivity to market forces, can actually spur private sector innovation and investment in the energy sector.

Take the issue of fuel-efficiency standards. Had we steadily raised those standards over the past two decades, when gas was cheap, U.S. automakers might have invested in new, fuel-efficient models instead of gas-guzzling SUVs—making them more competitive as gas prices rose. Instead, we're seeing Japanese competitors run circles around Detroit. Toyota plans to sell one hundred thousand of their popular Priuses in 2006, while GM's hybrid won't even hit the market until 2007. And we can expect companies like Toyota to outcompete U.S automakers in the burgeoning Chinese market since China already has higher fuel-efficiency standards than we do.

The bottom line is that fuel-efficient cars and alternative fuels like E85, a fuel formulated with 85 percent ethanol, represent the future of the auto industry. It is a future American car companies can attain if we start making some tough choices now. For years U.S. automakers and the UAW have resisted higher fuel-efficiency standards because retooling costs money, and Detroit is already struggling under huge retiree health-care costs and stiff competition. So during my first year in the Senate I proposed legislation I called "Health Care for Hybrids." The bill makes a deal with U.S. automakers: In exchange for federal financial assistance in meeting the health-care costs of retired autoworkers, the Big Three would reinvest these savings into developing more fuel-efficient vehicles.

Aggressively investing in alternative fuel sources can also lead to the creation of thousands of new jobs. Ten or twenty years down the road, that old Maytag plant in Galesburg could reopen its doors as a cellulosic ethanol refinery. Down the street, scientists might be busy in a research lab working on a new hydrogen cell. And across the way, a new auto company could be busy churning out hybrid cars. The new jobs created could be filled by American workers trained with new skills and a world-class education, from elementary school to college.

But we can't afford to hesitate much longer. I got a glimpse of what a nation's dependence on foreign energy can do in the summer of 2005, when Senator Dick Lugar and I visited Ukraine and met with the country's newly elected president, Viktor Yushchenko. The story of Yushchenko's election had made headlines around the world: Running against a ruling party that for years had catered to the wishes of neighboring Russia, Yushchenko survived an assassination attempt, a stolen election, and threats from Moscow, before the Ukrainian people finally rose up in an "Orange Revolution"—a series of peaceful mass demonstrations that ultimately led to Yushchenko's installation as president.

It should have been a heady time in the former Soviet state, and indeed, everywhere we went there was talk of democratic liberalization and economic reform. But in our conversations with Yushchenko and his cabinet, we soon discovered that Ukraine had a major problem—it continued to be entirely dependent on Russia for all its oil and natural gas. Already, Russia had indicated that it would end Ukraine's ability to purchase this energy at below-world-market prices, a move that would lead to a tripling of home heating oil prices during the winter months leading up to parliamentary elections. Pro-Russian forces inside the country were biding their time, aware that for all the soaring rhetoric, the orange banners, the demonstrations, and Yushchenko's courage, Ukraine still found itself at the mercy of its former patron.

A nation that can't control its energy sources can't control its future. Ukraine may have little choice in the matter, but the wealthiest and most powerful nation on earth surely does.

EDUCATION. SCIENCE AND technology. Energy. Investments in these three key areas would go a long way in making America more competitive. Of course, none of these investments will yield results overnight. All will be subject to controversy. Investment in R & D and education will cost money at a time when our federal budget is already stretched. Increasing the fuel efficiency of American cars or instituting performance pay for public-school teachers will involve overcoming the suspicions of workers who already feel embattled. And arguments over the wisdom of school vouchers or the viability of hydrogen fuel cells won't go away anytime soon.

But while the means we use to accomplish these ends should be subject to vigorous and open debate, the ends themselves shouldn't be in dispute. If we fail to act, our competitive position in the world will decline. If we act boldly, then our economy will be less vulnerable to economic disruption, our trade balance will improve, the pace of U.S. technological innovation will accelerate, and the American worker will be in a stronger position to adapt to the global economy.

Still, will that be enough? Assuming we're able to bridge some of our ideological differences and keep the U.S. economy growing, will I be able to look squarely in the eyes of those workers in Galesburg and tell them that globalization can work for them and their children?

That was the question on my mind during the 2005 debate on the Central American Free Trade Agreement, or CAFTA. Viewed in isolation, the agreement posed little threat to American workers—the combined economies of the Central American countries involved were roughly the same as that of New Haven, Connecticut. It opened up new markets for U.S. agricultural producers, and promised much-needed foreign investment in poor countries like Honduras and the Dominican Republic. There were some problems with the agreement, but overall, CAFTA was probably a net plus for the U.S. economy.

When I met with representatives from organized labor, though, they were having none of it. As far as they were concerned, NAFTA had been a disaster for U.S. workers, and CAFTA just promised more of the same. What was needed, they said, was not just free trade but fair trade: stronger labor protections in countries that trade with the United States, including rights to unionize and bans on child labor; improved environmental standards in these same countries; an end to unfair government subsidies to foreign exporters and nontariff barriers on U.S. exports; stronger protections for U.S. intellectual property; and—in the case of China in particular—an end to an artificially devalued currency that put U.S. companies at a perpetual disadvantage.

Like most Democrats, I strongly support all these things. And yet, I felt obliged to say to the union reps that none of these measures would change the underlying realities of globalization. Stronger labor or environmental provisions in a trade bill can help put pressure on countries to keep improving worker conditions, as can efforts to obtain agreements from U.S. retailers to sell goods produced at a fair wage. But they won't eliminate the enormous gap in hourly wages between U.S. workers and workers in Honduras, Indonesia, Mozambique, or Bangladesh, countries where work in a dirty factory or overheated sweatshop is often considered a step up on the economic ladder.

Likewise, China's willingness to let its currency rise might modestly raise the price on goods manufactured there, thereby making U.S. goods somewhat more competitive. But when all is said and done, China will still have more surplus labor in its countryside than half the entire population of the United States—which means Wal-Mart will be keeping suppliers there busy for a very, very long time.

We need a new approach to the trade question, I would say, one that acknowledges these realities.

And my union brothers and sisters would nod and say that they were interested in talking to me about my ideas—but in the meantime, could they mark me as a "no" vote on CAFTA?

In fact, the basic debate surrounding free trade has hardly changed since the early 1980s, with labor and its allies generally losing the fight. The conventional wisdom among policy makers, the press, and the business community these days is that free trade makes everyone better off. At any given time, so the argument goes, some U.S. jobs may be lost to trade and cause localized pain and hardship—but for every one thousand manufacturing jobs lost due to a plant closure, the same or an even greater number of jobs will be created in the new and expanding service sectors of the economy.

As the pace of globalization has picked up, though, it's not just unions that are worrying about the long-term prospects for U.S. workers. Economists have noted that throughout the world—including China and India—it seems to take more economic growth each year to produce the same number of jobs, a consequence of ever-increasing automation and higher productivity.

Some analysts question whether a U.S. economy more dominated by services can expect to see the same productivity growth,
and hence rising living standards, as we've seen in the past. In
fact, over the past five years, statistics consistently show that the
wages of American jobs being lost are higher than the wages of
American jobs being created.

And while upgrading the education levels of American workers will improve their ability to adapt to the global economy, a
better education alone won't necessarily protect them from growing competition. Even if the United States produced twice as
many computer programmers per capita as China, India, or any
Eastern European country, the sheer number of new entrants
into the global marketplace means a lot more programmers overseas than there are in the United States—all of them available at
one-fifth the salary to any business with a broadband link.

In other words, free trade may well grow the worldwide economic pie—but there's no law that says workers in the United
States will continue to get a bigger and bigger slice.

Given these realities, it's easy to understand why some might
want to put a stop to globalization—to freeze the status quo and
insulate ourselves from economic disruption. On a stop to New
York during the CAFTA debate, I mentioned some of the studies
I'd been reading to Robert Rubin, the former U.S. Treasury secretary under Clinton whom I had gotten to know during my
campaign. It would be hard to find a Democrat more closely
identified with globalization than Rubin—not only had he been
one of Wall Street's most influential bankers for decades, but for
much of the nineties he had helped chart the course of world finance. He also happens to be one of the more thoughtful and
unassuming people I know. So I asked him whether at least some
of the fears I'd heard from the Maytag workers in Galesburg
were well founded—that there was no way to avoid a long-term
decline in U.S. living standards if we opened ourselves up entirely to competition with much cheaper labor around the world.

"That's a complicated question," Rubin said. "Most economists will tell you that there's no inherent limit to the number of good new jobs that the U.S. economy can generate, because there's no limit to human ingenuity. People invent new industries, new needs and wants. I think the economists are probably right. Historically, it's been the case. Of course, there's no guarantee that the pattern holds this time. With the pace of technological change, the size of the countries we're competing against, and the cost differentials with those countries, we may see a different dynamic emerge. So I suppose it's possible that even if we do everything right, we could still face some challenges."

I suggested that the folks in Galesburg might not find his answer reassuring.

"I said it's possible, not probable," he said. "I tend to be cautiously optimistic that if we get our fiscal house in order and improve our educational system, their children will do just fine. Anyway, there's one thing that I would tell the people in Galesburg *is* certain. Any efforts at protectionism will be counterproductive—and it will make their children worse off in the bargain."

I appreciated Rubin's acknowledgment that American workers might have legitimate cause for concern when it came to globalization; in my experience, most labor leaders have thought deeply about the issue and can't be dismissed as kneejerk protectionists.

Still, it was hard to deny Rubin's basic insight: We can try to slow globalization, but we can't stop it. The U.S. economy is now so integrated with the rest of the world, and digital commerce so widespread, that it's hard to even imagine, much less enforce, an effective regime of protectionism. A tariff on imported steel may give temporary relief to U.S. steel producers, but it will make every U.S. manufacturer that uses steel in its products less competitive on the world market. It's tough to "buy American" when a video game sold by a U.S. company has been developed by Japanese software engineers and packaged in Mexico. U.S. Border Patrol agents can't interdict the services of a call center in India, or stop an electrical engineer in Prague from sending his work via email to a company in Dubuque. When it comes to trade, there are few borders left.

This doesn't mean, however, that we should just throw up our hands and tell workers to fend for themselves. I would make this point to President Bush toward the end of the CAFTA debate, when I and a group of other senators were invited to the White House for discussions. I told the President that I believed in the benefits of trade, and that I had no doubt the White House could squeeze out the votes for this particular agreement. But I said that resistance to CAFTA had less to do with the specifics of the agreement and more to do with the growing insecurities of the American worker. Unless we found strategies to allay those fears, and sent a strong signal to American workers that the federal government was on their side, protectionist sentiment would only grow.

The President listened politely and said that he'd be interested in hearing my ideas. In the meantime, he said, he hoped he could count on my vote.

He couldn't. I ended up voting against CAFTA, which passed the Senate by a vote of 55 to 45. My vote gave me no satisfaction, but I felt it was the only way to register a protest against what I considered to be the White House's inattention to the losers from free trade. Like Bob Rubin, I am optimistic about the long-term prospects for the U.S. economy and the ability of U.S. workers to compete in a free trade environment—but only if we distribute the costs and benefits of globalization more fairly across the population.

THE LAST TIME we faced an economic transformation as disruptive as the one we face today, FDR led the nation to a new social compact—a bargain between government, business, and workers that resulted in widespread prosperity and economic security for more than fifty years. For the average American worker, that security rested on three pillars: the ability to find a job that paid enough to support a family and save for emergencies; a package of health and retirement benefits from his employer; and a government safety net—Social Security, Medicaid and Medicare, unemployment insurance, and to a lesser extent federal bankruptcy and pension protections—that could cushion the fall of those who suffered setbacks in their lives.

Certainly the impulse behind this New Deal compact involved a sense of social solidarity: the idea that employers should do right by their workers, and that if fate or miscalculation caused any one of us to stumble, the larger American community would be there to lift us up.

But this compact also rested on an understanding that a system of sharing risks and rewards can actually improve the workings of the market. FDR understood that decent wages and benefits for workers could create the middle-class base of consumers that would stabilize the U.S. economy and drive its expansion. And FDR recognized that we would all be more likely to take risks in our lives—to change jobs or start new businesses or welcome competition from other countries—if we knew that we would have some measure of protection should we fail.

That's what Social Security, the centerpiece of New Deal legislation, has provided—a form of social insurance that protects us from risk. We buy private insurance for ourselves in the marketplace all the time, because as self-reliant as we may be, we recognize that things don't always work out as planned—a child gets sick, the company we work for shuts its doors, a parent contracts Alzheimer's, the stock market portfolio turns south. The bigger the pool of insured, the more risk is spread, the more coverage provided, and the lower the cost. Sometimes, though, we can't buy insurance for certain risks on the marketplace—usually because companies find it unprofitable. Sometimes the insurance we get through our job isn't enough, and we can't afford to buy more on our own. Sometimes an unexpected tragedy strikes and it turns out we didn't have enough insurance. For all these reasons, we ask the government to step in and create an insurance pool for us—a pool that includes all of the American people.

Today the social compact FDR helped construct is beginning to crumble. In response to increased foreign competition and pressure from a stock market that insists on quarterly boosts in profitability, employers are automating, downsizing, and off-shoring, all of which makes workers more vulnerable to job loss and gives them less leverage to demand increased pay or benefits. Although the federal government offers a generous tax break for companies that provide health insurance, companies have shifted the skyrocketing costs onto employees in the form of higher premiums, copayments, and deductibles; meanwhile, half of small businesses, where millions of Americans work, can't afford to offer their employees any insurance at all. In similar fashion, companies are shifting from the traditional defined-benefit pension plan to 401(k)s, and in some cases using bankruptcy court to shed existing pension obligations.

The cumulative impact on families is severe. The wages of the average American worker have barely kept pace with inflation over the past two decades. Since 1988, the average family's health insurance costs have quadrupled. Personal savings rates have never been lower. And levels of personal debt have never been higher.

Rather than use the government to lessen the impact of these trends, the Bush Administration's response has been to encourage them. That's the basic idea behind the Ownership Society: If we free employers of any obligations to their workers and dismantle what's left of New Deal, government-run social insurance programs, then the magic of the marketplace will take care of the rest. If the guiding philosophy behind the traditional system of social insurance could be described as "We're all in it together," the philosophy behind the Ownership Society seems to be "You're on your own."

It's a tempting idea, one that's elegant in its simplicity and that frees us of any obligations we have toward one another. There's only one problem with it. It won't work—at least not for those who are already falling behind in the global economy.

Take the Administration's attempt to privatize Social Security. The Administration argues that the stock market can provide individuals a better return on investment, and in the aggregate at least they are right; historically, the market outperforms Social Security's cost-of-living adjustments. But individual investment decisions will always produce winners and losers—those who bought Microsoft early and those who bought Enron late. What would the Ownership Society do with the losers? Unless we're willing to see seniors starve on the street, we're going to have to cover their retirement expenses one way or another—and since we don't know in advance which of us will be losers, it makes sense for all of us to chip in to a pool that gives us at least some guaranteed income in our golden years. That doesn't mean we shouldn't encourage individuals to pursue higher-risk, higher-return investment strategies. They should. It just means that they should do so with savings other than those put into Social Security.

The same principles are at work when it comes to the Administration's efforts to encourage a shift from employer- or government-based health-care plans to individual Health Savings Accounts. The idea might make sense if the lump sum each individual received were enough to buy a decent health-care plan through his employer, and if that lump sum kept pace with inflation of health-care costs. But what if you work for an employer who doesn't offer a health-care plan? Or what if the Administration's theory on health-care inflation turns out to be wrong—if it turns out that health-care costs aren't due to people's cavalier attitude toward their health or an irrational desire to purchase more than they need? Then "freedom to choose" will mean that employees bear the brunt of future increases in health care, and the amount of money in their Health Savings Accounts will buy less and less coverage each year.

In other words, the Ownership Society doesn't even try to spread the risks and rewards of the new economy among all Americans. Instead, it simply magnifies the uneven risks and rewards of today's winner-take-all economy. If you are healthy or wealthy or just plain lucky, then you will become more so. If you are poor or sick or catch a bad break, you will have nobody to look to for help. That's not a recipe for sustained economic growth or the maintenance of a strong American middle class. It's certainly not a recipe for social cohesion. It runs counter to those values that say we have a stake in each other's success.

It's not who we are as a people.

FORTUNATELY, THERE'S AN alternative approach, one that recasts FDR's social compact to meet the needs of a new century. In each area where workers are vulnerable—wages, job loss, retirement, and health care—there are good ideas, some old and some new, that would go a long way toward making Americans more secure.

Let's start with wages. Americans believe in work—not just as a means of supporting themselves but as a means of giving their lives purpose and direction, order and dignity. The old welfare program, Aid to Families with Dependent Children, too often failed to honor this core value, which helps explain not only its unpopularity with the public but also why it often isolated the very people it was supposed to help.

On the other hand, Americans also believe that if we work full-time, we should be able to support ourselves and our kids. For many people on the bottom rungs of the economy—mainly low-skilled workers in the rapidly growing service sector—this basic promise isn't being fulfilled.

Government policies can help these workers, with little impact on market efficiency. For starters, we can raise the minimum wage. It may be true—as some economists argue—that any big jumps in the minimum wage discourage employers from hiring more workers. But when the minimum wage hasn't been changed in nine years and has less purchasing power in real dollars than it did in 1955, so that someone working full-time today in a minimum-wage job doesn't earn enough to rise out of poverty, such arguments carry less force. The Earned Income Tax Credit, a program championed by Ronald Reagan that provides low-wage workers with supplemental income through the tax code, should also be expanded and streamlined so more families can take advantage of it.

To help all workers adapt to a rapidly changing economy, it's also time to update the existing system of unemployment insurance and trade adjustment assistance. In fact, there are a slew of good ideas out there on how to create a more comprehensive system of adjustment assistance. We could extend such assistance to service industries, create flexible education accounts that workers could use to retrain, or provide retraining assistance for workers in sectors of the economy vulnerable to dislocation before they lose their jobs. And in an economy where the job you lose often paid more than the new job you gain, we could also try the concept of wage insurance, which provides 50 percent of the difference between a worker's old wage and his new wage for anywhere from one to two years.

Finally, to help workers gain higher wages and better benefits, we need once again to level the playing field between organized labor and employers. Since the early 1980s, unions have been steadily losing ground, not just because of changes in the economy but also because today's labor laws—and the make-up of the National Labor Relations Board—have provided workers with very little protection. Each year, more than twenty thousand workers are fired or lose wages simply for trying to organize and join unions. That needs to change. We should have tougher penalties to prevent employers from firing or discriminating against workers involved in organizing efforts. Employers should have to recognize a union if a majority of employees sign authorization cards choosing the union to represent them. And federal mediation should be available to help an employer and a new union reach agreement on a contract within a reasonable amount of time.

Business groups may argue that a more unionized workforce will rob the U.S. economy of flexibility and its competitive edge. But it's precisely because of a more competitive global environment that we can expect unionized workers to want to cooperate with employers—so long as they are getting their fair share of higher productivity.

Just as government policies can boost workers' wages without hurting the competitiveness of U.S. firms, so can we strengthen their ability to retire with dignity. We should start with a commitment to preserve Social Security's essential character and shore up its solvency. The problems with the Social Security trust fund are real but manageable. In 1983, when facing a similar problem, Ronald Reagan and House Speaker Tip O'Neill got together and shaped a bipartisan plan that stabilized the system for the next sixty years. There's no reason we can't do the same today.

With respect to the private retirement system, we should acknowledge that defined-benefit pension plans have been declining, but insist that companies fulfill any outstanding promises to their workers and retirees. Bankruptcy laws should be amended to move pension beneficiaries to the front of the creditor line so that companies can't just file for Chapter 11 to stiff workers. Moreover, new rules should force companies to properly fund their pension funds, in part so taxpayers don't end up footing the bill.

And if Americans are going to depend on defined-contribution plans like 401(k)s to supplement Social Security, then the government should step in to make them more broadly available to all Americans and more effective in encouraging savings. Former Clinton economic adviser Gene Sperling has suggested the creation of a universal 401(k), in which the government would match contributions made into a new retirement account by low- and moderate-income families. Other experts have suggested the simple (and cost-free) step of having employers automatically enroll their employees in their 401(k) plans at the maximum allowable level; people could still choose to contribute less than the maximum or not participate at all, but evidence shows that by changing the default rule, employee participation rates go up dramatically. As a complement to Social Security, we should take the best and most affordable of these ideas and begin moving toward a beefed-up, universally available pension system that not only promotes savings but gives all Americans a bigger stake in the fruits of globalization.

As vital as it may be to raise the wages of American workers and improve their retirement security, perhaps our most pressing task is to fix our broken health-care system. Unlike Social Security, the two main government-funded health-care programs—Medicare and Medicaid—really are broken; without any changes, by 2050 these two entitlements, along with Social Security, could grow to consume as large a share of our national economy as the entire federal budget does today. The addition of a hugely expensive prescription drug benefit that provides limited coverage and does nothing to control the cost of drugs has only made the problem worse. And the private system has evolved into a patchwork of inefficient bureaucracies, endless paperwork, overburdened providers, and dissatisfied patients.

In 1993, President Clinton took a stab at creating a system of universal coverage, but was stymied. Since then, the public debate has been deadlocked, with some on the right arguing for a strong dose of market discipline through Health Savings Accounts, others on the left arguing for a single-payer national health-care plan similar to those that exist in Europe and Canada, and experts across the political spectrum recommending a series of sensible but incremental reforms to the existing system.

It's time we broke this impasse by acknowledging a few simple truths.

Given the amount of money we spend on health care (more per capita than any other nation), we should be able to provide basic coverage to every single American. But we can't sustain current rates of health-care inflation every year; we have to contain costs for the entire system, including Medicare and Medicaid.

With Americans changing jobs more frequently, more likely to go through spells of unemployment, and more likely to work part-time or to be self-employed, health insurance can't just run through employers anymore. It needs to be portable.

The market alone can't solve our health-care woes—in part because the market has proven incapable of creating large enough insurance pools to keep costs to individuals affordable, in part because health care is not like other products or services (when your child gets sick, you don't go shopping for the best bargain).

And finally, whatever reforms we implement should provide strong incentives for improved quality, prevention, and more efficient delivery of care.

With these principles in mind, let me offer just one example of what a serious health-care reform plan might look like. We could start by having a nonpartisan group like the National Academy of Science's Institute of Medicine (IOM) determine what a basic, high-quality health-care plan should look like and how much it should cost. In designing this model plan, the IOM would examine which existing health-care programs deliver the best care in the most cost-effective manner. In particular, the model plan would emphasize coverage of primary care, prevention, catastrophic care, and the management of chronic conditions like asthma and diabetes. Overall, 20 percent of all patients account for 80 percent of the care, and if we can prevent diseases from occurring or manage their effects through simple interventions like making sure patients control their diets or take their medicines regularly, we can dramatically improve patient outcomes and save the system a great deal of money.

Next, we would allow anyone to purchase this model health-care plan either through an existing insurance pool like the one set up for federal employees, or through a series of new pools set up in every state. Private insurers like Blue Cross Blue Shield and Aetna would compete to provide coverage to participants in these pools, but whatever plan they offered would have to meet the criteria for high quality and cost controls set forth by IOM.

To further drive down costs, we would require that insurers and providers who participate in Medicare, Medicaid, or the new health plans have electronic claims, electronic records, and up-to-date patient error reporting systems—all of which would dramatically cut down on administrative costs, and the number of medical errors and adverse events (which in turn would reduce costly medical malpractice lawsuits). This simple step alone could cut overall health-care costs by up to 10 percent, with some experts pointing to even greater savings.

With the money we save through increased preventive care and lower administrative and malpractice costs, we would provide a subsidy to low-income families who wanted to purchase the model plan through their state pool, and immediately mandate coverage for all uninsured children. If necessary, we could also help pay for these subsidies by restructuring the tax break that employers use to provide health care to their employees: They would continue to get a tax break for the plans typically offered to workers, but we could examine a tax break for fancy, gold-plated executive health-care plans that fail to provide any additional health benefits.

The point of this exercise is not to suggest that there's an easy formula for fixing our health-care system—there isn't. Many details would have to be addressed before we moved forward on a plan like the one outlined above; in particular, we would have to make sure that the creation of a new state pool does not cause employers to drop the health-care plans that they are already providing their employees. And, there may be other more cost-effective and elegant ways to improve the health-care system.

The point is that if we commit ourselves to making sure everybody has decent health care, there are ways to accomplish it without breaking the federal treasury or resorting to rationing.

If we want Americans to accept the rigors of globalization, then we will need to make that commitment. One night five years ago, Michelle and I were awakened by the sound of our younger daughter, Sasha, crying in her room. Sasha was only three months old at the time, so it wasn't unusual for her to wake up in the middle of the night. But there was something about the way she was crying, and her refusal to be comforted, that concerned us. Eventually we called our pediatrician, who agreed to meet us at his office at the crack of dawn. After examining her, he told us that she might have meningitis and sent us immediately to the emergency room.

It turned out that Sasha did have meningitis, although a form that responded to intravenous antibiotics. Had she not been diagnosed in time, she could have lost her hearing or possibly even died. As it was, Michelle and I spent three days with our baby in the hospital, watching nurses hold her down while a doctor performed a spinal tap, listening to her scream, praying she didn't take a turn for the worse.

Sasha is fine now, as healthy and happy as a five-year-old should be. But I still shudder when I think of those three days; how my world narrowed to a single point, and how I was not interested in anything or anybody outside the four walls of that hospital room—not my work, not my schedule, not my future. And I am reminded that unlike Tim Wheeler, the steelworker I met in Galesburg whose son needed a liver transplant, unlike millions of Americans who've gone through a similar ordeal, I had a job and insurance at the time.

Americans are willing to compete with the world. We work harder than the people of any other wealthy nation. We are willing to tolerate more economic instability and are willing to take more personal risks to get ahead. But we can only compete if our government makes the investments that give us a fighting chance—and if we know that our families have some net beneath which they cannot fall.

That's a bargain with the American people worth making.

INVESTMENTS TO MAKE America more competitive, and a new American social compact—if pursued in concert, these broad concepts point the way to a better future for our children and grandchildren. But there's one last piece to the puzzle, a lingering question that presents itself in every single policy debate in Washington.

How do we pay for it?

At the end of Bill Clinton's presidency, we had an answer. For the first time in almost thirty years, we enjoyed big budget surpluses and a rapidly declining national debt. In fact, Federal Reserve Chairman Alan Greenspan expressed concern that the debt might get paid down too fast, thereby limiting the Reserve System's ability to manage monetary policy. Even after the dot-com bubble burst and the economy was forced to absorb the shock of 9/11, we had the chance to make a down payment on sustained economic growth and broader opportunity for all Americans.

But that's not the path we chose. Instead, we were told by our President that we could fight two wars, increase our military budget by 74 percent, protect the homeland, spend more on education, initiate a new prescription drug plan for seniors, and initiate successive rounds of massive tax cuts, all at the same time. We were told by our congressional leaders that they could make up for lost revenue by cutting out government waste and fraud, even as the number of pork barrel projects increased by an astonishing 64 percent.

The result of this collective denial is the most precarious budget situation that we've seen in years. We now have an annual budget deficit of almost $300 billion, not counting more than $180 billion we borrow every year from the Social Security Trust Fund, all of which adds directly to our national debt. That debt now stands at $9 trillion—approximately $30,000 for every man, woman, and child in the country.

It's not the debt itself that's most troubling. Some debt might have been justified if we had spent the money investing in those things that would make us more competitive—overhauling our schools, or increasing the reach of our broadband system, or installing E85 pumps in gas stations across the country. We might have used the surplus to shore up Social Security or restructure our health-care system. Instead, the bulk of the debt is a direct result of the President's tax cuts, 47.4 percent of which went to the top 5 percent of the income bracket, 36.7 percent of which went to the top 1 percent, and 15 percent of which went to the top one-tenth of 1 percent, typically people making $1.6 million a year or more.

In other words, we ran up the national credit card so that the biggest beneficiaries of the global economy could keep an even bigger share of the take.

So far we've been able to get away with this mountain of debt because foreign central banks—particularly China's—want us to keep buying their exports. But this easy credit won't continue forever. At some point, foreigners will stop lending us money, interest rates will go up, and we will spend most of our nation's output paying them back.

If we're serious about avoiding such a future, then we'll have to start digging ourselves out of this hole. On paper, at least, we know what to do. We can cut and consolidate nonessential programs. We can rein in spending on health-care costs. We can eliminate tax credits that have outlived their usefulness and close loopholes that let corporations get away without paying taxes. And we can restore a law that was in place during the Clinton presidency—called Paygo—that prohibits money from leaving the federal treasury, either in the form of new spending or tax cuts, without some way of compensating for the lost revenue.

If we take all of these steps, emerging from this fiscal situation will still be difficult. We will probably have to postpone some investments that we know are needed to improve our competitive position in the world, and we will have to prioritize the help that we give to struggling American families.

But even as we make these difficult choices, we should ponder the lesson of the past six years and ask ourselves whether our budgets and our tax policy really reflect the values that we profess to hold.

"IF THERE'S CLASS warfare going on in America, then my class is winning."

I was sitting in the office of Warren Buffett, chairman of Berkshire Hathaway and the second richest man in the world. I had heard about the famous simplicity of Buffett's tastes—how he still lived in the same modest home that he'd bought in 1967, and how he had sent all his children to the Omaha public schools.

Still, I had been a little surprised when I walked into a non-descript office building in Omaha and entered what looked like an insurance agent's office, with mock wood paneling, a few decorative pictures on the wall, and no one in sight. "Come on back," a woman's voice had called out, and I'd turned the corner to find the Oracle of Omaha himself, chuckling about something with his daughter, Susie, and his assistant, Debbie, his suit a bit rumpled, his bushy eyebrows sticking out high over his glasses.

Buffett had invited me to Omaha to discuss tax policy. More

specifically, he wanted to know why Washington continued to cut taxes for people in his income bracket when the country was broke.

"I did a calculation the other day," he said as we sat down in his office. "Though I've never used tax shelters or had a tax planner, after including the payroll taxes we each pay, I'll pay a lower effective tax rate this year than my receptionist. In fact, I'm pretty sure I pay a lower rate than the average American. And if the President has his way, I'll be paying even less."

Buffett's low rates were a consequence of the fact that, like most wealthy Americans, almost all his income came from dividends and capital gains, investment income that since 2003 has been taxed at only 15 percent. The receptionist's salary, on the other hand, was taxed at almost twice that rate once FICA was included. From Buffett's perspective, the discrepancy was unconscionable.

"The free market's the best mechanism ever devised to put resources to their most efficient and productive use," he told me. "The government isn't particularly good at that. But the market isn't so good at making sure that the wealth that's produced is being distributed fairly or wisely. Some of that wealth has to be plowed back into education, so that the next generation has a fair chance, and to maintain our infrastructure, and provide some sort of safety net for those who lose out in a market economy. And it just makes sense that those of us who've benefited most from the market should pay a bigger share."

We spent the next hour talking about globalization, executive compensation, the worsening trade deficit, and the national debt. He was especially exercised over Bush's proposed elimination of the estate tax, a step he believed would encourage an aristocracy of wealth rather than merit.

"When you get rid of the estate tax," he said, "you're basically handing over command of the country's resources to people who didn't earn it. It's like choosing the 2020 Olympic team by picking the children of all the winners at the 2000 Games."

Before I left, I asked Buffett how many of his fellow billionaires shared his views. He laughed.

"I'll tell you, not very many," he said. "They have this idea that it's 'their money' and they deserve to keep every penny of it. What they don't factor in is all the public investment that lets us live the way we do. Take me as an example. I happen to have a talent for allocating capital. But my ability to use that talent is completely dependent on the society I was born into. If I'd been born into a tribe of hunters, this talent of mine would be pretty worthless. I can't run very fast. I'm not particularly strong. I'd probably end up as some wild animal's dinner.

"But I was lucky enough to be born in a time and place where society values my talent, and gave me a good education to develop that talent, and set up the laws and the financial system to let me do what I love doing—and make a lot of money doing it. The least I can do is help pay for all that."

It may be surprising to some to hear the world's foremost capitalist talk in this way, but Buffett's views aren't necessarily a sign of a soft heart. Rather, they reflect an understanding that how well we respond to globalization won't be just a matter of identifying the right policies. It will also have to do with a change in spirit, a willingness to put our common interests and the interests of future generations ahead of short-term expediency.

More particularly, we will have to stop pretending that all cuts in spending are equivalent, or that all tax increases are the same. Ending corporate subsidies that serve no discernible economic purpose is one thing; reducing health-care benefits to poor children is something else entirely. At a time when ordinary families are feeling hit from all sides, the impulse to keep their taxes as low as possible is honorable and right. What's less honorable has been the willingness of the rich and the powerful to ride this antitax sentiment for their own purposes, or the way the President, Congress, lobbyists, and conservative commentators have been able to successfully conflate in the mind of voters the very real tax burdens of the middle class and the very manageable tax burdens of the wealthy.

Nowhere has this confusion been more evident than in the debate surrounding the proposed repeal of the estate tax. As currently structured, a husband and wife can pass on $4 million without paying any estate tax; in 2009, under current law, that figure goes up to $7 million. For this reason, the tax currently affects only the wealthiest one-half of 1 percent of the population, and will affect only one-third of 1 percent in 2009. And since completely repealing the estate tax would cost the U.S. Treasury around $1 trillion, it would be hard to find a tax cut that was less responsive to the needs of ordinary Americans or the long-term interests of the country.

Nevertheless, after some shrewd marketing by the President and his allies, 70 percent of the country now opposes the "death tax." Farm groups come to visit my office, insisting that the estate tax will mean the end of the family farm, despite the Farm Bureau's inability to point to a single farm in the country lost as a result of the "death tax." Meanwhile, I've had corporate CEOs explain to me that it's easy for Warren Buffett to favor an estate tax—even if his estate is taxed at 90 percent, he could still have a few billion to pass on to his kids—but that the tax is grossly unfair to those with estates worth "only" $10 or $15 million.

So let's be clear. The rich in America have little to complain about. Between 1971 and 2001, while the median wage and salary income of the average worker showed literally no gain, the income of the top hundredth of a percent went up almost 500 percent. The distribution of wealth is even more skewed, and levels of inequality are now higher than at any time since the Gilded Age. These trends were already at work throughout the nineties. Clinton's tax policies simply slowed them down a bit. Bush's tax cuts made them worse.

I point out these facts not—as Republican talking points would have it—to stir up class envy. I admire many Americans of great wealth and don't begrudge their success in the least. I know that many if not most have earned it through hard work, building businesses and creating jobs and providing value to their customers. I simply believe that those of us who have benefited most from this new economy can best afford to shoulder the obligation of ensuring every American child has a chance for that same success. And perhaps I possess a certain Midwestern sensibility that I inherited from my mother and her parents, a sensibility that Warren Buffett seems to share: that at a certain point one has enough, that you can derive as much pleasure from a Picasso hanging in a museum as from one that's hanging in your den, that you can get an awfully good meal in a restaurant for less than twenty dollars, and that once your drapes cost more than the average American's yearly salary, then you can afford to pay a bit more in taxes.

More than anything, it is that sense—that despite great differences in wealth, we rise and fall together—that we can't afford to lose. As the pace of change accelerates, with some rising and many falling, that sense of common kinship becomes harder to maintain. Jefferson was not entirely wrong to fear Hamilton's vision for the country, for we have always been in a constant balancing act between self-interest and community, markets and democracy, the concentration of wealth and power and the opening up of opportunity. We've lost that balance in Washington, I think. With all of us scrambling to raise money for campaigns, with unions weakened and the press distracted and lobbyists for the powerful pressing their full advantage, there are few countervailing voices to remind us of who we are and where we've come from, and to affirm our bonds with one another.

That was the subtext of a debate in early 2006, when a bribery scandal triggered new efforts to curb the influence of lobbyists in Washington. One of the proposals would have ended the practice of letting senators fly on private jets at the cheaper first-class commercial rate. The provision had little chance of passage. Still, my staff suggested that as the designated Democratic spokesperson on ethics reform, I should initiate a self-imposed ban on the practice.

It was the right thing to do, but I won't lie; the first time I was scheduled for a four-city swing in two days flying commercial, I felt some pangs of regret. The traffic to O'Hare was terrible. When I got there, the flight to Memphis had been delayed. A kid spilled orange juice on my shoe.

Then, while waiting in line, a man came up to me, maybe in his mid-thirties, dressed in chinos and a golf shirt, and told me that he hoped Congress would do something about stem cell research this year. I have early-stage Parkinson's disease, he said, and a son who's three years old. I probably won't ever get to play catch with him. I know it may be too late for me, but there's no reason somebody else has to go through what I'm going through.

These are the stories you miss, I thought to myself, when you fly on a private jet.

Chapter 6

Faith

TWO DAYS AFTER I won the Democratic nomination in my U.S. Senate race, I received an email from a doctor at the University of Chicago Medical School.

"Congratulations on your overwhelming and inspiring primary win," the doctor wrote. "I was happy to vote for you, and I will tell you that I am seriously considering voting for you in the general election. I write to express my concerns that may, in the end, prevent me from supporting you."

The doctor described himself as a Christian who understood his commitments to be comprehensive and "totalizing." His faith led him to strongly oppose abortion and gay marriage, but he said his faith also led him to question the idolatry of the free market and the quick resort to militarism that seemed to characterize much of President Bush's foreign policy.

The reason the doctor was considering voting for my opponent was not my position on abortion as such. Rather, he had read an entry that my campaign had posted on my website, suggesting that I would fight "right-wing ideologues who want to take away a woman's right to choose." He went on to write:

> I sense that you have a strong sense of justice and of the precarious position of justice in any polity, and I know that you have championed the plight of the voiceless. I also sense

that you are a fair-minded person with a high regard for reason. . . . Whatever your convictions, if you truly believe that those who oppose abortion are all ideologues driven by perverse desires to inflict suffering on women, then you, in my judgment, are not fair-minded. . . . You know that we enter times that are fraught with possibilities for good and for harm, times when we are struggling to make sense of a common polity in the context of plurality, when we are unsure of what grounds we have for making any claims that involve others. . . . I do not ask at this point that you oppose abortion, only that you speak about this issue in fair-minded words.

I checked my website and found the offending words. They were not my own; my staff had posted them to summarize my prochoice position during the Democratic primary, at a time when some of my opponents were questioning my commitment to protect *Roe v. Wade.* Within the bubble of Democratic Party politics, this was standard boilerplate, designed to fire up the base. The notion of engaging the other side on the issue was pointless, the argument went; any ambiguity on the issue implied weakness, and faced with the single-minded, give-no-quarter approach of antiabortion forces, we simply could not afford weakness.

Rereading the doctor's letter, though, I felt a pang of shame. Yes, I thought, there were those in the antiabortion movement for whom I had no sympathy, those who jostled or blocked women who were entering clinics, shoving photographs of mangled fetuses in the women's faces and screaming at the top of their lungs; those who bullied and intimidated and occasionally resorted to violence.

But those antiabortion protesters weren't the ones who occasionally appeared at my campaign rallies. The ones I encountered usually showed up in the smaller, downstate communities that we visited, their expressions weary but determined as they stood in silent vigil outside whatever building in which the rally was taking place, their handmade signs or banners held before them like shields. They didn't yell or try to disrupt our events, although they still made my staff jumpy. The first time a group of protesters showed up, my advance team went on red alert; five minutes before my arrival at the meeting hall, they called the car I was in and suggested that I slip in through the rear entrance to avoid a confrontation.

"I don't want to go through the back," I told the staffer driving me. "Tell them we're coming through the front."

We turned into the library parking lot and saw seven or eight protesters gathered along a fence: several older women and what looked to be a family—a man and woman with two young children. I got out of the car, walked up to the group, and introduced myself. The man shook my hand hesitantly and told me his name. He looked to be about my age, in jeans, a plaid shirt, and a St. Louis Cardinals cap. His wife shook my hand as well, but the older women kept their distance. The children, maybe nine or ten years old, stared at me with undisguised curiosity.

"You folks want to come inside?" I asked.

"No, thank you," the man said. He handed me a pamphlet. "Mr. Obama, I want you to know that I agree with a lot of what you have to say."

"I appreciate that."

"And I know you're a Christian, with a family of your own."

"That's true."

"So how can you support murdering babies?"

I told him I understood his position but had to disagree with it. I explained my belief that few women made the decision to terminate a pregnancy casually; that any pregnant woman felt the full force of the moral issues involved and wrestled with her conscience when making that heart-wrenching decision; that I feared a ban on abortion would force women to seek unsafe

abortions, as they had once done in this country and as they continued to do in countries that prosecute abortion doctors and the
women who seek their services. I suggested that perhaps we
could agree on ways to reduce the number of women who felt
the need to have abortions in the first place.

The man listened politely and then pointed to statistics on the
pamphlet listing the number of unborn children that, according
to him, were sacrificed every year. After a few minutes, I said I
had to go inside to greet my supporters and asked again if the
group wanted to come in. Again the man declined. As I turned to
go, his wife called out to me.

"I will pray for you," she said. "I pray that you have a change
of heart."

Neither my mind nor my heart changed that day, nor did they
in the days to come. But I did have that family in mind as I wrote
back to the doctor and thanked him for his email. The next day,
I circulated the email to my staff and had the language on my
website changed to state in clear but simple terms my prochoice
position. And that night, before I went to bed, I said a prayer of
my own—that I might extend the same presumption of good
faith to others that the doctor had extended to me.

IT IS A truism that we Americans are a religious people. According to the most recent surveys, 95 percent of Americans believe
in God, more than two-thirds belong to a church, 37 percent call
themselves committed Christians, and substantially more people
believe in angels than believe in evolution. Nor is religion confined to places of worship. Books proclaiming the end of days
sell millions of copies, Christian music fills the *Billboard* charts,
and new megachurches seem to spring up daily on the outskirts
of every major metropolis, providing everything from day care to
singles mixers to yoga and Pilates classes. Our President rou-

tinely remarks on how Christ changed his heart, and football players point to the heavens after every touchdown, as if God were calling plays from the celestial sidelines.

Of course, such religiosity is hardly new. The Pilgrims came to our shores to escape religious persecution and practice without impediment to their brand of strict Calvinism. Evangelical revivalism has repeatedly swept across the nation, and waves of successive immigrants have used their faith to anchor their lives in a strange new world. Religious sentiment and religious activism have sparked some of our most powerful political movements, from abolition to civil rights to the prairie populism of William Jennings Bryan.

Still, if fifty years ago you had asked the most prominent cultural commentators of the time just what the future of religion in America might be, they undoubtedly would have told you it was on the decline. The old-time religion was withering away, it was argued, a victim of science, higher levels of education in the general population, and the marvels of technology. Respectable folks might still attend church every Sunday; Bible-thumpers and faith healers might still work the Southern revival circuit; the fear of "godless communism" might help feed McCarthyism and the Red Scare. But for the most part, traditional religious practice—and certainly religious fundamentalism—was considered incompatible with modernity, at most a refuge of the poor and uneducated from the hardships of life. Even Billy Graham's monumental crusades were treated as a curious anachronism by pundits and academics, vestiges of an earlier time that had little to do with the serious work of managing a modern economy or shaping foreign policy.

By the time the sixties rolled around, many mainstream Protestant and Catholic leaders had concluded that if America's religious institutions were to survive, they would have to make themselves "relevant" to changing times—by accommodating church doctrine to science, and by articulating a social gospel that addressed the material issues of economic inequality, racism, sexism, and American militarism.

What happened? In part, the cooling of religious enthusiasm among Americans was always exaggerated. On this score, at least, the conservative critique of "liberal elitism" has a strong measure of truth: Ensconced in universities and large urban centers, academics, journalists, and purveyors of popular culture simply failed to appreciate the continuing role that all manner of religious expression played in communities across the country. Indeed, the failure of the country's dominant cultural institutions to acknowledge America's religious impulse helped foster a degree of religious entrepreneurship unmatched elsewhere in the industrialized world. Pushed out of sight but still throbbing with vitality throughout the heartland and the Bible Belt, a parallel universe emerged, a world not only of revivals and thriving ministries but also of Christian television, radio, universities, publishers, and entertainment, all of which allowed the devout to ignore the popular culture as surely as they were being ignored.

The reluctance on the part of many evangelicals to be drawn into politics—their inward focus on individual salvation and willingness to render unto Caesar what is his—might have endured indefinitely had it not been for the social upheavals of the sixties. In the minds of Southern Christians, the decision of a distant federal court to dismantle segregation seemed of a piece with its decisions to eliminate prayer in schools—a multipronged assault on the pillars of traditional Southern life. Across America, the women's movement, the sexual revolution, the increasing assertiveness of gays and lesbians, and most powerfully the Supreme Court's decision in *Roe v. Wade* seemed a direct challenge to the church's teachings about marriage, sexuality, and the proper roles of men and women. Feeling mocked and under attack, conservative Christians found it no longer possible to insulate themselves from the country's broader political and cultural trends.

And although it was Jimmy Carter who would first introduce the language of evangelical Christianity into modern national politics, it was the Republican Party, with its increasing emphasis on tradition, order, and "family values," that was best positioned to harvest this crop of politically awakened evangelicals and mobilize them against the liberal orthodoxy.

The story of how Ronald Reagan, Jerry Falwell, Pat Robertson, Ralph Reed, and finally Karl Rove and George W. Bush mobilized this army of Christian foot soldiers need not be repeated here. Suffice it to say that today white evangelical Christians (along with conservative Catholics) are the heart and soul of the Republican Party's grassroots base—a core following continually mobilized by a network of pulpits and media outlets that technology has only amplified. It is their issues—abortion, gay marriage, prayer in schools, intelligent design, Terri Schiavo, the posting of the Ten Commandments in the courthouse, home schooling, voucher plans, and the makeup of the Supreme Court—that often dominate the headlines and serve as one of the major fault lines in American politics. The single biggest gap in party affiliation among white Americans is not between men and women, or between those who reside in so-called red states and those who reside in blue states, but between those who attend church regularly and those who don't. Democrats, meanwhile, are scrambling to "get religion," even as a core segment of our constituency remains stubbornly secular in orientation, and fears—rightly, no doubt—that the agenda of an assertively Christian nation may not make room for them or their life choices.

But the growing political influence of the Christian right tells only part of the story. The Moral Majority and the Christian Coalition may have tapped into the discontent of many evangelical Christians, but what is more remarkable is the ability of evangelical Christianity not only to survive but to thrive in modern, high-tech America. At a time when mainline Protestant churches are all losing membership at a rapid clip, nondenominational evangelical churches are growing by leaps and bounds, eliciting levels of commitment and participation from their membership that no other American institution can match. Their fervor has gone mainstream.

There are various explanations for this success, from the skill of evangelicals in marketing religion to the charisma of their leaders. But their success also points to a hunger for the product they are selling, a hunger that goes beyond any particular issue or cause. Each day, it seems, thousands of Americans are going about their daily rounds—dropping off the kids at school, driving to the office, flying to a business meeting, shopping at the mall, trying to stay on their diets—and coming to the realization that something is missing. They are deciding that their work, their possessions, their diversions, their sheer busyness are not enough. They want a sense of purpose, a narrative arc to their lives, something that will relieve a chronic loneliness or lift them above the exhausting, relentless toll of daily life. They need an assurance that somebody out there cares about them, is listening to them—that they are not just destined to travel down a long highway toward nothingness.

If I have any insight into this movement toward a deepening religious commitment, perhaps it's because it's a road I have traveled.

I was not raised in a religious household. My maternal grandparents, who hailed from Kansas, had been steeped in religion as children: My grandfather had been raised by devout Baptist grandparents after his father had gone AWOL and his mother committed suicide, while my grandmother's parents—who occupied a slightly higher station in the hierarchy of small-town, Great Depression society (her father worked for an oil refinery, her mother was a schoolteacher)—were practicing Methodists.

But for perhaps the same reasons that my grandparents would

end up leaving Kansas and migrating to Hawaii, religious faith never really took root in their hearts. My grandmother was always too rational and too stubborn to accept anything she couldn't see, feel, touch, or count. My grandfather, the dreamer in our family, possessed the sort of restless soul that might have found refuge in religious belief had it not been for those other characteristics—an innate rebelliousness, a complete inability to discipline his appetites, and a broad tolerance of other people's weaknesses—that precluded him from getting too serious about anything.

This combination of traits—my grandmother's flinty rationalism, my grandfather's joviality and incapacity to judge others or himself too strictly—got passed on to my mother. Her own experiences as a bookish, sensitive child growing up in small towns in Kansas, Oklahoma, and Texas only reinforced this inherited skepticism. Her memories of the Christians who populated her youth were not fond ones. Occasionally, for my benefit, she would recall the sanctimonious preachers who would dismiss three-quarters of the world's people as ignorant heathens doomed to spend the afterlife in eternal damnation—and who in the same breath would insist that the earth and the heavens had been created in seven days, all geologic and astrophysical evidence to the contrary. She remembered the respectable church ladies who were always so quick to shun those unable to meet their standards of propriety, even as they desperately concealed their own dirty little secrets; the church fathers who uttered racial epithets and chiseled their workers out of any nickel that they could.

For my mother, organized religion too often dressed up closed-mindedness in the garb of piety, cruelty and oppression in the cloak of righteousness.

This isn't to say that she provided me with no religious instruction. In her mind, a working knowledge of the world's great religions was a necessary part of any well-rounded education. In our household the Bible, the Koran, and the Bhagavad Gita sat on the shelf alongside books of Greek and Norse and African mythology. On Easter or Christmas Day my mother might drag me to church, just as she dragged me to the Buddhist temple, the Chinese New Year celebration, the Shinto shrine, and ancient Hawaiian burial sites. But I was made to understand that such religious samplings required no sustained commitment on my part—no introspective exertion or self-flagellation. Religion was an expression of human culture, she would explain, not its wellspring, just one of the many ways—and not necessarily the best way—that man attempted to control the unknowable and understand the deeper truths about our lives.

In sum, my mother viewed religion through the eyes of the anthropologist that she would become; it was a phenomenon to be treated with a suitable respect, but with a suitable detachment as well. Moreover, as a child I rarely came in contact with those who might offer a substantially different view of faith. My father was almost entirely absent from my childhood, having been divorced from my mother when I was two years old; in any event, although my father had been raised a Muslim, by the time he met my mother he was a confirmed atheist, thinking religion to be so much superstition, like the mumbo-jumbo of witch doctors that he had witnessed in the Kenyan villages of his youth.

When my mother remarried, it was to an Indonesian with an equally skeptical bent, a man who saw religion as not particularly useful in the practical business of making one's way in the world, and who had grown up in a country that easily blended its Islamic faith with remnants of Hinduism, Buddhism, and ancient animist traditions. During the five years that we would live with my stepfather in Indonesia, I was sent first to a neighborhood Catholic school and then to a predominantly Muslim school; in both cases, my mother was less concerned with me learning the catechism or puzzling out the meaning of the muezzin's call to evening prayer than she was with whether I was properly learning my multiplication tables.

And yet for all her professed secularism, my mother was in many ways the most spiritually awakened person that I've ever known. She had an unswerving instinct for kindness, charity, and love, and spent much of her life acting on that instinct, sometimes to her detriment. Without the help of religious texts or outside authorities, she worked mightily to instill in me the values that many Americans learn in Sunday school: honesty, empathy, discipline, delayed gratification, and hard work. She raged at poverty and injustice, and scorned those who were indifferent to both.

Most of all, she possessed an abiding sense of wonder, a reverence for life and its precious, transitory nature that could properly be described as devotional. During the course of the day, she might come across a painting, read a line of poetry, or hear a piece of music, and I would see tears well up in her eyes. Sometimes, as I was growing up, she would wake me up in the middle of the night to have me gaze at a particularly spectacular moon, or she would have me close my eyes as we walked together at twilight to listen to the rustle of leaves. She loved to take children—any child—and sit them in her lap and tickle them or play games with them or examine their hands, tracing out the miracle of bone and tendon and skin and delighting at the truths to be found there. She saw mysteries everywhere and took joy in the sheer strangeness of life.

It is only in retrospect, of course, that I fully understand how deeply this spirit of hers influenced me—how it sustained me despite the absence of a father in the house, how it buoyed me through the rocky shoals of my adolescence, and how it invisibly guided the path I would ultimately take. My fierce ambitions might have been fueled by my father—by my knowledge of his achievements and failures, by my unspoken desire to somehow earn his love, and by my resentments and anger toward him. But it was my mother's fundamental faith—in the goodness of people

and in the ultimate value of this brief life we've each been given—
that channeled those ambitions. It was in search of confirmation
of her values that I studied political philosophy, looking for both
a language and systems of action that could help build community and make justice real. And it was in search of some practical
application of those values that I accepted work after college as a
community organizer for a group of churches in Chicago that
were trying to cope with joblessness, drugs, and hopelessness in
their midst.

I have recorded in a previous book the ways in which my
early work in Chicago helped me grow into my manhood—how
my work with the pastors and laypeople there deepened my resolve to lead a public life, how they fortified my racial identity
and confirmed my belief in the capacity of ordinary people to do
extraordinary things. But my experiences in Chicago also forced
me to confront a dilemma that my mother never fully resolved in
her own life: the fact that I had no community or shared traditions in which to ground my most deeply held beliefs. The Christians with whom I worked recognized themselves in me; they
saw that I knew their Book and shared their values and sang
their songs. But they sensed that a part of me remained removed,
detached, an observer among them. I came to realize that without a vessel for my beliefs, without an unequivocal commitment
to a particular community of faith, I would be consigned at some
level to always remain apart, free in the way that my mother was
free, but also alone in the same ways she was ultimately alone.

There are worse things than such freedom. My mother would
live happily as a citizen of the world, stitching together a community of friends wherever she found herself, satisfying her need
for meaning in her work and in her children. In such a life I, too,
might have contented myself had it not been for the particular
attributes of the historically black church, attributes that helped
me shed some of my skepticism and embrace the Christian faith.

For one thing, I was drawn to the power of the African American religious tradition to spur social change. Out of necessity, the black church had to minister to the whole person. Out of necessity, the black church rarely had the luxury of separating individual salvation from collective salvation. It had to serve as the center of the community's political, economic, and social as well as spiritual life; it understood in an intimate way the biblical call to feed the hungry and clothe the naked and challenge powers and principalities. In the history of these struggles, I was able to see faith as more than just a comfort to the weary or a hedge against death; rather, it was an active, palpable agent in the world. In the day-to-day work of the men and women I met in church each day, in their ability to "make a way out of no way" and maintain hope and dignity in the direst of circumstances, I could see the Word made manifest.

And perhaps it was out of this intimate knowledge of hardship, the grounding of faith in struggle, that the historically black church offered me a second insight: that faith doesn't mean that you don't have doubts, or that you relinquish your hold on this world. Long before it became fashionable among television evangelists, the typical black sermon freely acknowledged that all Christians (including the pastors) could expect to still experience the same greed, resentment, lust, and anger that everyone else experienced. The gospel songs, the happy feet, and the tears and shouts all spoke of a release, an acknowledgment, and finally a channeling of those emotions. In the black community, the lines between sinner and saved were more fluid; the sins of those who came to church were not so different from the sins of those who didn't, and so were as likely to be talked about with humor as with condemnation. You needed to come to church precisely because you were of this world, not apart from it; rich, poor, sinner, saved, you needed to embrace Christ precisely because you had sins to wash away—because you were human and needed an ally in your difficult journey, to make the peaks and valleys smooth and render all those crooked paths straight.

It was because of these newfound understandings—that religious commitment did not require me to suspend critical thinking, disengage from the battle for economic and social justice, or otherwise retreat from the world that I knew and loved—that I was finally able to walk down the aisle of Trinity United Church of Christ one day and be baptized. It came about as a choice and not an epiphany; the questions I had did not magically disappear. But kneeling beneath that cross on the South Side of Chicago, I felt God's spirit beckoning me. I submitted myself to His will, and dedicated myself to discovering His truth.

DISCUSSIONS OF FAITH are rarely heavy-handed within the confines of the Senate. No one is quizzed on his or her religious affiliation; I have rarely heard God's name invoked during debate on the floor. The Senate chaplain, Barry Black, is a wise and worldly man, former chief of navy chaplains, an African American who grew up in one of the toughest neighborhoods in Baltimore and carries out his limited duties—offering the morning prayer, hosting voluntary Bible study sessions, providing spiritual counseling to those who seek it—with a constant spirit of warmth and inclusiveness. The Wednesday-morning prayer breakfast is entirely optional, bipartisan, and ecumenical (Senator Norm Coleman, who is Jewish, is currently chief organizer on the Republican side); those who choose to attend take turns selecting a passage from Scripture and leading group discussion. Hearing the sincerity, openness, humility, and good humor with which even the most overtly religious senators—men like Rick Santorum, Sam Brownback, or Tom Coburn—share their personal faith journeys during these breakfasts, one is tempted to assume that the impact of faith on politics is largely salutary, a check on personal ambition, a ballast against the buffeting winds of today's head-lines and political expediency.

Beyond the Senate's genteel confines, though, any discussion of religion and its role in politics can turn a bit less civil. Take my Republican opponent in 2004, Ambassador Alan Keyes, who deployed a novel argument for attracting voters in the waning days of the campaign.

"Christ would not vote for Barack Obama," Mr. Keyes proclaimed, "because Barack Obama has voted to behave in a way that it is inconceivable for Christ to have behaved."

This wasn't the first time that Mr. Keyes had made such pronouncements. After my original Republican opponent had been forced to withdraw in the wake of some awkward disclosures from his divorce file, the Illinois Republican Party, unable to settle on a local candidate, had decided to recruit Mr. Keyes for the task. The fact that Mr. Keyes hailed from Maryland, had never lived in Illinois, had never won an election, and was regarded by many in the national Republican Party as insufferable didn't deter the Illinois GOP leadership. One Republican colleague of mine in the state senate provided me with a blunt explanation of their strategy: "We got our own Harvard-educated conservative black guy to go up against the Harvard-educated liberal black guy. He may not win, but at least he can knock that halo off your head."

Mr. Keyes himself was not lacking in confidence. A Ph.D. from Harvard, a protégé of Jeane Kirkpatrick, and U.S. ambassador to the UN Economic and Social Council under Ronald Reagan, he had burst into the public eye first as a two-time candidate for a U.S. Senate seat from Maryland and then as a two-time candidate for the GOP presidential nomination. He had been clobbered in all four races, but those losses had done nothing to diminish Mr. Keyes's reputation in the eyes of his supporters; for them, electoral failure seemed only to confirm his uncompromising devotion to conservative principles.

There was no doubt that the man could talk. At the drop of a hat Mr. Keyes could deliver a grammatically flawless disquisition on virtually any topic. On the stump, he could wind himself up into a fiery intensity, his body rocking, his brow running with sweat, his fingers jabbing the air, his high-pitched voice trembling with emotion as he called the faithful to do battle against the forces of evil.

Unfortunately for him, neither his intellect nor his eloquence could overcome certain defects as a candidate. Unlike most politicians, for example, Mr. Keyes made no effort to conceal what he clearly considered to be his moral and intellectual superiority. With his erect bearing, almost theatrically formal manner, and a hooded gaze that made him appear perpetually bored, he came off as a cross between a Pentecostal preacher and William F. Buckley.

Moreover, that self-assuredness disabled in him the instincts for self-censorship that allow most people to navigate the world without getting into constant fistfights. Mr. Keyes said whatever popped into his mind, and with dogged logic would follow over a cliff just about any idea that came to him. Already disadvantaged by a late start, a lack of funds, and his status as a carpetbagger, he proceeded during the course of a mere three months to offend just about everybody. He labeled all homosexuals—including Dick Cheney's daughter—"selfish hedonists," and insisted that adoption by gay couples inevitably resulted in incest. He called the Illinois press corps a tool of the "anti-marriage, anti-life agenda." He accused me of taking a "slaveholder's position" in my defense of abortion rights and called me a "hardcore, academic Marxist" for my support of universal health care and other social programs—and then added for good measure that because I was not the descendant of slaves I was not really African American. At one point he even managed to alienate the conservative Republicans who recruited him to Illinois by recommending—perhaps in a play for black votes—reparations in the form of a complete abolition of the income tax for all blacks with slave ancestry. ("This is a disaster!" sputtered one comment posted on the discussion board of Illinois's hard-right website, the Illinois Leader. "WHAT ABOUT THE WHITE GUYS!!!")

In other words, Alan Keyes was an ideal opponent; all I had to do was keep my mouth shut and start planning my swearing-in ceremony. And yet, as the campaign progressed, I found him getting under my skin in a way that few people ever have. When our paths crossed during the campaign, I often had to suppress the rather uncharitable urge to either taunt him or wring his neck. Once, when we bumped into each other at an Indian Independence Day parade, I poked him in the chest while making a point, a bit of alpha-male behavior that I hadn't engaged in since high school and which an observant news crew gamely captured; the moment was replayed in slow motion on TV that evening. In the three debates that were held before the election, I was frequently tongue-tied, irritable, and uncharacteristically tense—a fact that the public (having by that point written Mr. Keyes off) largely missed, but one that caused no small bit of distress to some of my supporters. "Why are you letting this guy give you fits?" they would ask me. For them, Mr. Keyes was a kook, an extremist, his arguments not even worth entertaining.

What they didn't understand was that I could not help but take Mr. Keyes seriously. For he claimed to speak for my religion—and although I might not like what came out of his mouth, I had to admit that some of his views had many adherents within the Christian church.

His argument went something like this: America was founded on the twin principles of God-given liberty and Christian faith. Successive liberal administrations had hijacked the federal government to serve a godless materialism and had thereby steadily chipped away—through regulation, socialistic welfare programs, gun laws, compulsory attendance at public schools, and the income tax ("the slave tax," as Mr. Keyes called it)—at individual

liberty and traditional values. Liberal judges had further con-
tributed to this moral decay by perverting the First Amendment
to mean the separation of church and state, and by validating all
sorts of aberrant behavior—particularly abortion and homosexuality—that threatened to destroy the nuclear family. The answer
to American renewal, then, was simple: Restore religion generally—and Christianity in particular—to its rightful place at the
center of our public and private lives, align the law with religious
precepts, and drastically restrict the power of federal government to legislate in areas prescribed neither by the Constitution
nor by God's commandments.

In other words, Alan Keyes presented the essential vision of
the religious right in this country, shorn of all caveat, compromise, or apology. Within its own terms, it was entirely coherent,
and provided Mr. Keyes with the certainty and fluency of an Old
Testament prophet. And while I found it simple enough to dis-
pose of his constitutional and policy arguments, his readings of
Scripture put me on the defensive.

Mr. Obama says he's a Christian, Mr. Keyes would say, and
yet he supports a lifestyle that the Bible calls an abomination.

Mr. Obama says he's a Christian, but he supports the destruction of innocent and sacred life.

What could I say? That a literal reading of the Bible was folly?
That Mr. Keyes, a Roman Catholic, should disregard the Pope's
teachings? Unwilling to go there, I answered with the usual liberal response in such debates—that we live in a pluralistic society, that I can't impose my religious views on another, that I was
running to be a U.S. senator from Illinois and not the minister
of Illinois. But even as I answered, I was mindful of Mr. Keyes's
implicit accusation—that I remained steeped in doubt, that my
faith was adulterated, that I was not a true Christian.

IN A SENSE, my dilemma with Mr. Keyes mirrors the broader dilemma that liberalism has faced in answering the religious right. Liberalism teaches us to be tolerant of other people's religious beliefs, so long as those beliefs don't cause anyone harm or impinge on another's right to believe differently. To the extent that religious communities are content to keep to themselves and faith is neatly confined as a matter of individual conscience, such tolerance is not tested.

But religion is rarely practiced in isolation; organized religion, at least, is a very public affair. The faithful may feel compelled by their religion to actively evangelize wherever they can. They may feel that a secular state promotes values that directly offend their beliefs. They may want the larger society to validate and reinforce their views.

And when the religiously motivated assert themselves politically to achieve these aims, liberals get nervous. Those of us in public office may try to avoid the conversation about religious values altogether, fearful of offending anyone and claiming that— regardless of our personal beliefs—constitutional principles tie our hands on issues like abortion or school prayer. (Catholic politicians of a certain generation seem particularly cautious, perhaps because they came of age when large segments of America still questioned whether John F. Kennedy would end up taking orders from the Pope.) Some on the left (although not those in public office) go further, dismissing religion in the public square as inherently irrational, intolerant, and therefore dangerous— and noting that, with its emphasis on personal salvation and the policing of private morality, religious talk has given conservatives cover to ignore questions of public morality, like poverty or corporate malfeasance.

Such strategies of avoidance may work for progressives when the opponent is Alan Keyes. But over the long haul, I think we make a mistake when we fail to acknowledge the power of faith in the lives of the American people, and so avoid joining a serious debate about how to reconcile faith with our modern, pluralistic democracy.

To begin with, it's bad politics. There are a whole lot of religious people in America, including the majority of Democrats. When we abandon the field of religious discourse—when we ignore the debate about what it means to be a good Christian or Muslim or Jew; when we discuss religion only in the negative sense of where or how it should not be practiced, rather than in the positive sense of what it tells us about our obligations toward one another; when we shy away from religious venues and religious broadcasts because we assume that we will be unwelcome—others will fill the vacuum. And those who do are likely to be those with the most insular views of faith, or who cynically use religion to justify partisan ends.

More fundamentally, the discomfort of some progressives with any hint of religiosity has often inhibited us from effectively addressing issues in moral terms. Some of the problem is rhetorical: Scrub language of all religious content and we forfeit the imagery and terminology through which millions of Americans understand both their personal morality and social justice. Imagine Lincoln's Second Inaugural Address without reference to "the judgments of the Lord," or King's "I Have a Dream" speech without reference to "all of God's children." Their summoning of a higher truth helped inspire what had seemed impossible and move the nation to embrace a common destiny. Of course organized religion doesn't have a monopoly on virtue, and one not need be religious to make moral claims or appeal to a common good. But we should not avoid making such claims or appeals—or abandon any reference to our rich religious traditions—in order to avoid giving offense.

Our failure as progressives to tap into the moral underpinnings of the nation is not just rhetorical, though. Our fear of getting "preachy" may also lead us to discount the role that values and culture play in addressing some of our most urgent social problems.

After all, the problems of poverty and racism, the uninsured and the unemployed, are not simply technical problems in search of the perfect ten-point plan. They are also rooted in societal indifference and individual callousness—the desire among those at the top of the social ladder to maintain their wealth and status whatever the cost, as well as the despair and self-destructiveness among those at the bottom of the social ladder.

Solving these problems will require changes in government policy; it will also require changes in hearts and minds. I believe in keeping guns out of our inner cities, and that our leaders must say so in the face of the gun manufacturers' lobby. But I also believe that when a gangbanger shoots indiscriminately into a crowd because he feels somebody disrespected him, we have a problem of morality. Not only do we need to punish that man for his crime, but we need to acknowledge that there's a hole in his heart, one that government programs alone may not be able to repair. I believe in vigorous enforcement of our nondiscrimination laws; I also believe that a transformation of conscience and a genuine commitment to diversity on the part of the nation's CEOs could bring quicker results than a battalion of lawyers. I think we should put more of our tax dollars into educating poor girls and boys, and give them the information about contraception that can prevent unwanted pregnancies, lower abortion rates, and help ensure that every child is loved and cherished. But I also think faith can fortify a young woman's sense of self, a young man's sense of responsibility, and the sense of reverence all young people should have for the act of sexual intimacy.

I am not suggesting that every progressive suddenly latch on to religious terminology or that we abandon the fight for institutional change in favor of "a thousand points of light." I recognize how often appeals to private virtue become excuses for inaction. Moreover, nothing is more transparent than inauthentic expressions of faith—such as the politician who shows up at a black church around election time and claps (off rhythm) to the gospel choir or sprinkles in a few biblical citations to spice up a thoroughly dry policy speech.

I am suggesting that if we progressives shed some of our own biases, we might recognize the values that both religious and secular people share when it comes to the moral and material direction of our country. We might recognize that the call to sacrifice on behalf of the next generation, the need to think in terms of "thou" and not just "I," resonates in religious congregations across the country. We need to take faith seriously not simply to block the religious right but to engage all persons of faith in the larger project of American renewal.

Some of this is already beginning to happen. Megachurch pastors like Rick Warren and T. D. Jakes are wielding their enormous influence to confront AIDS, Third World debt relief, and the genocide in Darfur. Self-described "progressive evangelicals" like Jim Wallis and Tony Campolo are lifting up the biblical injunction to help the poor as a means of mobilizing Christians against budget cuts to social programs and growing inequality. And across the country, individual churches like my own are sponsoring day-care programs, building senior centers, and helping ex-offenders reclaim their lives.

But to build on these still tentative partnerships between the religious and secular worlds, more work will need to be done. The tensions and suspicions on each side of the religious divide will have to be squarely addressed, and each side will need to accept some ground rules for collaboration.

The first and most difficult step for some evangelical Christians is to acknowledge the critical role that the establishment clause has played not only in the development of our democracy but also in the robustness of our religious practice. Contrary to the claims of many on the Christian right who rail against the separation of church and state, their argument is not with a

handful of liberal sixties judges. It is with the drafters of the Bill
of Rights and the forebears of today's evangelical church.

Many of the leading lights of the Revolution, most notably
Franklin and Jefferson, were deists who—while believing in an
Almighty God—questioned not only the dogmas of the Christian church but the central tenets of Christianity itself (including
Christ's divinity). Jefferson and Madison in particular argued for
what Jefferson called a "wall of separation" between church and
state, as a means of protecting individual liberty in religious belief and practice, guarding the state against sectarian strife, and
defending organized religion against the state's encroachment or
undue influence.

Of course, not all the Founding Fathers agreed; men like
Patrick Henry and John Adams forwarded a variety of proposals
to use the arm of the state to promote religion. But while it was
Jefferson and Madison who pushed through the Virginia statute
of religious freedom that would become the model for the First
Amendment's religion clauses, it wasn't these students of the Enlightenment who proved to be the most effective champions of a
separation between church and state.

Rather, it was Baptists like Reverend John Leland and other
evangelicals who provided the popular support needed to get
these provisions ratified. They did so because they were out-
siders; because their style of exuberant worship appealed to
the lower classes; because their evangelization of all comers—
including slaves—threatened the established order; because they
were no respecters of rank and privilege; and because they were
consistently persecuted and disdained by the dominant Anglican
Church in the South and the Congregationalist orders of the
North. Not only did they rightly fear that any state-sponsored
religion might encroach on their ability, as religious minorities,
to practice their faith; they also believed that religious vitality inevitably withers when compelled or supported by the state. In
the words of the Reverend Leland, "It is error alone, that stands

in need of government to support it; truth can and will do better without . . . it."

Jefferson and Leland's formula for religious freedom worked. Not only has America avoided the sorts of religious strife that continue to plague the globe, but religious institutions have continued to thrive—a phenomenon that some observers attribute directly to the absence of a state-sponsored church, and hence a premium on religious experimentation and volunteerism. Moreover, given the increasing diversity of America's population, the dangers of sectarianism have never been greater. Whatever we once were, we are no longer just a Christian nation; we are also a Jewish nation, a Muslim nation, a Buddhist nation, a Hindu nation, and a nation of nonbelievers.

But let's even assume that we only had Christians within our borders. Whose Christianity would we teach in the schools? James Dobson's or Al Sharpton's? Which passages of Scripture should guide our public policy? Should we go with Leviticus, which suggests that slavery is all right and eating shellfish is an abomination? How about Deuteronomy, which suggests stoning your child if he strays from the faith? Or should we just stick to the Sermon on the Mount—a passage so radical that it's doubtful that our Defense Department would survive its application?

This brings us to a different point—the manner in which religious views should inform public debate and guide elected officials. Surely, secularists are wrong when they ask believers to leave their religion at the door before entering the public square; Frederick Douglass, Abraham Lincoln, William Jennings Bryan, Dorothy Day, Martin Luther King, Jr.—indeed, the majority of great reformers in American history—not only were motivated by faith but repeatedly used religious language to argue their causes. To say that men and women should not inject their "personal morality" into public-policy debates is a practical absurdity; our law is by definition a codification of morality, much of it grounded in the Judeo-Christian tradition.

What our deliberative, pluralistic democracy does demand is that the religiously motivated translate their concerns into universal, rather than religion-specific, values. It requires that their proposals must be subject to argument and amenable to reason. If I am opposed to abortion for religious reasons and seek to pass a law banning the practice, I cannot simply point to the teachings of my church or invoke God's will and expect that argument to carry the day. If I want others to listen to me, then I have to explain why abortion violates some principle that is accessible to people of all faiths, including those with no faith at all.

For those who believe in the inerrancy of the Bible, as many evangelicals do, such rules of engagement may seem just one more example of the tyranny of the secular and material worlds over the sacred and eternal. But in a pluralistic democracy, we have no choice. Almost by definition, faith and reason operate in different domains and involve different paths to discerning truth. Reason—and science—involves the accumulation of knowledge based on realities that we can all apprehend. Religion, by contrast, is based on truths that are not provable through ordinary human understanding—the "belief in things not seen." When science teachers insist on keeping creationism or intelligent design out of their classrooms, they are not asserting that scientific knowledge is superior to religious insight. They are simply insisting that each path to knowledge involves different rules and that those rules are not interchangeable.

Politics is hardly a science, and it too infrequently depends on reason. But in a pluralistic democracy, the same distinctions apply. Politics, like science, depends on our ability to persuade each other of common aims based on a common reality. Moreover, politics (unlike science) involves compromise, the art of the possible. At some fundamental level, religion does not allow for compromise. It insists on the impossible. If God has spoken, then followers are expected to live up to God's edicts, regardless of the consequences. To base one's life on such uncompromising commitments may be sublime; to base our policy making on such commitments would be a dangerous thing.

The story of Abraham and Isaac offers a simple but powerful example. According to the Bible, Abraham is ordered by God to offer up his "only son, Isaac, whom you love," as a burnt offering. Without argument, Abraham takes Isaac to the mountaintop, binds him to an altar, and raises his knife, prepared to act as God has commanded.

Of course, we know the happy ending—God sends down an angel to intercede at the very last minute. Abraham has passed God's test of devotion. He becomes a model of fidelity to God, and his great faith is rewarded through future generations. And yet it is fair to say that if any of us saw a twenty-first-century Abraham raising the knife on the roof of his apartment building, we would call the police; we would wrestle him down; even if we saw him lower the knife at the last minute, we would expect the Department of Children and Family Services to take Isaac away and charge Abraham with child abuse. We would do so because God doesn't reveal Himself or His angels to all of us in a single moment. We do not hear what Abraham hears, do not see what Abraham sees, true as those experiences may be. So the best we can do is act in accordance with those things that are possible for all of us to know, understanding that a part of what we know to be true—as individuals or communities of faith—will be true for us alone.

Finally, any reconciliation between faith and democratic pluralism requires some sense of proportion. This is not entirely foreign to religious doctrine; even those who claim the Bible's inerrancy make distinctions between Scriptural edicts, based on a sense that some passages—the Ten Commandments, say, or a belief in Christ's divinity—are central to Christian faith, while others are more culturally specific and may be modified to accommodate modern life. The American people intuitively understand this, which is why the majority of Catholics practice birth control and some of those opposed to gay marriage nevertheless are opposed to a constitutional amendment banning it. Religious leadership need not accept such wisdom in counseling their flocks, but they should recognize this wisdom in their politics.

If a sense of proportion should guide Christian activism, then it must also guide those who police the boundaries between church and state. Not every mention of God in public is a breach in the wall of separation; as the Supreme Court has properly recognized, context matters. It is doubtful that children reciting the Pledge of Allegiance feel oppressed as a consequence of muttering the phrase "under God"; I didn't. Allowing the use of school property for meetings by voluntary student prayer groups should not be a threat, any more than its use by the high school Republican Club should threaten Democrats. And one can envision certain faith-based programs—targeting ex-offenders or substance abusers—that offer a uniquely powerful way of solving problems and hence merit carefully tailored support.

THESE BROAD PRINCIPLES for discussing faith within a democracy are not all-inclusive. It would be helpful, for example, if in debates about matters touching on religion—as in all of democratic discourse—we could resist the temptation to impute bad faith to those who disagree with us. In judging the persuasiveness of various moral claims, we should be on the lookout for inconsistency in how such claims are applied: As a general rule, I am more prone to listen to those who are as outraged by the indecency of homelessness as they are by the indecency of music videos. And we need to recognize that sometimes our argument is less about what is right than about who makes the final determination—whether we need the coercive arm of the state to enforce our values, or whether the subject is one best left to individual conscience and evolving norms.

Of course, even steadfast application of these principles won't resolve every conflict. The willingness of many who oppose abortion to make an exception for rape and incest indicates a willingness to bend principle for the sake of practical considerations; the willingness of even the most ardent prochoice advocates to accept some restrictions on late-term abortion marks a recognition that a fetus is more than a body part and that society has some interest in its development. Still, between those who believe that life begins at conception and those who consider the fetus an extension of the woman's body until birth, a point is rapidly reached at which compromise is not possible. At that point, the best we can do is ensure that persuasion rather than violence or intimidation determines the political outcome—and that we refocus at least some of our energies on reducing the number of unwanted pregnancies through education (including about abstinence), contraception, adoption, or any other strategies that have broad support and have been proven to work.

For many practicing Christians, the same inability to compromise may apply to gay marriage. I find such a position troublesome, particularly in a society in which Christian men and women have been known to engage in adultery or other violations of their faith without civil penalty. All too often I have sat in a church and heard a pastor use gay bashing as a cheap parlor trick—"It was Adam and Eve, not Adam and Steve!" he will shout, usually when the sermon is not going so well. I believe that American society can choose to carve out a special place for the union of a man and a woman as the unit of child rearing most common to every culture. I am not willing to have the state deny American citizens a civil union that confers equivalent rights on such basic matters as hospital visitation or health insurance coverage simply because the people they love are of the same sex—nor am I willing to accept a reading of the Bible that considers an obscure line in Romans to be more defining of Christianity than the Sermon on the Mount.

Perhaps I am sensitive on this issue because I have seen the pain my own carelessness has caused. Before my election, in the middle of my debates with Mr. Keyes, I received a phone message from one of my strongest supporters. She was a small-business owner, a mother, and a thoughtful, generous person. She was also a lesbian who had lived in a monogamous relationship with her partner for the last decade.

She knew when she decided to support me that I was opposed to same-sex marriage, and she had heard me argue that, in the absence of any meaningful consensus, the heightened focus on marriage was a distraction from other, attainable measures to prevent discrimination against gays and lesbians. Her phone message in this instance had been prompted by a radio interview she had heard in which I had referenced my religious traditions in explaining my position on the issue. She told me that she had been hurt by my remarks; she felt that by bringing religion into the equation, I was suggesting that she, and others like her, were somehow bad people.

I felt bad, and told her so in a return call. As I spoke to her I was reminded that no matter how much Christians who oppose homosexuality may claim that they hate the sin but love the sinner, such a judgment inflicts pain on good people—people who are made in the image of God, and who are often truer to Christ's message than those who condemn them. And I was reminded that it is my obligation, not only as an elected official in a pluralistic society but also as a Christian, to remain open to the possibility that my unwillingness to support gay marriage is misguided, just as I cannot claim infallibility in my support of abortion rights. I must admit that I may have been infected with society's prejudices and predilections and attributed them to God; that Jesus' call to love one another might demand a different conclusion; and that in years hence I may be seen as someone who was on the wrong side of history. I don't believe such doubts make me a bad Christian. I believe they make me human, limited in my understandings of God's purpose and therefore prone to sin. When I read the Bible, I do so with the belief that it is not a static text but the Living Word and that I must be continually open to new revelations—whether they come from a lesbian friend or a doctor opposed to abortion.

THIS IS NOT to say that I'm unanchored in my faith. There are some things that I'm absolutely sure about—the Golden Rule, the need to battle cruelty in all its forms, the value of love and charity, humility and grace.

Those beliefs were driven home two years ago when I flew down to Birmingham, Alabama, to deliver a speech at the city's Civil Rights Institute. The institute is right across the street from the Sixteenth Street Baptist Church, the site where, in 1963, four young children—Addie Mae Collins, Carole Robertson, Cynthia Wesley, and Denise McNair—lost their lives when a bomb planted by white supremacists exploded during Sunday school, and before my talk I took the opportunity to visit the church. The young pastor and several deacons greeted me at the door and showed me the still-visible scar along the wall where the bomb went off. I saw the clock at the back of the church, still frozen at 10:22 a.m. I studied the portraits of the four little girls.

After the tour, the pastor, deacons, and I held hands and said a prayer in the sanctuary. Then they left me to sit in one of the pews and gather my thoughts. What must it have been like for those parents forty years ago, I wondered, knowing that their precious daughters had been snatched away by violence at once so casual and so vicious? How could they endure the anguish unless they were certain that some purpose lay behind their children's murders, that some meaning could be found in immeasurable loss? Those parents would have seen the mourners pour in from all across the nation, would have read the condolences from across the globe, would have watched as Lyndon Johnson announced on national television that the time had come to overcome, would have seen Congress finally pass the Civil Rights Act of 1964. Friends and strangers alike would have assured them that their daughters had not died in vain—that they had awakened the conscience of a nation and helped liberate a people; that the bomb had burst a dam to let justice roll down like water and righteousness like a mighty stream. And yet would even that knowledge be enough to console your grief, to keep you from madness and eternal rage—unless you also knew that your child had gone on to a better place?

My thoughts turned to my mother and her final days, after cancer had spread through her body and it was clear that there was no coming back. She had admitted to me during the course of her illness that she was not ready to die; the suddenness of it all had taken her by surprise, as if the physical world she loved so much had turned on her, betrayed her. And although she fought valiantly, endured the pain and chemotherapy with grace and good humor to the very end, more than once I saw fear flash across her eyes. More than fear of pain or fear of the unknown, it was the sheer loneliness of death that frightened her, I think— the notion that on this final journey, on this last adventure, she would have no one to fully share her experiences with, no one who could marvel with her at the body's capacity to inflict pain on itself, or laugh at the stark absurdity of life once one's hair starts falling out and one's salivary glands shut down.

I carried such thoughts with me as I left the church and made my speech. Later that night, back home in Chicago, I sat at the dinner table, watching Malia and Sasha as they laughed and bickered and resisted their string beans before their mother chased them up the stairs and to their baths. Alone in the kitchen washing the dishes, I imagined my two girls growing up, and I felt the ache that every parent must feel at one time or another, that desire to snatch up each moment of your child's presence and never let go—to preserve every gesture, to lock in for all eternity the sight of their curls or the feel of their fingers clasped around yours. I thought of Sasha asking me once what happened when we die—"I don't want to die, Daddy," she had added matter-of-factly—and I had hugged her and said, "You've got a long, long way before you have to worry about that," which had seemed to satisfy her. I wondered whether I should have told her the truth, that I wasn't sure what happens when we die, any more than I was sure of where the soul resides or what existed before the Big Bang. Walking up the stairs, though, I knew what I hoped for—that my mother was together in some way with those four little girls, capable in some fashion of embracing them, of finding joy in their spirits.

I know that tucking in my daughters that night, I grasped a little bit of heaven.

Chapter 7

Race

T HE FUNERAL WAS held in a big church, a gleaming, geometric structure spread out over ten well-manicured acres. Reputedly, it had cost $35 million to build, and every dollar showed—there was a banquet hall, a conference center, a 1,200-car parking lot, a state-of-the-art sound system, and a TV production facility with digital editing equipment.

Inside the church sanctuary, some four thousand mourners had already gathered, most of them African American, many of them professionals of one sort or another: doctors, lawyers, accountants, educators, and real estate brokers. On the stage, senators, governors, and captains of industry mingled with black leaders like Jesse Jackson, John Lewis, Al Sharpton, and T. D. Jakes. Outside, under a bright October sun, thousands more stood along the quiet streets: elderly couples, solitary men, young women with strollers, some waving to the motorcades that occasionally passed, others standing in quiet contemplation, all of them waiting to pay their final respects to the diminutive, gray-haired woman who lay in the casket within.

The choir sang; the pastor said an opening prayer. Former President Bill Clinton rose to speak, and began to describe what it had been like for him as a white Southern boy to ride in segregated buses, how the civil rights movement that Rosa Parks helped spark had liberated him and his white neighbors from their own bigotry. Clinton's ease with his black audience, their almost giddy affection for him, spoke of reconciliation, of forgiveness, a partial mending of the past's grievous wounds.

In many ways, seeing a man who was both the former leader of the free world and a son of the South acknowledge the debt he owed a black seamstress was a fitting tribute to the legacy of Rosa Parks. Indeed, the magnificent church, the multitude of black elected officials, the evident prosperity of so many of those in attendance, and my own presence onstage as a United States senator—all of it could be traced to that December day in 1955 when, with quiet determination and unruffled dignity, Mrs. Parks had refused to surrender her seat on a bus. In honoring Rosa Parks, we honored others as well, the thousands of women and men and children across the South whose names were absent from the history books, whose stories had been lost in the slow eddies of time, but whose courage and grace had helped liberate a people.

And yet, as I sat and listened to the former President and the procession of speakers that followed, my mind kept wandering back to the scenes of devastation that had dominated the news just two months earlier, when Hurricane Katrina struck the Gulf Coast and New Orleans was submerged. I recalled images of teenage mothers weeping or cursing in front of the New Orleans Superdome, their listless infants hoisted to their hips, and old women in wheelchairs, heads lolled back from the heat, their withered legs exposed under soiled dresses. I thought about the news footage of a solitary body someone had laid beside a wall, motionless beneath the flimsy dignity of a blanket; and the scenes of shirtless young men in sagging pants, their legs churning through the dark waters, their arms draped with whatever goods they had managed to grab from nearby stores, the spark of chaos in their eyes.

I had been out of the country when the hurricane first hit the Gulf, on my way back from a trip to Russia. One week after the initial tragedy, though, I traveled to Houston, joining Bill and Hillary Clinton, as well as George H. W. Bush and his wife, Barbara, as they announced fund-raising efforts on behalf of the hurricane's victims and visited with some of the twenty-five thousand evacuees who were now sheltered in the Houston Astrodome and adjoining Reliant Center.

The city of Houston had done an impressive job setting up emergency facilities to accommodate so many people, working with the Red Cross and FEMA to provide them with food, clothing, shelter, and medical care. But as we walked along the rows of cots that now lined the Reliant Center, shaking hands, playing with children, listening to people's stories, it was obvious that many of Katrina's survivors had been abandoned long before the hurricane struck. They were the faces of any inner-city neighborhood in any American city, the faces of black poverty—the jobless and almost jobless, the sick and soon to be sick, the frail and the elderly. A young mother talked about handing off her children to a bus full of strangers. Old men quietly described the houses they had lost and the absence of any insurance or family to fall back on. A group of young men insisted that the levees had been blown up by those who wished to rid New Orleans of black people. One tall, gaunt woman, looking haggard in an Astros T-shirt two sizes too big, clutched my arm and pulled me toward her.

"We didn't have nothin' before the storm," she whispered. "Now we got less than nothin'."

In the days that followed, I returned to Washington and worked the phones, trying to secure relief supplies and contributions. In Senate Democratic Caucus meetings, my colleagues and I discussed possible legislation. I appeared on the Sunday morning news shows, rejecting the notion that the Administration had acted slowly because Katrina's victims were black—"the incompetence was color-blind," I said—but insisting that the Administration's inadequate planning showed a degree of remove from, and indifference toward, the problems of inner-city poverty that had to be addressed. Late one afternoon we joined Republican senators in what the Bush Administration deemed a classified briefing on the federal response. Almost the entire Cabinet was there, along with the chairman of the Joint Chiefs, and for an hour Secretaries Chertoff, Rumsfeld, and the rest bristled with confidence—and displayed not the slightest bit of remorse—as they recited the number of evacuations made, military rations distributed, National Guard troops deployed. A few nights later, we watched President Bush in that eerie, floodlit square, acknowledging the legacy of racial injustice that the tragedy had helped expose and proclaiming that New Orleans would rise again.

And now, sitting at the funeral of Rosa Parks, nearly two months after the storm, after the outrage and shame that Americans across the country had felt during the crisis, after the speeches and emails and memos and caucus meetings, after television specials and essays and extended newspaper coverage, it felt as if nothing had happened. Cars remained on rooftops. Bodies were still being discovered. Stories drifted back from the Gulf that the big contractors were landing hundreds of millions of dollars' worth of contracts, circumventing prevailing wage and affirmative action laws, hiring illegal immigrants to keep their costs down. The sense that the nation had reached a transformative moment—that it had had its conscience stirred out of a long slumber and would launch a renewed war on poverty—had quickly died away.

Instead, we sat in church, eulogizing Rosa Parks, reminiscing about past victories, entombed in nostalgia. Already, legislation was moving to place a statue of Mrs. Parks under the Capitol dome. There would be a commemorative stamp bearing her likeness, and countless streets, schools, and libraries across America would no doubt bear her name. I wondered what Rosa Parks would make of all of this—whether stamps or statues could summon her spirit, or whether honoring her memory demanded something more.

I thought about what that woman in Houston had whispered to me, and wondered how we might be judged, in those days after the levee broke.

WHEN I MEET people for the first time, they sometimes quote back to me a line in my speech at the 2004 Democratic National Convention that seemed to strike a chord: "There is not a black America and white America and Latino America and Asian America—there's the United States of America." For them, it seems to capture a vision of America finally freed from the past of Jim Crow and slavery, Japanese internment camps and Mexican braceros, workplace tensions and cultural conflict—an America that fulfills Dr. King's promise that we be judged not by the color of our skin but by the content of our character.

In a sense I have no choice but to believe in this vision of America. As the child of a black man and a white woman, someone who was born in the racial melting pot of Hawaii, with a sister who's half Indonesian but who's usually mistaken for Mexican or Puerto Rican, and a brother-in-law and niece of Chinese descent, with some blood relatives who resemble Margaret Thatcher and others who could pass for Bernie Mac, so that family get-togethers over Christmas take on the appearance of a UN General Assembly meeting, I've never had the option of restricting my loyalties on the basis of race, or measuring my worth on the basis of tribe.

Moreover, I believe that part of America's genius has always been its ability to absorb newcomers, to forge a national identity out of the disparate lot that arrived on our shores. In this we've been aided by a Constitution that—despite being marred by the original sin of slavery—has at its very core the idea of equal citizenship under the law; and an economic system that, more than any other, has offered opportunity to all comers, regardless of status or title or rank. Of course, racism and nativist sentiments have repeatedly undermined these ideals; the powerful and the privileged have often exploited or stirred prejudice to further their own ends. But in the hands of reformers, from Tubman to Douglass to Chavez to King, these ideals of equality have gradually shaped how we understand ourselves and allowed us to form a multicultural nation the likes of which exists nowhere else on earth.

Finally, those lines in my speech describe the demographic realities of America's future. Already, Texas, California, New Mexico, Hawaii, and the District of Columbia are majority minority. Twelve other states have populations that are more than a third Latino, black, and/or Asian. Latino Americans now number forty-two million and are the fastest-growing demographic group, accounting for almost half of the nation's population growth between 2004 and 2005; the Asian American population, though far smaller, has experienced a similar surge and is expected to increase by more than 200 percent over the next forty-five years. Shortly after 2050, experts project, America will no longer be a majority white country—with consequences for our economics, our politics, and our culture that we cannot fully anticipate.

Still, when I hear commentators interpreting my speech to mean that we have arrived at a "postracial politics" or that we already live in a color-blind society, I have to offer a word of caution. To say that we are one people is not to suggest that race no longer matters—that the fight for equality has been won, or that the problems that minorities face in this country today are largely self-inflicted. We know the statistics: On almost every single socioeconomic indicator, from infant mortality to life expectancy to employment to home ownership, black and Latino Americans in particular continue to lag far behind their white counterparts. In corporate boardrooms across America, minorities are grossly underrepresented; in the United States Senate, there are only three Latinos and two Asian members (both from Hawaii), and as I write today I am the chamber's sole African American. To suggest that our racial attitudes play no part in these disparities is to turn a blind eye to both our history and our experience—and to relieve ourselves of the responsibility to make things right.

Moreover, while my own upbringing hardly typifies the African American experience—and although, largely through luck and circumstance, I now occupy a position that insulates me from most of the bumps and bruises that the average black man must endure—I can recite the usual litany of petty slights that during my forty-five years have been directed my way: security guards tailing me as I shop in department stores, white couples who toss me their car keys as I stand outside a restaurant waiting for the valet, police cars pulling me over for no apparent reason. I know what it's like to have people tell me I can't do something because of my color, and I know the bitter swill of swallowed-back anger. I know as well that Michelle and I must be continually vigilant against some of the debilitating story lines that our daughters may absorb—from TV and music and friends and the streets— about who the world thinks they are, and what the world imagines they should be.

To think clearly about race, then, requires us to see the world on a split screen—to maintain in our sights the kind of America that we want while looking squarely at America as it is, to acknowledge the sins of our past and the challenges of the present without becoming trapped in cynicism or despair. I have witnessed a profound shift in race relations in my lifetime. I have felt it as surely as one feels a change in the temperature. When I hear some in the black community deny those changes, I think it not only dishonors those who struggled on our behalf but also robs us of our agency to complete the work they began. But as much as I insist that things have gotten better, I am mindful of this truth as well: Better isn't good enough.

MY CAMPAIGN for the U.S. Senate indicates some of the changes that have taken place in both the white and black communities of Illinois over the past twenty-five years. By the time I ran, Illinois already had a history of blacks elected to statewide office, including a black state comptroller and attorney general (Roland Burris), a United States senator (Carol Moseley Braun), and a sitting secretary of state, Jesse White, who had been the state's leading vote-getter only two years earlier. Because of the pioneering success of these public officials, my own campaign was no longer a novelty—I might not have been favored to win, but the fact of my race didn't foreclose the possibility.

Moreover, the types of voters who ultimately gravitated to my campaign defied the conventional wisdom. On the day I announced my candidacy for the U.S. Senate, for example, three of my white state senate colleagues showed up to endorse me. They weren't what we in Chicago call "Lakefront Liberals"— the so-called Volvo-driving, latte-sipping, white-wine-drinking Democrats that Republicans love to poke fun at and might be expected to embrace a lost cause such as mine. Instead, they were three middle-aged, working-class guys—Terry Link of Lake County, Denny Jacobs of the Quad Cities, and Larry Walsh of Will County—all of whom represented mostly white, mostly working-class or suburban communities outside Chicago.

It helped that these men knew me well; the four of us had served together in Springfield during the previous seven years and had maintained a weekly poker game whenever we were in session. It also helped that each of them prided himself on his independence, and was therefore willing to stick with me despite pressure from more favored white candidates.

But it wasn't just our personal relationships that led them to support me (although the strength of my friendships with these men—all of whom grew up in neighborhoods and at a time in which hostility toward blacks was hardly unusual—itself said something about the evolution of race relations). Senators Link, Jacobs, and Walsh are hard-nosed, experienced politicians; they had no interest in backing losers or putting their own positions at risk. The fact was, they all thought that I'd "sell" in their districts—once their constituents met me and could get past the name.

They didn't make such a judgment blind. For seven years they had watched me interact with their constituents, in the state capitol or on visits to their districts. They had seen white mothers hand me their children for pictures and watched white World War II vets shake my hand after I addressed their convention. They sensed what I'd come to know from a lifetime of experience: that whatever preconceived notions white Americans may continue to hold, the overwhelming majority of them these days are able—if given the time—to look beyond race in making their judgments of people.

This isn't to say that prejudice has vanished. None of us— black, white, Latino, or Asian—is immune to the stereotypes that our culture continues to feed us, especially stereotypes about black criminality, black intelligence, or the black work ethic. In general, members of every minority group continue to be measured largely by the degree of our assimilation—how closely speech patterns, dress, or demeanor conform to the dominant white culture—and the more that a minority strays from these external markers, the more he or she is subject to negative assumptions. If an internalization of antidiscrimination norms over the past three decades—not to mention basic decency—prevents most whites from consciously acting on such stereotypes in their daily interactions with persons of other races, it's unrealistic to believe that these stereotypes don't have some cumulative impact on the often snap decisions of who's hired and who's promoted, on who's arrested and who's prosecuted, on how you feel about the customer who just walked into your store or about the demographics of your children's school.

I maintain, however, that in today's America such prejudices are far more loosely held than they once were—and hence are subject to refutation. A black teenage boy walking down the street may elicit fear in a white couple, but if he turns out to be their son's friend from school he may be invited over for dinner. A black man may have trouble catching a cab late at night, but if he is a capable software engineer Microsoft will have no qualms about hiring him.

I cannot prove these assertions; surveys of racial attitudes are notoriously unreliable. And even if I'm right, it's cold comfort to many minorities. After all, spending one's days refuting stereotypes can be a wearying business. It's the added weight that many minorities, especially African Americans, so often describe in their daily round—the feeling that as a group we have no store of goodwill in America's accounts, that as individuals we must prove ourselves anew each day, that we will rarely get the benefit of the doubt and will have little margin for error. Making a way through such a world requires the black child to fight off the additional hesitation that she may feel when she stands at the threshold of a mostly white classroom on the first day of school; it requires the Latina woman to fight off self-doubt as she prepares for a job interview at a mostly white company.

Most of all, it requires fighting off the temptation to stop making the effort. Few minorities can isolate themselves entirely from white society—certainly not in the way that whites can successfully avoid contact with members of other races. But it is possible for minorities to pull down the shutters psychologically, to protect themselves by assuming the worst. "Why should I have to make the effort to disabuse whites of their ignorance about us?" I've had some blacks tell me. "We've been trying for three hundred years, and it hasn't worked yet."

To which I suggest that the alternative is surrender—to what has been instead of what might be.

One of the things I value most in representing Illinois is the way it has disrupted my own assumptions about racial attitudes. During my Senate campaign, for example, I traveled with Illinois's senior senator, Dick Durbin, on a thirty-nine-city tour of southern Illinois. One of our scheduled stops was a town called Cairo, at the very southern tip of the state, where the Mississippi and Ohio Rivers meet, a town made famous during the late sixties and early seventies as the site of some of the worst racial conflict anywhere outside of the Deep South. Dick had first visited Cairo during this period, when as a young attorney working for then Lieutenant Governor Paul Simon, he had been sent to investigate what might be done to lessen the tensions there. As we drove down to Cairo, Dick recalled that visit: how, upon his arrival, he'd been warned not to use the telephone in his motel room because the switchboard operator was a member of the White Citizens Council; how white store owners had closed their businesses rather than succumb to boycotters' demands to hire blacks; how black residents told him of their efforts to integrate the schools, their fear and frustration, the stories of lynching and jailhouse suicides, shootings and riots.

By the time we pulled into Cairo, I didn't know what to expect. Although it was midday, the town felt abandoned, a handful of stores open along the main road, a few elderly couples coming out of what appeared to be a health clinic. Turning a corner, we arrived at a large parking lot, where a crowd of a couple of hundred were milling about. A quarter of them were black, almost all the rest white.

They were all wearing blue buttons that read OBAMA FOR U.S. SENATE.

Ed Smith, a big, hearty guy who was the Midwest regional manager of the Laborers' International Union and who'd grown up in Cairo, strode up to our van with a big grin on his face.

"Welcome," he said, shaking our hands as we got off the bus. "Hope you're hungry, 'cause we got a barbecue going and my mom's cooking."

I don't presume to know exactly what was in the minds of the white people in the crowd that day. Most were my age and older and so would at least have remembered, if not been a direct part of, those grimmer days thirty years before. No doubt many of them were there because Ed Smith, one of the most powerful men in the region, wanted them to be there; others may have been there for the food, or just to see the spectacle of a U.S. senator and a candidate for the Senate campaign in their town.

I do know that the barbecue was terrific, the conversation spirited, the people seemingly glad to see us. For an hour or so we ate, took pictures, and listened to people's concerns. We discussed what might be done to restart the area's economy and get more money into the schools; we heard about sons and daughters on their way to Iraq and the need to tear down an old hospital that had become a blight on downtown. And by the time we left, I felt a relationship had been established between me and the people I'd met—nothing transformative, but perhaps enough to weaken some of our biases and reinforce some of our better impulses. In other words, a quotient of trust had been built.

Of course, such trust between the races is often tentative. It can wither without a sustaining effort. It may last only so long as minorities remain quiescent, silent to injustice; it can be blown asunder by a few well-timed negative ads featuring white workers displaced by affirmative action, or the news of a police shooting of an unarmed black or Latino youth.

But I also believe that moments like the one in Cairo ripple from their immediate point: that people of all races carry these moments into their homes and places of worship; that such moments shade a conversation with their children or their coworkers and can wear down, in slow, steady waves, the hatred and suspicion that isolation breeds.

Recently, I was back in southern Illinois, driving with one of my downstate field directors, a young white man named Robert Stephan, after a long day of speeches and appearances in the area. It was a beautiful spring night, the broad waters and dusky banks of the Mississippi shimmering under a full, low-flung moon. The waters reminded me of Cairo and all the other towns up and down the river, the settlements that had risen and fallen with the barge traffic and the often sad, tough, cruel histories that had been deposited there at the confluence of the free and enslaved, the world of Huck and the world of Jim.

I mentioned to Robert the progress we'd made on tearing down the old hospital in Cairo—our office had started meeting with the state health department and local officials—and told him about my first visit to the town. Because Robert had grown up in the southern part of the state, we soon found ourselves talking about the racial attitudes of his friends and neighbors. Just the previous week, he said, a few local guys with some influence had invited him to join them at a small social club in Alton, a couple of blocks from the house where he'd been raised. Robert had never been to the place, but it seemed nice enough. The food had been served, the group was making some small talk, when Robert noticed that of the fifty or so people in the room not a single person was black. Since Alton's population is about a quarter African American, Robert thought this odd, and asked the men about it.

It's a private club, one of them said.

At first, Robert didn't understand—had no blacks tried to join? When they said nothing, he said, It's 2006, for God's sake.

The men shrugged. It's always been that way, they told him. No blacks allowed.

Which is when Robert dropped his napkin on his plate, said good night, and left.

I suppose I could spend time brooding over those men in the club, file it as evidence that white people still maintain a simmering hostility toward those who look like me. But I don't want to confer on such bigotry a power it no longer possesses.

I choose to think about Robert instead, and the small but difficult gesture he made. If a young man like Robert can make the effort to cross the currents of habit and fear in order to do what he knows is right, then I want to be sure that I'm there to meet him on the other side and help him onto shore.

MY ELECTION WASN'T just aided by the evolving racial attitudes of Illinois's white voters. It reflected changes in Illinois's African American community as well.

One measure of these changes could be seen in the types of early support my campaign received. Of the first $500,000 that I raised during the primary, close to half came from black businesses and professionals. It was a black-owned radio station, WVON, that first began to mention my campaign on the Chicago airwaves, and a black-owned weekly newsmagazine, *N'Digo,* that first featured me on its cover. One of the first times I needed a corporate jet for the campaign, it was a black friend who lent me his.

Such capacity simply did not exist a generation ago. Although Chicago has always had one of the more vibrant black business communities in the country, in the sixties and seventies only a handful of self-made men—John Johnson, the founder of *Ebony* and *Jet;* George Johnson, the founder of Johnson Products; Ed Gardner, the founder of Soft Sheen; and Al Johnson, the first black in the country to own a GM franchise—would have been considered wealthy by the standards of white America.

Today not only is the city filled with black doctors, dentists, lawyers, accountants, and other professionals, but blacks also occupy some of the highest management positions in corporate Chicago. Blacks own restaurant chains, investment banks, PR agencies, real estate investment trusts, and architectural firms.

They can afford to live in neighborhoods of their choosing and send their children to the best private schools. They are actively recruited to join civic boards and generously support all manner of charities.

Statistically, the number of African Americans who occupy the top fifth of the income ladder remains relatively small. Moreover, every black professional and businessperson in Chicago can tell you stories of the roadblocks they still experience on account of race. Few African American entrepreneurs have either the inherited wealth or the angel investors to help launch their businesses or cushion them from a sudden economic downturn. Few doubt that if they were white they would be further along in reaching their goals.

And yet you won't hear these men and women use race as a crutch or point to discrimination as an excuse for failure. In fact, what characterizes this new generation of black professionals is their rejection of any limits to what they can achieve. When a friend who had been the number one bond salesman at Merrill Lynch's Chicago office decided to start his own investment bank, his goal wasn't to grow it into the top black firm—he wanted it to become the top firm, period. When another friend decided to leave an executive position at General Motors to start his own parking service company in partnership with Hyatt, his mother thought he was crazy. "She couldn't imagine anything better than having a management job at GM," he told me, "because those jobs were unattainable for her generation. But I knew I wanted to build something of my own."

That simple notion—that one isn't confined in one's dreams— is so central to our understanding of America that it seems almost commonplace. But in black America, the idea represents a radical break from the past, a severing of the psychological shackles of slavery and Jim Crow. It is perhaps the most important legacy of the civil rights movement, a gift from those leaders like John Lewis and Rosa Parks who marched, rallied, and endured threats, arrests, and beatings to widen the doors of freedom. And it is also a testament to that generation of African American mothers and fathers whose heroism was less dramatic but no less important: parents who worked all their lives in jobs that were too small for them, without complaint, scrimping and saving to buy a small home; parents who did without so that their children could take dance classes or the school-sponsored field trip; parents who coached Little League games and baked birthday cakes and badgered teachers to make sure that their children weren't tracked into the less challenging programs; parents who dragged their children to church every Sunday, whupped their children's behinds when they got out of line, and looked out for all the children on the block during long summer days and into the night. Parents who pushed their children to achieve and fortified them with a love that could withstand whatever the larger society might throw at them.

It is through this quintessentially American path of upward mobility that the black middle class has grown fourfold in a generation, and that the black poverty rate was cut in half. Through a similar process of hard work and commitment to family, Latinos have seen comparable gains: From 1979 to 1999, the number of Latino families considered middle class has grown by more than 70 percent. In their hopes and expectations, these black and Latino workers are largely indistinguishable from their white counterparts. They are the people who make our economy run and our democracy flourish—the teachers, mechanics, nurses, computer technicians, assembly-line workers, bus drivers, postal workers, store managers, plumbers, and repairmen who constitute America's vital heart.

And yet, for all the progress that's been made in the past four decades, a stubborn gap remains between the living standards of black, Latino, and white workers. The average black wage is 75 percent of the average white wage; the average Latino wage is 71 percent of the average white wage. Black median net worth is about $6,000, and Latino median net worth is about $8,000, compared to $88,000 for whites. When laid off from their job or confronted with a family emergency, blacks and Latinos have less savings to draw on, and parents are less able to lend their children a helping hand. Even middle-class blacks and Latinos pay more for insurance, are less likely to own their own homes, and suffer poorer health than Americans as a whole. More minorities may be living the American dream, but their hold on that dream remains tenuous.

How we close this persistent gap—and how much of a role government should play in achieving that goal—remains one of the central controversies of American politics. But there should be some strategies we can all agree on. We might start with completing the unfinished business of the civil rights movement— namely, enforcing nondiscrimination laws in such basic areas as employment, housing, and education. Anyone who thinks that such enforcement is no longer needed should pay a visit to one of the suburban office parks in their area and count the number of blacks employed there, even in the relatively unskilled jobs, or stop by a local trade union hall and inquire as to the number of blacks in the apprenticeship program, or read recent studies showing that real estate brokers continue to steer prospective black homeowners away from predominantly white neighborhoods. Unless you live in a state without many black residents, I think you'll agree that something's amiss.

Under recent Republican Administrations, such enforcement of civil rights laws has been tepid at best, and under the current Administration, it's been essentially nonexistent—unless one counts the eagerness of the Justice Department's Civil Rights Division to label university scholarship or educational enrichment programs targeted at minority students as "reverse discrimination," no matter how underrepresented minority students may be in a particular institution or field, and no matter how incidental the program's impact on white students.

This should be a source of concern across the political spectrum, even to those who oppose affirmative action. Affirmative action programs, when properly structured, can open up opportunities otherwise closed to qualified minorities without diminishing opportunities for white students. Given the dearth of black and Latino Ph.D. candidates in mathematics and the physical sciences, for example, a modest scholarship program for minorities interested in getting advanced degrees in these fields (a recent target of a Justice Department inquiry) won't keep white students out of such programs, but can broaden the pool of talent that America will need for all of us to prosper in a technology-based economy. Moreover, as a lawyer who's worked on civil rights cases, I can say that where there's strong evidence of prolonged and systematic discrimination by large corporations, trade unions, or branches of municipal government, goals and timetables for minority hiring may be the only meaningful remedy available.

Many Americans disagree with me on this as a matter of principle, arguing that our institutions should never take race into account, even if it is to help victims of past discrimination. Fair enough—I understand their arguments, and don't expect the debate to be settled anytime soon. But that shouldn't stop us from at least making sure that when two equally qualified people— one minority and one white—apply for a job, house, or loan, and the white person is consistently preferred, then the government, through its prosecutors and through its courts, should step in to make things right.

We should also agree that the responsibility to close the gap can't come from government alone; minorities, individually and collectively, have responsibilities as well. Many of the social or cultural factors that negatively affect black people, for example, simply mirror in exaggerated form problems that afflict America as a whole: too much television (the average black household has the television on more than eleven hours per day), too much consumption of poisons (blacks smoke more and eat more fast food), and a lack of emphasis on educational achievement.

Then there's the collapse of the two-parent black household, a phenomenon that is occurring at such an alarming rate when compared to the rest of American society that what was once a difference in degree has become a difference in kind, a phenomenon that reflects a casualness toward sex and child rearing among black men that renders black children more vulnerable—and for which there is simply no excuse.

Taken together, these factors impede progress. Moreover, although government action can help change behavior (encouraging supermarket chains with fresh produce to locate in black neighborhoods, to take just one small example, would go a long way toward changing people's eating habits), a transformation in attitudes has to begin in the home, and in neighborhoods, and in places of worship. Community-based institutions, particularly the historically black church, have to help families reinvigorate in young people a reverence for educational achievement, encourage healthier lifestyles, and reenergize traditional social norms surrounding the joys and obligations of fatherhood.

Ultimately, though, the most important tool to close the gap between minority and white workers may have little to do with race at all. These days, what ails working-class and middle-class blacks and Latinos is not fundamentally different from what ails their white counterparts: downsizing, outsourcing, automation, wage stagnation, the dismantling of employer-based health-care and pension plans, and schools that fail to teach young people the skills they need to compete in a global economy. (Blacks in particular have been vulnerable to these trends, since they are more reliant on blue-collar manufacturing jobs and are less likely to live in suburban communities where new jobs are being generated.) And what would help minority workers are the same things that would help white workers: the opportunity to earn a living wage, the education and training that lead to such jobs, labor laws and tax laws that restore some balance to the distribution of the nation's wealth, and health-care, child care, and retirement systems that working people can count on.

This pattern—of a rising tide lifting minority boats—has certainly held true in the past. The progress made by the previous generation of Latinos and African Americans occurred primarily because the same ladders of opportunity that built the white middle class were for the first time made available to minorities as well. They benefited, as all people did, from an economy that was growing and a government interested in investing in its people. Not only did tight labor markets, access to capital, and programs like Pell Grants and Perkins Loans benefit blacks directly; growing incomes and a sense of security among whites made them less resistant to minority claims for equality.

The same formula holds true today. As recently as 1999, the black unemployment rate fell to record lows and black income rose to record highs not because of a surge in affirmative action hiring or a sudden change in the black work ethic but because the economy was booming and government took a few modest measures—like the expansion of the Earned Income Tax Credit—to spread the wealth around. If you want to know the secret of Bill Clinton's popularity among African Americans, you need look no further than these statistics.

But these same statistics should also force those of us interested in racial equality to conduct an honest accounting of the costs and benefits of our current strategies. Even as we continue to defend affirmative action as a useful, if limited, tool to expand opportunity to underrepresented minorities, we should consider spending a lot more of our political capital convincing America to make the investments needed to ensure that all children perform at grade level and graduate from high school—a goal that, if met, would do more than affirmative action to help those black and Latino children who need it the most. Similarly, we should support targeted programs to eliminate existing health disparities between minorities and whites (some evidence suggests that even when income and levels of insurance are factored out, minorities may still be receiving worse care), but a plan for universal health-care coverage would do more to eliminate health disparities between whites and minorities than any race-specific programs we might design.

An emphasis on universal, as opposed to race-specific, programs isn't just good policy; it's also good politics. I remember once sitting with one of my Democratic colleagues in the Illinois state senate as we listened to another fellow senator—an African American whom I'll call John Doe who represented a largely inner-city district—launch into a lengthy and passionate peroration on why the elimination of a certain program was a case of blatant racism. After a few minutes, the white senator (who had one of the chamber's more liberal voting records) turned to me and said, "You know what the problem is with John? Whenever I hear him, he makes me feel more white."

In defense of my black colleague, I pointed out that it's not always easy for a black politician to gauge the right tone to take—too angry? not angry enough?—when discussing the enormous hardships facing his or her constituents. Still, my white colleague's comment was instructive. Rightly or wrongly, white guilt has largely exhausted itself in America; even the most fair-minded of whites, those who would genuinely like to see racial inequality ended and poverty relieved, tend to push back against suggestions of racial victimization—or race-specific claims based on the history of race discrimination in this country.

Some of this has to do with the success of conservatives in fanning the politics of resentment—by wildly overstating, for example, the adverse effects of affirmative action on white workers. But mainly it's a matter of simple self-interest. Most white Americans figure that they haven't engaged in discrimination themselves and have plenty of their own problems to worry about.

They also know that with a national debt approaching $9 trillion and annual deficits of almost $300 billion, the country has precious few resources to help them with those problems.

As a result, proposals that solely benefit minorities and dissect Americans into "us" and "them" may generate a few short-term concessions when the costs to whites aren't too high, but they can't serve as the basis for the kinds of sustained, broad-based political coalitions needed to transform America. On the other hand, universal appeals around strategies that help all Americans (schools that teach, jobs that pay, health care for everyone who needs it, a government that helps out after a flood), along with measures that ensure our laws apply equally to everyone and hence uphold broadly held American ideals (like better enforcement of existing civil rights laws), can serve as the basis for such coalitions—even if such strategies disproportionately help minorities.

Such a shift in emphasis is not easy: Old habits die hard, and there is always a fear on the part of many minorities that unless racial discrimination, past and present, stays on the front burner, white America will be let off the hook and hard-fought gains may be reversed. I understand these fears—nowhere is it ordained that history moves in a straight line, and during difficult economic times it is possible that the imperatives of racial equality get shunted aside.

Still, when I look at what past generations of minorities have had to overcome, I am optimistic about the ability of this next generation to continue their advance into the economic mainstream. For most of our recent history, the rungs on the opportunity ladder may have been more slippery for blacks; the admittance of Latinos into firehouses and corporate suites may have been grudging. But despite all that, the combination of economic growth, government investment in broad-based programs to encourage upward mobility, and a modest commitment to enforce the simple principle of nondiscrimination was sufficient to pull the large majority of blacks and Latinos into the socioeconomic main-stream within a generation.

We need to remind ourselves of this achievement. What's remarkable is not the number of minorities who have failed to climb into the middle class but the number who succeeded against the odds; not the anger and bitterness that parents of color have transmitted to their children but the degree to which such emotions have ebbed. That knowledge gives us something to build on. It tells us that more progress can be made.

IF UNIVERSAL STRATEGIES that target the challenges facing all Americans can go a long way toward closing the gap between blacks, Latinos, and whites, there are two aspects of race relations in America that require special attention—issues that fan the flames of racial conflict and undermine the progress that's been made. With respect to the African American community, the issue is the deteriorating condition of the inner-city poor. With respect to Latinos, it is the problem of undocumented workers and the political firestorm surrounding immigration.

One of my favorite restaurants in Chicago is a place called MacArthur's. It's away from the Loop, on the west end of the West Side on Madison Street, a simple, brightly lit space with booths of blond wood that seat maybe a hundred people. On any day of the week, about that many people can be found lining up—families, teenagers, groups of matronly women and elderly men—all waiting their turn, cafeteria-style, for plates filled with fried chicken, catfish, hoppin' John, collard greens, meatloaf, cornbread, and other soul-food standards. As these folks will tell you, it's well worth the wait.

The restaurant's owner, Mac Alexander, is a big, barrel-chested man in his early sixties, with thinning gray hair, a mustache, and a slight squint behind his glasses that gives him a pensive, professorial air. He's an army vet, born in Lexington, Mississippi, who lost his left leg in Vietnam; after his convalescence, he and his wife moved to Chicago, where he took business courses while working in a warehouse. In 1972, he opened Mac's Records, and helped found the Westside Business Improvement Association, pledging to fix up what he calls his "little corner of the world."

By any measure he has succeeded. His record store grew; he opened up the restaurant and hired local residents to work there; he started buying and rehabbing run-down buildings and renting them out. It's because of the efforts of men and women like Mac that the view along Madison Street is not as grim as the West Side's reputation might suggest. There are clothing stores and pharmacies and what seems like a church on every block. Off the main thoroughfare you will find the same small bungalows— with neatly trimmed lawns and carefully tended flower beds— that make up many of Chicago's neighborhoods.

But travel a few blocks farther in any direction and you will also experience a different side of Mac's world: the throngs of young men on corners casting furtive glances up and down the street; the sound of sirens blending with the periodic thump of car stereos turned up full blast; the dark, boarded-up buildings and hastily scrawled gang signs; the rubbish everywhere, swirling in winter winds. Recently, the Chicago Police Department installed permanent cameras and flashing lights atop the lampposts of Madison, bathing each block in a perpetual blue glow. The folks who live along Madison didn't complain; flashing blue lights are a familiar enough sight. They're just one more reminder of what everybody knows—that the community's immune system has broken down almost entirely, weakened by drugs and gunfire and despair; that despite the best efforts of folks like Mac, a virus has taken hold, and a people is wasting away.

"Crime's nothing new on the West Side," Mac told me one afternoon as we walked to look at one of his buildings. "I mean, back in the seventies, the police didn't really take the idea of looking after black neighborhoods seriously. As long as trouble didn't spill out into the white neighborhoods, they didn't care. First store I opened, on Lake and Damen, I must've had eight, nine break-ins in a row.

"The police are more responsive now," Mac said. "The commander out here, he's a good brother, does the best he can. But he's just as overwhelmed as everybody else. See, these kids out here, they just don't care. Police don't scare 'em, jail doesn't scare 'em—more than half of the young guys out here already got a record. If the police pick up ten guys standing on a corner, another ten'll take their place in an hour.

"That's the thing that's changed . . . the attitude of these kids. You can't blame them, really, because most of them have nothing at home. Their mothers can't tell them nothing—a lot of these women are still children themselves. Father's in jail. Nobody around to guide the kids, keep them in school, teach them respect. So these boys just raise themselves, basically, on the streets. That's all they know. The gang, that's their family. They don't see any jobs out here except the drug trade. Don't get me wrong, we've still got a lot of good families around here . . . not a lot of money necessarily, but doing their best to keep their kids out of trouble. But they're just too outnumbered. The longer they stay, the more they feel their kids are at risk. So the minute they get a chance, they move out. And that just leaves things worse."

Mac shook his head. "I don't know. I keep thinking we can turn things around. But I'll be honest with you, Barack—it's hard not to feel sometimes like the situation is hopeless. Hard—and getting harder."

I hear a lot of such sentiments in the African American community these days, a frank acknowledgment that conditions in the heart of the inner city are spinning out of control. Sometimes the conversation will center on statistics—the infant mortality rate (on par with Malaysia among poor black Americans), or black male unemployment (estimated at more than a third in some Chicago neighborhoods), or the number of black men who can expect to go through the criminal justice system at some point in their lives (one in three nationally).

But more often the conversation focuses on personal stories, offered as evidence of a fundamental breakdown within a portion of our community and voiced with a mixture of sadness and incredulity. A teacher will talk about what it's like to have an eight-year-old shout obscenities and threaten her with bodily harm. A public defender will describe a fifteen-year-old's harrowing rap sheet or the nonchalance with which his clients predict they will not live to see their thirtieth year. A pediatrician will describe the teenage parents who don't think there's anything wrong with feeding their toddlers potato chips for breakfast, or who admit to having left their five- or six-year-old alone at home.

These are the stories of those who didn't make it out of history's confinement, of the neighborhoods within the black community that house the poorest of the poor, serving as repositories for all the scars of slavery and violence of Jim Crow, the internalized rage and the forced ignorance, the shame of men who could not protect their women or support their families, the children who grew up being told they wouldn't amount to anything and had no one there to undo the damage.

There was a time, of course, when such deep intergenerational poverty could still shock a nation—when the publication of Michael Harrington's *The Other America* or Bobby Kennedy's visits to the Mississippi Delta could inspire outrage and a call to action. Not anymore. Today the images of the so-called underclass are ubiquitous, a permanent fixture in American popular culture—in film and TV, where they're the foil of choice for the forces of law and order; in rap music and videos, where the gangsta life is glorified and mimicked by white and black teenagers alike (although white teenagers, at least, are aware that theirs is just a pose); and on the nightly news, where the depredation to be found in the inner city always makes for good copy. Rather than evoke our sympathy, our familiarity with the lives of the black poor has bred spasms of fear and outright contempt. But mostly it's bred indifference. Black men filling our prisons, black children unable to read or caught in a gangland shooting, the black homeless sleeping on grates and in the parks of our nation's capital—we take these things for granted, as part of the natural order, a tragic situation, perhaps, but not one for which we are culpable, and certainly not something subject to change.

This concept of a black underclass—separate, apart, alien in its behavior and in its values—has also played a central role in modern American politics. It was partly on behalf of fixing the black ghetto that Johnson's War on Poverty was launched, and it was on the basis of that war's failures, both real and perceived, that conservatives turned much of the country against the very concept of the welfare state. A cottage industry grew within conservative think tanks, arguing not only that cultural pathologies—rather than racism or structural inequalities built into our economy—were responsible for black poverty but also that government programs like welfare, coupled with liberal judges who coddled criminals, actually made these pathologies worse. On television, images of innocent children with distended bellies were replaced with those of black looters and muggers; news reports focused less on the black maid struggling to make ends meet and more on the "welfare queen" who had babies just to collect a check. What was needed, conservatives argued, was a stern dose of discipline—more police, more prisons, more personal responsibility, and an end to welfare. If such strategies could not transform the black ghetto, at least they would contain it and keep hardworking taxpayers from throwing good money after bad.

That conservatives won over white public opinion should come as no surprise. Their arguments tapped into a distinction

between the "deserving" and "undeserving" poor that has a long
and varied history in America, an argument that has often been
racially or ethnically tinged and that has gained greater currency
during those periods—like the seventies and eighties—when economic times are tough. The response of liberal policy makers and
civil rights leaders didn't help; in their urgency to avoid blaming
the victims of historical racism, they tended to downplay or ignore evidence that entrenched behavioral patterns among the
black poor really were contributing to intergenerational poverty.
(Most famously, Daniel Patrick Moynihan was accused of racism
in the early sixties when he raised alarms about the rise of out-
of-wedlock births among the black poor.) This willingness to dismiss the role that values played in shaping the economic success
of a community strained credulity and alienated working-class
whites—particularly since some of the most liberal policy makers lived lives far removed from urban disorder.

The truth is that such rising frustration with conditions in the
inner city was hardly restricted to whites. In most black neighborhoods, law-abiding, hardworking residents have been demanding more aggressive police protection for years, since they
are far more likely to be victims of crime. In private—around
kitchen tables, in barbershops, and after church—black folks
can often be heard bemoaning the eroding work ethic, inadequate parenting, and declining sexual mores with a fervor that
would make the Heritage Foundation proud.

In that sense, black attitudes regarding the sources of chronic
poverty are far more conservative than black politics would care
to admit. What you won't hear, though, are blacks using such
terms as "predator" in describing a young gang member, or
"underclass" in describing mothers on welfare—language that
divides the world between those who are worthy of our concern
and those who are not. For black Americans, such separation
from the poor is never an option, and not just because the color

of our skin—and the conclusions the larger society draws from our color—makes all of us only as free, only as respected, as the least of us.

It's also because blacks know the back story to the inner city's dysfunction. Most blacks who grew up in Chicago remember the collective story of the great migration from the South, how after arriving in the North blacks were forced into ghettos because of racial steering and restrictive covenants and stacked up in public housing, where the schools were substandard and the parks were underfunded and police protection was nonexistent and the drug trade was tolerated. They remember how the plum patronage jobs were reserved for other immigrant groups and the blue-collar jobs that black folks relied on evaporated, so that families that had been intact began to crack under the pressure and ordinary children slipped through those cracks, until a tipping point was reached and what had once been the sad exception somehow became the rule. They know what drove that homeless man to drink because he is their uncle. That hardened criminal—they remember when he was a little boy, so full of life and capable of love, for he is their cousin.

In other words, African Americans understand that culture matters but that culture is shaped by circumstance. We know that many in the inner city are trapped by their own self-destructive behaviors but that those behaviors are not innate. And because of that knowledge, the black community remains convinced that if America finds its will to do so, then circumstances for those trapped in the inner city can be changed, individual attitudes among the poor will change in kind, and the damage can gradually be undone, if not for this generation then at least for the next.

Such wisdom might help us move beyond ideological bickering and serve as the basis of a renewed effort to tackle the problems of inner-city poverty. We could begin by acknowledging that perhaps the single biggest thing we could do to reduce such poverty is to encourage teenage girls to finish high school and avoid having children out of wedlock. In this effort, school- and community-based programs that have a proven track record of reducing teen pregnancy need to be expanded, but parents, clergy, and community leaders also need to speak out more consistently on the issue.

We should also acknowledge that conservatives—and Bill Clinton—were right about welfare as it was previously structured: By detaching income from work, and by making no demands on welfare recipients other than a tolerance for intrusive bureaucracy and an assurance that no man lived in the same house as the mother of his children, the old AFDC program sapped people of their initiative and eroded their self-respect. Any strategy to reduce intergenerational poverty has to be centered on work, not welfare—not only because work provides independence and income but also because work provides order, structure, dignity, and opportunities for growth in people's lives.

But we also need to admit that work alone does not ensure that people can rise out of poverty. Across America, welfare reform has sharply reduced the number of people on the public dole; it has also swelled the ranks of the working poor, with women churning in and out of the labor market, locked into jobs that don't pay a living wage, forced every day to scramble for adequate child care, affordable housing, and accessible health care, only to find themselves at the end of each month wondering how they can stretch the last few dollars that they have left to cover the food bill, the gas bill, and the baby's new coat.

Strategies like an expanded Earned Income Tax Credit that help all low-wage workers can make an enormous difference in the lives of these women and their children. But if we're serious about breaking the cycle of intergenerational poverty, then many of these women will need some extra help with the basics that those living outside the inner city often take for granted. They need more police and more effective policing in their neighborhoods, to provide them and their children some semblance of personal security. They need access to community-based health centers that emphasize prevention—including reproductive health care, nutritional counseling, and in some cases treatment for substance abuse. They need a radical transformation of the schools their children attend, and access to affordable child care that will allow them to hold a full-time job or pursue their education.

And in many cases they need help learning to be effective parents. By the time many inner-city children reach the school system, they're already behind—unable to identify basic numbers, colors, or the letters in the alphabet, unaccustomed to sitting still or participating in a structured environment, and often burdened by undiagnosed health problems. They're unprepared not because they're unloved but because their mothers don't know how to provide what they need. Well-structured government programs— prenatal counseling, access to regular pediatric care, parenting programs, and quality early-childhood-education programs— have a proven ability to help fill the void.

Finally, we need to tackle the nexus of unemployment and crime in the inner city so that the men who live there can begin fulfilling their responsibilities. The conventional wisdom is that most unemployed inner-city men could find jobs if they really wanted to work; that they inevitably prefer drug dealing, with its attendant risks but potential profits, to the low-paying jobs that their lack of skills warrants. In fact, economists who've studied the issue—and the young men whose fates are at stake—will tell you that the costs and benefits of the street life don't match the popular mythology: At the bottom or even the middle ranks of the industry, drug dealing is a minimum-wage affair. For many inner-city men, what prevents gainful employment is not simply the absence of motivation to get off the streets but the absence of a job history or any marketable skills—and, increasingly, the stigma of a prison record.

Ask Mac, who has made it part of his mission to provide young men in his neighborhood a second chance. Ninety-five percent of his male employees are ex-felons, including one of his best cooks, who has been in and out of prison for the past twenty years for various drug offenses and one count of armed robbery. Mac starts them out at eight dollars an hour and tops them out at fifteen dollars an hour. He has no shortage of applicants. Mac's the first one to admit that some of the guys come in with issues—they aren't used to getting to work on time, and a lot of them aren't used to taking orders from a supervisor—and his turnover can be high. But by not accepting excuses from the young men he employs ("I tell them I got a business to run, and if they don't want the job I got other folks who do"), he finds that most are quick to adapt. Over time they become accustomed to the rhythms of ordinary life: sticking to schedules, working as part of a team, carrying their weight. They start talking about getting their GEDs, maybe enrolling in the local community college.

They begin to aspire to something better.

It would be nice if there were thousands of Macs out there, and if the market alone could generate opportunities for all the inner-city men who need them. But most employers aren't willing to take a chance on ex-felons, and those who are willing are often prevented from doing so. In Illinois, for example, ex-felons are prohibited from working not only in schools, nursing homes, and hospitals—restrictions that sensibly reflect our unwillingness to compromise the safety of our children or aging parents—but some are also prohibited from working as barbers and nail technicians.

Government could kick-start a transformation of circumstances for these men by working with private-sector contractors to hire and train ex-felons on projects that can benefit the community as a whole: insulating homes and offices to make them energy-efficient, perhaps, or laying the broadband lines needed to thrust entire communities into the Internet age. Such programs would cost money, of course—although, given the annual cost of incarcerating an inmate, any drop in recidivism would help the program pay for itself. Not all of the hard-core unemployed would prefer entry-level jobs to life on the streets, and no program to help ex-felons will eliminate the need to lock up hardened criminals, those whose habits of violence are too deeply entrenched.

Still, we can assume that with lawful work available for young men now in the drug trade, crime in many communities would drop; that as a consequence more employers would locate businesses in these neighborhoods and a self-sustaining economy would begin to take root; and that over the course of ten or fifteen years norms would begin to change, young men and women would begin to imagine a future for themselves, marriage rates would rise, and children would have a more stable world in which to grow up.

What would that be worth to all of us—an America in which crime has fallen, more children are cared for, cities are reborn, and the biases, fear, and discord that black poverty feeds are slowly drained away? Would it be worth what we've spent in the past year in Iraq? Would it be worth relinquishing demands for estate tax repeal? It's hard to quantify the benefits of such changes—precisely because the benefits would be immeasurable.

IF THE PROBLEMS of inner-city poverty arise from our failure to face up to an often tragic past, the challenges of immigration spark fears of an uncertain future. The demographics of America are changing inexorably and at lightning speed, and the claims of new immigrants won't fit neatly into the black-and-white paradigm of discrimination and resistance and guilt and recrimination. Indeed, even black and white newcomers—from Ghana and Ukraine, Somalia and Romania—arrive on these shores unburdened by the racial dynamics of an earlier era.

During the campaign, I would see firsthand the faces of this new America—in the Indian markets along Devon Avenue, in the sparkling new mosque in the southwest suburbs, in an Armenian wedding and a Filipino ball, in the meetings of the Korean American Leadership Council and the Nigerian Engineers Association. Everywhere I went, I found immigrants anchoring themselves to whatever housing and work they could find, washing dishes or driving cabs or toiling in their cousin's dry cleaners, saving money and building businesses and revitalizing dying neighborhoods, until they moved to the suburbs and raised children with accents that betrayed not the land of their parents but their Chicago birth certificates, teenagers who listened to rap and shopped at the mall and planned for futures as doctors and lawyers and engineers and even politicians.

Across the country, this classic immigrant story is playing itself out, the story of ambition and adaptation, hard work and education, assimilation and upward mobility. Today's immigrants, however, are living out this story in hyperdrive. As beneficiaries of a nation more tolerant and more worldly than the one immigrants faced generations ago, a nation that has come to revere its immigrant myth, they are more confident in their place here, more assertive of their rights. As a senator, I receive countless invitations to address these newest Americans, where I am often quizzed on my foreign policy views—where do I stand on Cyprus, say, or the future of Taiwan? They may have policy concerns specific to fields in which their ethnic groups are heavily represented— Indian American pharmacists might complain about Medicare reimbursements, Korean small-business owners might lobby for changes in the tax code.

But mostly they want affirmation that they, too, are Americans. Whenever I appear before immigrant audiences, I can count on some good-natured ribbing from my staff after my speech; according to them, my remarks always follow a three-part structure: "I am your friend," "[Fill in the home country] has been a cradle of civilization," and "You embody the American dream." They're right, my message is simple, for what I've come to understand is that my mere presence before these newly minted Americans serves notice that they matter, that they are voters critical to my success and full-fledged citizens deserving of respect.

Of course, not all my conversations in immigrant communities follow this easy pattern. In the wake of 9/11, my meetings with Arab and Pakistani Americans, for example, have a more urgent quality, for the stories of detentions and FBI questioning and hard stares from neighbors have shaken their sense of security and belonging. They have been reminded that the history of immigration in this country has a dark underbelly; they need specific assurances that their citizenship really means something, that America has learned the right lessons from the Japanese internments during World War II, and that I will stand with them should the political winds shift in an ugly direction.

It's in my meetings with the Latino community, though, in neighborhoods like Pilsen and Little Village, towns like Cicero and Aurora, that I'm forced to reflect on the meaning of America, the meaning of citizenship, and my sometimes conflicted feelings about all the changes that are taking place.

Of course, the presence of Latinos in Illinois—Puerto Ricans, Colombians, Salvadorans, Cubans, and most of all Mexicans—dates back generations, when agricultural workers began making their way north and joined ethnic groups in factory jobs throughout the region. Like other immigrants, they assimilated into the culture, although like African Americans, their upward mobility was often hampered by racial bias. Perhaps for that reason, black and Latino political and civil rights leaders often made common cause. In 1983, Latino support was critical in the election of Chicago's first black mayor, Harold Washington. That support was reciprocated, as Washington helped elect a generation of young, progressive Latinos to the Chicago city council and the Illinois state legislature. Indeed, until their numbers finally justified their own organization, Latino state legislators were official members of the Illinois Legislative Black Caucus.

It was against this backdrop, shortly after my arrival in Chicago, that my own ties to the Latino community were formed. As a young organizer, I often worked with Latino leaders on issues that affected both black and brown residents, from failing schools to illegal dumping to unimmunized children. My interest went beyond politics; I would come to love the Mexican and Puerto Rican sections of the city—the sounds of salsa and merengue pulsing out of apartments on hot summer nights, the solemnity of Mass in churches once filled with Poles and Italians and Irish, the frantic, happy chatter of soccer matches in the park, the cool humor of the men behind the counter at the sandwich shop, the elderly women who would grasp my hand and laugh at my pathetic efforts at Spanish. I made lifelong friends and allies in those neighborhoods; in my mind, at least, the fates of black and brown were to be perpetually intertwined, the cornerstone of a coalition that could help America live up to its promise.

By the time I returned from law school, though, tensions between blacks and Latinos in Chicago had started to surface. Between 1990 and 2000, the Spanish-speaking population in Chicago rose by 38 percent, and with this surge in population the Latino community was no longer content to serve as junior partner in any black-brown coalition. After Harold Washington died, a new cohort of Latino elected officials, affiliated with Richard M. Daley and remnants of the old Chicago political machine, came onto the scene, men and women less interested in high-minded principles and rainbow coalitions than in translating growing political power into contracts and jobs. As black businesses and commercial strips struggled, Latino businesses thrived, helped in part by financial ties to home countries and by a customer base held captive by language barriers. Everywhere, it seemed, Mexican and Central American workers came to dominate low-wage work that had once gone to blacks—as waiters and busboys, as hotel maids and as bellmen—and made inroads in the construction trades that had long excluded black labor. Blacks began to grumble and feel threatened; they wondered if once again they were about to be passed over by those who'd just arrived.

I shouldn't exaggerate the schism. Because both communities share a host of challenges, from soaring high school dropout rates to inadequate health insurance, blacks and Latinos continue to find common cause in their politics. As frustrated as blacks may get whenever they pass a construction site in a black neighborhood and see nothing but Mexican workers, I rarely hear them blame the workers themselves; usually they reserve their wrath for the contractors who hire them. When pressed, many blacks will express a grudging admiration for Latino immigrants—for their strong work ethic and commitment to family, their willingness to start at the bottom and make the most of what little they have.

Still, there's no denying that many blacks share the same anxieties as many whites about the wave of illegal immigration flooding our Southern border—a sense that what's happening now is fundamentally different from what has gone on before. Not all these fears are irrational. The number of immigrants added to the labor force every year is of a magnitude not seen in this country for over a century. If this huge influx of mostly low-skill workers provides some benefits to the economy as a whole—especially by keeping our workforce young, in contrast to an increasingly geriatric Europe and Japan—it also threatens to depress further the wages of blue-collar Americans and put strains on an already overburdened safety net. Other fears of native-born Americans are disturbingly familiar, echoing the xenophobia once directed at Italians, Irish, and Slavs fresh off the boat—fears that Latinos are inherently too different, in culture and in temperament, to assimilate fully into the American way of life; fears that, with the demographic changes now taking place, Latinos will wrest control away from those accustomed to wielding political power.

For most Americans, though, concerns over illegal immigration go deeper than worries about economic displacement and are more subtle than simple racism. In the past, immigration occurred on America's terms; the welcome mat could be extended selectively, on the basis of the immigrant's skills or color or the needs of industry. The laborer, whether Chinese or Russian or Greek, found himself a stranger in a strange land, severed from his home country, subject to often harsh constraints, forced to adapt to rules not of his own making.

Today it seems those terms no longer apply. Immigrants are entering as a result of a porous border rather than any systematic government policy; Mexico's proximity, as well as the desperate poverty of so many of its people, suggests the possibility that border crossing cannot even be slowed, much less stopped. Satellites, calling cards, and wire transfers, as well as the sheer size of the burgeoning Latino market, make it easier for today's immigrant to maintain linguistic and cultural ties to the land of his or her birth (the Spanish-language Univision now boasts the highest-rated newscast in Chicago). Native-born Americans suspect that it is they, and not the immigrant, who are being forced to adapt. In this way, the immigration debate comes to signify not a loss of jobs but a loss of sovereignty, just one more example—like September 11, avian flu, computer viruses, and factories moving to China—that America seems unable to control its own destiny.

IT WAS IN this volatile atmosphere—with strong passions on both sides of the debate—that the U.S. Senate considered a comprehensive immigration reform bill in the spring of 2006. With hundreds of thousands of immigrants protesting in the streets and a group of self-proclaimed vigilantes called the Minutemen rushing to defend the Southern border, the political stakes were high for Democrats, Republicans, and the President.

Under the leadership of Ted Kennedy and John McCain, the Senate crafted a compromise bill with three major components. The bill provided much tougher border security and, through an amendment I wrote with Chuck Grassley, made it significantly more difficult for employers to hire workers here illegally. The bill also recognized the difficulty of deporting twelve million un-documented immigrants and instead created a long, eleven-year process under which many of them could earn their citizenship. Finally, the bill included a guest worker program that would allow two hundred thousand foreign workers to enter the country for temporary employment.

On balance, I thought the legislation was worth support-ing. Still, the guest worker provision of the bill troubled me; it was essentially a sop to big business, a means for them to employ immigrants without granting them citizenship rights—indeed, a means for business to gain the benefits of outsourcing without having to locate their operations overseas. To address this problem, I succeeded in including language requiring that any job first be offered to U.S. workers, and that employers not undercut American wages by paying guest workers less than they would pay U.S. workers. The idea was to ensure that businesses turned to temporary foreign workers only when there was a labor shortage.

It was plainly an amendment designed to help American work-ers, which is why all the unions vigorously supported it. But no sooner had the provision been included in the bill than some con-servatives, both inside and outside of the Senate, began attacking me for supposedly "requiring that foreign workers get paid more than U.S. workers."

On the floor of the Senate one day, I caught up with one of my Republican colleagues who had leveled this charge at me. I explained that the bill would actually protect U.S. workers, since employers would have no incentive to hire guest workers if they had to pay the same wages they paid U.S. workers. The Republican colleague, who had been quite vocal in his opposition to any bill that would legalize the status of undocumented immigrants, shook his head.

"My small business guys are still going to hire immigrants," he said. "All your amendment does is make them pay more for their help."

"But why would they hire immigrants over U.S. workers if they cost the same?" I asked him.

He smiled. "'Cause let's face it, Barack. These Mexicans are just willing to work harder than Americans do."

That the opponents of the immigration bill could make such statements privately, while publicly pretending to stand up for American workers, indicates the degree of cynicism and hypocrisy that permeates the immigration debate. But with the public in a sour mood, their fears and anxieties fed daily by Lou Dobbs and talk radio hosts around the country, I can't say I'm surprised that the compromise bill has been stalled in the House ever since it passed out of the Senate.

And if I'm honest with myself, I must admit that I'm not entirely immune to such nativist sentiments. When I see Mexican flags waved at proimmigration demonstrations, I sometimes feel a flush of patriotic resentment. When I'm forced to use a translator to communicate with the guy fixing my car, I feel a certain frustration.

Once, as the immigration debate began to heat up in the Capitol, a group of activists visited my office, asking that I sponsor a private relief bill that would legalize the status of thirty Mexican nationals who had been deported, leaving behind spouses or children with legal resident status. One of my staffers, Danny Sepulveda, a young man of Chilean descent, took the meeting, and explained to the group that although I was sympathetic to their plight and was one of the chief sponsors of the Senate immigration bill, I didn't feel comfortable, as a matter of principle, sponsoring legislation that would select thirty people out of the millions in similar situations for a special dispensation. Some in the group became agitated; they suggested that I didn't care about immigrant families and immigrant children, that I cared more about borders than about justice. One activist accused Danny of having forgotten where he came from—of not really being Latino.

When I heard what had happened, I was both angry and frustrated. I wanted to call the group and explain that American citizenship is a privilege and not a right; that without meaningful borders and respect for the law, the very things that brought them to America, the opportunities and protections afforded those who live in this country, would surely erode; and that anyway, I didn't put up with people abusing my staff—especially one who was championing their cause.

It was Danny who talked me out of the call, sensibly suggesting that it might be counterproductive. Several weeks later, on a Saturday morning, I attended a naturalization workshop at St. Pius Church in Pilsen, sponsored by Congressman Luis Gutierrez, the Service Employees International Union, and several of the immigrants' rights groups that had visited my office. About a thousand people had lined up outside the church, including young families, elderly couples, and women with strollers; inside, people sat silently in wooden pews, clutching the small American flags that the organizers had passed out, waiting to be called by one of the volunteers who would help them manage the start of what would be a years-long process to become citizens.

As I wandered down the aisle, some people smiled and waved; others nodded tentatively as I offered my hand and introduced myself. I met a Mexican woman who spoke no English but whose son was in Iraq; I recognized a young Colombian man who worked as a valet at a local restaurant and learned that he was studying accounting at the local community college. At one point a young girl, seven or eight, came up to me, her parents standing behind her, and asked me for an autograph; she was studying government in school, she said, and would show it to her class.

I asked her what her name was. She said her name was Cristina and that she was in the third grade. I told her parents they should be proud of her. And as I watched Cristina translate my words into Spanish for them, I was reminded that America has nothing to fear from these newcomers, that they have come here for the same reason that families came here 150 years ago—all those who fled Europe's famines and wars and unyielding hierarchies, all those who may not have had the right legal documents or connections or unique skills to offer but who carried with them a hope for a better life.

We have a right and duty to protect our borders. We can insist to those already here that with citizenship come obligations—to a common language, common loyalties, a common purpose, a common destiny. But ultimately the danger to our way of life is not that we will be overrun by those who do not look like us or do not yet speak our language. The danger will come if we fail to recognize the humanity of Cristina and her family—if we withhold from them the rights and opportunities that we take for granted, and tolerate the hypocrisy of a servant class in our midst; or more broadly, if we stand idly by as America continues to become increasingly unequal, an inequality that tracks racial lines and therefore feeds racial strife and which, as the country becomes more black and brown, neither our democracy nor our economy can long withstand.

That's not the future I want for Cristina, I said to myself as I watched her and her family wave good-bye. That's not the future I want for my daughters. Their America will be more dizzying in its diversity, its culture more polyglot. My daughters will learn Spanish and be the better for it. Cristina will learn about Rosa Parks and understand that the life of a black seamstress speaks to her own. The issues my girls and Cristina confront may lack the stark moral clarity of a segregated bus, but in one form or another their generation will surely be tested—just as Mrs. Parks was tested and the Freedom Riders were tested, just as we are all tested—by those voices that would divide us and have us turn on each other.

And when they are tested in that way, I hope Cristina and my daughters will have all read about the history of this country and will recognize they have been given something precious.

America is big enough to accommodate all their dreams.

Chapter 8

The World Beyond
Our Borders

INDONESIA IS A nation of islands—more than seventeen thousand in all, spread along the equator between the Indian and Pacific Oceans, between Australia and the South China Sea. Most Indonesians are of Malay stock and live on the larger islands of Java, Sumatra, Kalimantan, Sulawesi, and Bali. On the far eastern islands like Ambon and the Indonesian portion of New Guinea the people are, in varying degrees, of Melanesian ancestry. Indonesia's climate is tropical, and its rain forests were once teeming with exotic species like the orangutan and the Sumatran tiger. Today, those rain forests are rapidly dwindling, victim to logging, mining, and the cultivation of rice, tea, coffee, and palm oil. Deprived of their natural habitat, orangutans are now an endangered species; no more than a few hundred Sumatran tigers remain in the wild.

With more than 240 million people, Indonesia's population ranks fourth in the world, behind China, India, and the United States. More than seven hundred ethnic groups reside within the country's borders, and more than 742 languages are spoken there. Almost 90 percent of Indonesia's population practice Islam, making it the world's largest Muslim nation. Indonesia is OPEC's only Asian member, although as a consequence of aging infrastructure, depleted reserves, and high domestic consumption it is now a net importer of crude oil. The national language is Bahasa Indonesia. The capital is Jakarta. The currency is the rupiah.

Most Americans can't locate Indonesia on a map.

This fact is puzzling to Indonesians, since for the past sixty years the fate of their nation has been directly tied to U.S. foreign policy. Ruled by a succession of sultanates and often-splintering kingdoms for most of its history, the archipelago became a Dutch colony—the Dutch East Indies—in the 1600s, a status that would last for more than three centuries. But in the lead-up to World War II, the Dutch East Indies' ample oil reserves became a prime target of Japanese expansion; having thrown its lot in with the Axis powers and facing a U.S.-imposed oil embargo, Japan needed fuel for its military and industry. After the attack on Pearl Harbor, Japan moved swiftly to take over the Dutch colony, an occupation that would last for the duration of the war.

With the Japanese surrender in 1945, a budding Indonesian nationalist movement declared the country's independence. The Dutch had other ideas, and attempted to reclaim their former territory. Four bloody years of war ensued. Eventually the Dutch bowed to mounting international pressure (the U.S. government, already concerned with the spread of communism under the banner of anticolonialism, threatened the Netherlands with a cutoff of Marshall Plan funds) and recognized Indonesia's sovereignty. The principal leader of the independence movement, a charismatic, flamboyant figure named Sukarno, became Indonesia's first president.

Sukarno proved to be a major disappointment to Washington. Along with Nehru of India and Nasser of Egypt, he helped found the nonaligned movement, an effort by nations newly liberated from colonial rule to navigate an independent path between the West and the Soviet bloc. Indonesia's Communist Party, although never formally in power, grew in size and influence. Sukarno himself ramped up the anti-Western rhetoric, nationalizing key industries, rejecting U.S. aid, and strengthening ties with the Soviets and China. With U.S. forces knee-deep in Vietnam and the domino theory still a central tenet of U.S. foreign policy, the CIA began providing covert support to various insurgencies inside Indonesia, and cultivated close links with Indonesia's military officers, many of whom had been trained in the United States. In 1965, under the leadership of General Suharto, the military moved against Sukarno, and under emergency powers began a massive purge of communists and their sympathizers. According to estimates, between 500,000 and one million people were slaughtered during the purge, with 750,000 others imprisoned or forced into exile.

It was two years after the purge began, in 1967, the same year that Suharto assumed the presidency, that my mother and I arrived in Jakarta, a consequence of her remarriage to an Indonesian student whom she'd met at the University of Hawaii. I was six at the time, my mother twenty-four. In later years my mother would insist that had she known what had transpired in the preceding months, we never would have made the trip. But she didn't know—the full story of the coup and the purge was slow to appear in American newspapers. Indonesians didn't talk about it either. My stepfather, who had seen his student visa revoked while still in Hawaii and had been conscripted into the Indonesian army a few months before our arrival, refused to talk politics with my mother, advising her that some things were best forgotten.

And in fact, forgetting the past was easy to do in Indonesia. Jakarta was still a sleepy backwater in those days, with few buildings over four or five stories high, cycle rickshaws outnumbering cars, the city center and wealthier sections of town—with their colonial elegance and lush, well-tended lawns—quickly giving way to clots of small villages with unpaved roads and open sewers, dusty markets, and shanties of mud and brick and plywood and corrugated iron that tumbled down gentle banks to murky rivers where families bathed and washed laundry like pilgrims in the Ganges.

Our family was not well off in those early years; the Indonesian army didn't pay its lieutenants much. We lived in a modest house on the outskirts of town, without air-conditioning, refrigeration, or flush toilets. We had no car—my stepfather rode a motorcycle, while my mother took the local jitney service every morning to the U.S. embassy, where she worked as an English teacher. Without the money to go to the international school that most expatriate children attended, I went to local Indonesian schools and ran the streets with the children of farmers, servants, tailors, and clerks.

As a boy of seven or eight, none of this concerned me much. I remember those years as a joyous time, full of adventure and mystery—days of chasing down chickens and running from water buffalo, nights of shadow puppets and ghost stories and street vendors bringing delectable sweets to our door. As it was, I knew that relative to our neighbors we were doing fine—unlike many, we always had enough to eat.

And perhaps more than that, I understood, even at a young age, that my family's status was determined not only by our wealth but by our ties to the West. My mother might scowl at the attitudes she heard from other Americans in Jakarta, their condescension toward Indonesians, their unwillingness to learn anything about the country that was hosting them—but given the exchange rate, she was glad to be getting paid in dollars rather than the rupiahs her Indonesian colleagues at the embassy were paid. We might live as Indonesians lived—but every so often my mother would take me to the American Club, where I could jump in the pool and watch cartoons and sip Coca-Cola to my heart's content. Sometimes, when my Indonesian friends came to our house, I would show them books of photographs, of Disneyland or the Empire State Building, that my grandmother had sent me; sometimes we would thumb through the Sears Roebuck catalog and marvel at the treasures on display. All this, I knew, was part of my heritage and set me apart, for my mother and I were citizens of the United States, beneficiaries of its power, safe and secure under the blanket of its protection.

The scope of that power was hard to miss. The U.S. military conducted joint exercises with the Indonesian military and training programs for its officers. President Suharto turned to a cadre of American economists to design Indonesia's development plan, based on free-market principles and foreign investment. American development consultants formed a steady line outside government ministries, helping to manage the massive influx of foreign assistance from the U.S. Agency for International Development and the World Bank. And although corruption permeated every level of government—even the smallest interaction with a policeman or bureaucrat involved a bribe, and just about every commodity or product coming in and out of the country, from oil to wheat to automobiles, went through companies controlled by the president, his family, or members of the ruling junta—enough of the oil wealth and foreign aid was plowed back into schools, roads, and other infrastructure that Indonesia's general population saw its living standards rise dramatically; between 1967 and 1997, per capita income would go from $50 to $4,600 a year. As far as the United States was concerned, Indonesia had become a model of stability, a reliable supplier of raw materials and importer of Western goods, a stalwart ally and bulwark against communism.

I would stay in Indonesia long enough to see some of this newfound prosperity firsthand. Released from the army, my stepfather began working for an American oil company. We moved to a bigger house and got a car and a driver, a refrigerator, and a television set. But in 1971 my mother—concerned for my education and perhaps anticipating her own growing distance from my stepfather—sent me to live with my grandparents in Hawaii. A year later she and my sister would join me. My mother's ties to Indonesia would never diminish; for the next twenty years she would travel back and forth, working for international agencies for six or twelve months at a time as a specialist in women's development issues, designing programs to help village women start their own businesses or bring their produce to market. But while during my teenage years I would return to Indonesia three or four times on short visits, my life and attention gradually turned elsewhere.

What I know of Indonesia's subsequent history, then, I know mainly through books, newspapers, and the stories my mother told me. For twenty-five years, in fits and starts, Indonesia's economy continued to grow. Jakarta became a metropolis of almost nine million souls, with skyscrapers, slums, smog, and nightmare traffic. Men and women left the countryside to join the ranks of wage labor in manufacturing plants built by foreign investment, making sneakers for Nike and shirts for the Gap. Bali became the resort of choice for surfers and rock stars, with five-star hotels, Internet connections, and a Kentucky Fried Chicken franchise. By the early nineties, Indonesia was considered an "Asian tiger," the next great success story of a globalizing world.

Even the darker aspects of Indonesian life—its politics and human rights record—showed signs of improvement. When it came to sheer brutality, the post-1967 Suharto regime never reached the levels of Iraq under Saddam Hussein; with his subdued, placid style, the Indonesian president would never attract the attention that more demonstrative strongmen like Pinochet or the Shah of Iran did. By any measure, though, Suharto's rule was harshly repressive. Arrests and torture of dissidents were common, a free press nonexistent, elections a mere formality. When ethnically based secessionist movements sprang up in areas like Aceh, the army targeted not just guerrillas but civilians for swift retribution—murder, rape, villages set afire. And throughout the seventies and eighties, all this was done with the knowledge, if not outright approval, of U.S. administrations.

But with the end of the Cold War, Washington's attitudes began to change. The State Department began pressuring Indonesia to curb its human rights abuses. In 1992, after Indonesian military units massacred peaceful demonstrators in Dili, East Timor, Congress terminated military aid to the Indonesian government. By 1996, Indonesian reformists had begun taking to the streets, openly talking about corruption in high offices, the military's excesses, and the need for free and fair elections.

Then, in 1997, the bottom fell out. A run on currencies and securities throughout Asia engulfed an Indonesian economy already corroded by decades of corruption. The rupiah's value fell 85 percent in a matter of months. Indonesian companies that had borrowed in dollars saw their balance sheets collapse. In exchange for a $43 billion bailout, the Western-dominated International Monetary Fund, or IMF, insisted on a series of austerity measures (cutting government subsidies, raising interest rates) that would lead the price of such staples as rice and kerosene to nearly double. By the time the crisis was over, Indonesia's economy had contracted almost 14 percent. Riots and demonstrations grew so severe that Suharto was finally forced to resign, and in 1998 the country's first free elections were held, with some forty-eight parties vying for seats and some ninety-three million people casting their votes.

On the surface, at least, Indonesia has survived the twin shocks of financial meltdown and democratization. The stock market is booming, and a second national election went off without major incident, leading to a peaceful transfer of power. If corruption remains endemic and the military remains a potent force, there's been an explosion of independent newspapers and political parties to channel discontent.

On the other hand, democracy hasn't brought a return to prosperity. Per capita income is nearly 22 percent less than it was in 1997. The gap between rich and poor, always cavernous, appears to have worsened. The average Indonesian's sense of deprivation is amplified by the Internet and satellite TV, which beam in images of the unattainable riches of London, New York, Hong

Kong, and Paris in exquisite detail. And anti-American sentiment, almost nonexistent during the Suharto years, is now widespread, thanks in part to perceptions that New York speculators
and the IMF purposely triggered the Asian financial crisis. In a
2003 poll, most Indonesians had a higher opinion of Osama bin
Laden than they did of George W. Bush.

All of which underscores perhaps the most profound shift in
Indonesia—the growth of militant, fundamentalist Islam in the
country. Traditionally, Indonesians practiced a tolerant, almost
syncretic brand of the faith, infused with the Buddhist, Hindu,
and animist traditions of earlier periods. Under the watchful eye
of an explicitly secular Suharto government, alcohol was permitted, non-Muslims practiced their faith free from persecution, and
women—sporting skirts or sarongs as they rode buses or scoot-
ers on the way to work—possessed all the rights that men possessed. Today, Islamic parties make up one of the largest political
blocs, with many calling for the imposition of sharia, or Islamic
law. Seeded by funds from the Middle East, Wahhabist clerics,
schools, and mosques now dot the countryside. Many Indonesian
women have adopted the head coverings so familiar in the Muslim countries of North Africa and the Persian Gulf; Islamic mili-
tants and self-proclaimed "vice squads" have attacked churches,
nightclubs, casinos, and brothels. In 2002, an explosion in a Bali
nightclub killed more than two hundred people; similar suicide
bombings followed in Jakarta in 2004 and Bali in 2005. Members of Jemaah Islamiah, a militant Islamic organization with
links to Al Qaeda, were tried for the bombings; while three of
those connected to the bombings received death sentences, the
spiritual leader of the group, Abu Bakar Bashir, was released
after a twenty-six-month prison term.

It was on a beach just a few miles from the site of those
bombings that I stayed the last time I visited Bali. When I think
of that island, and all of Indonesia, I'm haunted by memories—
the feel of packed mud under bare feet as I wander through

paddy fields; the sight of day breaking behind volcanic peaks; the muezzin's call at night and the smell of wood smoke; the dickering at the fruit stands alongside the road; the frenzied sound of a gamelan orchestra, the musicians' faces lit by fire. I would like to take Michelle and the girls to share that piece of my life, to climb the thousand-year-old Hindu ruins of Prambanan or swim in a river high in Balinese hills.

But my plans for such a trip keep getting delayed. I'm chronically busy, and traveling with young children is always difficult. And, too, perhaps I am worried about what I will find there—that the land of my childhood will no longer match my memories. As much as the world has shrunk, with its direct flights and cell phone coverage and CNN and Internet cafés, Indonesia feels more distant now than it did thirty years ago.

I fear it's becoming a land of strangers.

IN THE FIELD of international affairs, it's dangerous to extrapolate from the experiences of a single country. In its history, geography, culture, and conflicts, each nation is unique. And yet in many ways Indonesia serves as a useful metaphor for the world beyond our borders—a world in which globalization and sectarianism, poverty and plenty, modernity and antiquity constantly collide.

Indonesia also provides a handy record of U.S. foreign policy over the past fifty years. In broad outline at least, it's all there: our role in liberating former colonies and creating international institutions to help manage the post–World War II order; our tendency to view nations and conflicts through the prism of the Cold War; our tireless promotion of American-style capitalism and multinational corporations; the tolerance and occasional encouragement of tyranny, corruption, and environmental degradation when it served our interests; our optimism once the Cold War ended that Big Macs and the Internet would lead to the end of historical conflicts; the growing economic power of Asia and the growing resentment of the United States as the world's sole superpower; the realization that in the short term, at least, democratization might lay bare, rather than alleviate, ethnic hatreds and religious divisions—and that the wonders of globalization might also facilitate economic volatility, the spread of pandemics, and terrorism.

In other words, our record is mixed—not just in Indonesia but across the globe. At times, American foreign policy has been farsighted, simultaneously serving our national interests, our ideals, and the interests of other nations. At other times American policies have been misguided, based on false assumptions that ignore the legitimate aspirations of other peoples, undermine our own credibility, and make for a more dangerous world.

Such ambiguity shouldn't be surprising, for American foreign policy has always been a jumble of warring impulses. In the earliest days of the Republic, a policy of isolationism often prevailed— a wariness of foreign intrigues that befitted a nation just emerging from a war of independence. "Why," George Washington asked in his famous Farewell Address, "by interweaving our destiny with that of any part of Europe, entangle our peace and prosperity in the toils of European ambition, rivalship, interest, humor or caprice?" Washington's view was reinforced by what he called America's "detached and distant situation," a geographic separation that would permit the new nation to "defy material injury from external annoyance."

Moreover, while America's revolutionary origins and republican form of government might make it sympathetic toward those seeking freedom elsewhere, America's early leaders cautioned against idealistic attempts to export our way of life; according to John Quincy Adams, America should not go "abroad in search of monsters to destroy" nor "become the dictatress of the world." Providence had charged America with the task of making a new world, not reforming the old; protected by an ocean and with the bounty of a continent, America could best serve the cause of freedom by concentrating on its own development, becoming a beacon of hope for other nations and people around the globe.

But if suspicion of foreign entanglements is stamped into our DNA, then so is the impulse to expand—geographically, commercially, and ideologically. Thomas Jefferson expressed early on the inevitability of expansion beyond the boundaries of the original thirteen states, and his timetable for such expansion was greatly accelerated with the Louisiana Purchase and the Lewis and Clark expedition. The same John Quincy Adams who warned against U.S. adventurism abroad became a tireless advocate of continental expansion and served as the chief architect of the Monroe Doctrine—a warning to European powers to keep out of the Western Hemisphere. As American soldiers and settlers moved steadily west and southwest, successive administrations described the annexation of territory in terms of "manifest destiny"—the conviction that such expansion was preordained, part of God's plan to extend what Andrew Jackson called "the area of freedom" across the continent.

Of course, manifest destiny also meant bloody and violent conquest—of Native American tribes forcibly removed from their lands and of the Mexican army defending its territory. It was a conquest that, like slavery, contradicted America's founding principles and tended to be justified in explicitly racist terms, a conquest that American mythology has always had difficulty fully absorbing but that other countries recognized for what it was— an exercise in raw power.

With the end of the Civil War and the consolidation of what's now the continental United States, that power could not be denied. Intent on expanding markets for its goods, securing raw materials for its industry, and keeping sea lanes open for its commerce, the nation turned its attention overseas. Hawaii was annexed, giving America a foothold in the Pacific. The Spanish-American War delivered Puerto Rico, Guam, and the Philippines into U.S. control; when some members of the Senate objected to the military occupation of an archipelago seven thousand miles away—an occupation that would involve thousands of U.S. troops crushing a Philippine independence movement—one senator argued that the acquisition would provide the United States with access to the China market and mean "a vast trade and wealth and power." America would never pursue the systematic colonization practiced by European nations, but it shed all inhibitions about meddling in the affairs of countries it deemed strategically important. Theodore Roosevelt, for example, added a corollary to the Monroe Doctrine, declaring that the United States would intervene in any Latin American or Caribbean country whose government it deemed not to America's liking. "The United States of America has not the option as to whether it will or it will not play a great part in the world," Roosevelt would argue. "It *must* play a great part. All that it can decide is whether it will play that part well or badly."

By the start of the twentieth century, then, the motives that drove U.S. foreign policy seemed barely distinguishable from those of the other great powers, driven by realpolitik and commercial interests. Isolationist sentiment in the population at large remained strong, particularly when it came to conflicts in Europe, and when vital U.S. interests did not seem directly at stake. But technology and trade were shrinking the globe; determining which interests were vital and which ones were not became increasingly difficult. During World War I, Woodrow Wilson avoided American involvement until the repeated sinking of American vessels by German U-boats and the imminent collapse of the European continent made neutrality untenable. When the war was over, America had emerged as the world's dominant power—but a power whose prosperity Wilson now understood to be linked to peace and prosperity in faraway lands.

It was in an effort to address this new reality that Wilson

sought to reinterpret the idea of America's manifest destiny. Making "the world safe for democracy" didn't just involve winning a war, he argued; it was in America's interest to encourage the self-determination of all peoples and provide the world a legal framework that could help avoid future conflicts. As part of the Treaty of Versailles, which detailed the terms of German surrender, Wilson proposed a League of Nations to mediate conflicts between nations, along with an international court and a set of international laws that would bind not just the weak but also the strong. "This is the time of all others when Democracy should prove its purity and its spiritual power to prevail," Wilson said. "It is surely the manifest destiny of the United States to lead in the attempt to make this spirit prevail."

Wilson's proposals were initially greeted with enthusiasm in the United States and around the world. The U.S. Senate, however, was less impressed. Republican Senate Leader Henry Cabot Lodge considered the League of Nations—and the very concept of international law—as an encroachment on American sovereignty, a foolish constraint on America's ability to impose its will around the world. Aided by traditional isolationists in both parties (many of whom had opposed American entry into World War I), as well as Wilson's stubborn unwillingness to compromise, the Senate refused to ratify U.S. membership in the League.

For the next twenty years, America turned resolutely inward—reducing its army and navy, refusing to join the World Court, standing idly by as Italy, Japan, and Nazi Germany built up their military machines. The Senate became a hotbed of isolationism, passing a Neutrality Act that prevented the United States from lending assistance to countries invaded by the Axis powers, and repeatedly ignoring the President's appeals as Hitler's armies marched across Europe. Not until the bombing of Pearl Harbor would America realize its terrible mistake. "There is no such thing as security for any nation—or any individual—in a world ruled by the principles of gangsterism," FDR would say in his national address after the attack. "We cannot measure our safety in terms of miles on any map any more."

In the aftermath of World War II, the United States would have a chance to apply these lessons to its foreign policy. With Europe and Japan in ruins, the Soviet Union bled white by its battles on the Eastern Front but already signaling its intentions to spread its brand of totalitarian communism as far as it could, America faced a choice. There were those on the right who argued that only a unilateral foreign policy and an immediate invasion of the Soviet Union could disable the emerging communist threat. And although isolationism of the sort that prevailed in the thirties was now thoroughly discredited, there were those on the left who downplayed Soviet aggression, arguing that given Soviet losses and the country's critical role in the Allied victory, Stalin should be accommodated.

America took neither path. Instead, the postwar leadership of President Truman, Dean Acheson, George Marshall, and George Kennan crafted the architecture of a new, postwar order that married Wilson's idealism to hardheaded realism, an acceptance of America's power with a humility regarding America's ability to control events around the world. Yes, these men argued, the world is a dangerous place, and the Soviet threat is real; America needed to maintain its military dominance and be prepared to use force in defense of its interests across the globe. But even the power of the United States was finite—and because the battle against communism was also a battle of ideas, a test of what system might best serve the hopes and dreams of billions of people around the world, military might alone could not ensure America's long-term prosperity or security.

What America needed, then, were stable allies—allies that shared the ideals of freedom, democracy, and the rule of law, and that saw themselves as having a stake in a market-based economic system. Such alliances, both military and economic, entered into freely and maintained by mutual consent, would be more lasting—and stir less resentment—than any collection of vassal states American imperialism might secure. Likewise, it was in America's interest to work with other countries to build up international institutions and promote international norms. Not because of a naive assumption that international laws and treaties alone would end conflicts among nations or eliminate the need for American military action, but because the more international norms were reinforced and the more America signaled a willingness to show restraint in the exercise of its power, the fewer the number of conflicts that would arise—and the more legitimate our actions would appear in the eyes of the world when we did have to move militarily.

In less than a decade, the infrastructure of a new world order was in place. There was a U.S. policy of containment with respect to communist expansion, backed not just by U.S. troops but also by security agreements with NATO and Japan; the Marshall Plan to rebuild war-shattered economies; the Bretton Woods agreement to provide stability to the world's financial markets and the General Agreement on Tariffs and Trade to establish rules governing world commerce; U.S. support for the independence of former European colonies; the IMF and World Bank to help integrate these newly independent nations into the world economy; and the United Nations to provide a forum for collective security and international cooperation.

Sixty years later, we can see the results of this massive postwar undertaking: a successful outcome to the Cold War, an avoidance of nuclear catastrophe, the effective end of conflict between the world's great military powers, and an era of unprecedented economic growth at home and abroad.

It's a remarkable achievement, perhaps the Greatest Generation's greatest gift to us after the victory over fascism. But like any system built by man, it had its flaws and contradictions; it could fall victim to the distortions of politics, the sins of hubris, the corrupting effects of fear. Because of the enormity of the Soviet threat, and the shock of communist takeovers in China and North Korea, American policy makers came to view nationalist movements, ethnic struggles, reform efforts, or left-leaning policies anywhere in the world through the lens of the Cold War—potential threats they felt outweighed our professed commitment to freedom and democracy. For decades we would tolerate and even aid thieves like Mobutu, thugs like Noriega, so long as they opposed communism. Occasionally U.S. covert operations would engineer the removal of democratically elected leaders in countries like Iran—with seismic repercussions that haunt us to this day.

America's policy of containment also involved an enormous military buildup, matching and then exceeding the Soviet and Chinese arsenals. Over time, the "iron triangle" of the Pentagon, defense contractors, and congressmen with large defense expenditures in their districts amassed great power in shaping U.S. foreign policy. And although the threat of nuclear war would preclude direct military confrontation with our superpower rivals, U.S policy makers increasingly viewed problems elsewhere in the world through a military lens rather than a diplomatic one.

Most important, the postwar system over time suffered from too much politics and not enough deliberation and domestic consensus building. One of America's strengths immediately following the war was a degree of domestic consensus surrounding foreign policy. There might have been fierce differences between Republicans and Democrats, but politics usually ended at the water's edge; professionals, whether in the White House, the Pentagon, the State Department, or the CIA, were expected to make decisions based on facts and sound judgment, not ideology or electioneering. Moreover, that consensus extended to the public at large; programs like the Marshall Plan, which involved a massive investment of U.S. funds, could not have gone forward without the American people's basic trust in their government, as well as a reciprocal faith on the part of government officials that the American people could be trusted with the facts that went into decisions that spent their tax dollars or sent their sons to war.

As the Cold War wore on, the key elements in this consensus began to erode. Politicians discovered that they could get votes by being tougher on communism than their opponents. Democrats were assailed for "losing China." McCarthyism destroyed careers and crushed dissent. Kennedy would blame Republicans for a "missile gap" that didn't exist on his way to beating Nixon, who himself had made a career of Red-baiting his opponents. Presidents Eisenhower, Kennedy, and Johnson would all find their judgment clouded by fear that they would be tagged as "soft on communism." The Cold War techniques of secrecy, snooping, and misinformation, used against foreign governments and foreign populations, became tools of domestic politics, a means to harass critics, build support for questionable policies, or cover up blunders. The very ideals that we had promised to export overseas were being betrayed at home.

All these trends came to a head in Vietnam. The disastrous consequences of that conflict—for our credibility and prestige abroad, for our armed forces (which would take a generation to recover), and most of all for those who fought—have been amply documented. But perhaps the biggest casualty of that war was the bond of trust between the American people and their government—and between Americans themselves. As a consequence of a more aggressive press corps and the images of body bags flooding into living rooms, Americans began to realize that the best and the brightest in Washington didn't always know what they were doing—and didn't always tell the truth. Increasingly, many on the left voiced opposition not only to the Vietnam War but also to the broader aims of American foreign policy. In their view, President Johnson, General Westmoreland, the CIA, the "military-industrial complex," and international institutions like the World Bank were all manifestations of American arrogance, jingoism,

racism, capitalism, and imperialism. Those on the right responded
in kind, laying responsibility not only for the loss of Vietnam but
also for the decline of America's standing in the world squarely
on the "blame America first" crowd—the protesters, the hippies,
Jane Fonda, the Ivy League intellectuals and liberal media who
denigrated patriotism, embraced a relativistic worldview, and
undermined American resolve to confront godless communism.

Admittedly, these were caricatures, promoted by activists and
political consultants. Many Americans remained somewhere in
the middle, still supportive of America's efforts to defeat communism but skeptical of U.S. policies that might involve large
numbers of American casualties. Throughout the seventies and
eighties, one could find Democratic hawks and Republican
doves; in Congress, there were men like Mark Hatfield of Ore-
gon and Sam Nunn of Georgia who sought to perpetuate the tradition of a bipartisan foreign policy. But the caricatures were
what shaped public impressions during election time, as Republicans increasingly portrayed Democrats as weak on defense, and
those suspicious of military and covert action abroad increasingly made the Democratic Party their political home.

It was against this backdrop—an era of division rather than
an era of consensus—that most Americans alive today formed
whatever views they may have on foreign policy. These were the
years of Nixon and Kissinger, whose foreign policies were tacti-
cally brilliant but were overshadowed by domestic policies and a
Cambodian bombing campaign that were morally rudderless.
They were the years of Jimmy Carter, a Democrat who—with
his emphasis on human rights—seemed prepared to once again
align moral concerns with a strong defense, until oil shocks, the
humiliation of the Iranian hostage crisis, and the Soviet Union's
invasion of Afghanistan made him seem naive and ineffective.

Looming perhaps largest of all was Ronald Reagan, whose
clarity about communism seemed matched by his blindness regarding other sources of misery in the world. I personally came

of age during the Reagan presidency—I was studying international affairs at Columbia, and later working as a community organizer in Chicago—and like many Democrats in those days I bemoaned the effect of Reagan's policies toward the Third World: his administration's support for the apartheid regime of South Africa, the funding of El Salvador's death squads, the invasion of tiny, hapless Grenada. The more I studied nuclear arms policy, the more I found Star Wars to be ill conceived; the chasm between Reagan's soaring rhetoric and the tawdry Iran-Contra deal left me speechless.

But at times, in arguments with some of my friends on the left, I would find myself in the curious position of defending aspects of Reagan's worldview. I didn't understand why, for example, progressives should be less concerned about oppression behind the Iron Curtain than they were about brutality in Chile. I couldn't be persuaded that U.S. multinationals and international terms of trade were single-handedly responsible for poverty around the world; nobody forced corrupt leaders in Third World countries to steal from their people. I might have arguments with the size of Reagan's military buildup, but given the Soviet invasion of Afghanistan, staying ahead of the Soviets militarily seemed a sensible thing to do. Pride in our country, respect for our armed services, a healthy appreciation for the dangers beyond our borders, an insistence that there was no easy equivalence between East and West—in all this I had no quarrel with Reagan. And when the Berlin Wall came tumbling down, I had to give the old man his due, even if I never gave him my vote.

Many people—including many Democrats—did give Reagan their vote, leading Republicans to argue that his presidency restored America's foreign policy consensus. Of course, that consensus was never really tested; Reagan's war against communism was mainly carried out through proxies and deficit spending, not the deployment of U.S. troops. As it was, the end of the Cold War made Reagan's formula seem ill suited to a new world.

George H. W. Bush's return to a more traditional, "realist" foreign policy would result in a steady management of the Soviet Union's dissolution and an able handling of the first Gulf War. But with the American public's attention focused on the domestic economy, his skill in building international coalitions or judiciously projecting American power did nothing to salvage his presidency.

By the time Bill Clinton came into office, conventional wisdom suggested that America's post–Cold War foreign policy would be more a matter of trade than tanks, protecting American copyrights rather than American lives. Clinton himself understood that globalization involved not only new economic challenges but also new security challenges. In addition to promoting free trade and bolstering the international financial system, his administration would work to end long-festering conflicts in the Balkans and Northern Ireland and advance democratization in Eastern Europe, Latin America, Africa, and the former Soviet Union. But in the eyes of the public, at least, foreign policy in the nineties lacked any overarching theme or grand imperatives. U.S. military action in particular seemed entirely a matter of choice, not necessity—the product of our desire to slap down rogue states, perhaps; or a function of humanitarian calculations regarding the moral obligations we owed to Somalis, Haitians, Bosnians, or other unlucky souls.

Then came September 11—and Americans felt their world turned upside down.

IN JANUARY 2006, I boarded a C-130 military cargo plane and took off for my first trip into Iraq. Two of my colleagues on the trip—Senator Evan Bayh of Indiana and Congressman Harold Ford, Jr. of Tennessee—had made the trip before, and they warned me that the landings in Baghdad could be a bit uncomfortable: To evade potential hostile fire, military flights in and out of Iraq's capital city engaged in a series of sometimes stomach-turning maneuvers. As our plane cruised through the hazy morning, though, it was hard to feel concerned. Strapped into canvas seats, most of my fellow passengers had fallen asleep, their heads bobbing against the orange webbing that ran down the center of the fuselage. One of the crew appeared to be playing a video game; another placidly thumbed through our flight plans.

It had been four and a half years since I'd first heard reports of a plane hitting the World Trade Center. I had been in Chicago at the time, driving to a state legislative hearing downtown. The reports on my car radio were sketchy, and I assumed that there must have been an accident, a small prop plane perhaps veering off course. By the time I arrived at my meeting, the second plane had already hit, and we were told to evacuate the State of Illinois Building. Up and down the streets, people gathered, staring at the sky and at the Sears Tower. Later, in my law office, a group of us sat motionless as the nightmare images unfolded across the TV screen—a plane, dark as a shadow, vanishing into glass and steel; men and women clinging to windowsills, then letting go; the shouts and sobs from below and finally the rolling clouds of dust blotting out the sun.

I spent the next several weeks as most Americans did—calling friends in New York and D.C., sending donations, listening to the President's speech, mourning the dead. And for me, as for most of us, the effect of September 11 felt profoundly personal. It wasn't just the magnitude of the destruction that affected me, or the memories of the five years I'd spent in New York— memories of streets and sights now reduced to rubble. Rather, it was the intimacy of imagining those ordinary acts that 9/11's victims must have performed in the hours before they were killed, the daily routines that constitute life in our modern world—the boarding of a plane, the jostling as we exit a commuter train, grabbing coffee and the morning paper at a newsstand, making small talk on the elevator. For most Americans, such routines represented a victory of order over chaos, the concrete expression of our belief that so long as we exercised, wore seat belts, had a job with benefits, and avoided certain neighborhoods, our safety was ensured, our families protected.

Now chaos had come to our doorstep. As a consequence, we would have to act differently, understand the world differently. We would have to answer the call of a nation. Within a week of the attacks, I watched the Senate vote 98–0 and the House vote 420–1 to give the President the authority to "use all necessary and appropriate force against those nations, organizations or persons" behind the attacks. Interest in the armed services and applications to join the CIA soared, as young people across America resolved to serve their country. Nor were we alone. In Paris, *Le Monde* ran the banner headline *"Nous sommes tous Américains"* ("We are all Americans"). In Cairo, local mosques offered prayers of sympathy. For the first time since its founding in 1949, NATO invoked Article 5 of its charter, agreeing that the armed attack on one of its members "shall be considered an attack against them all." With justice at our backs and the world by our side, we drove the Taliban government out of Kabul in just over a month; Al Qaeda operatives fled or were captured or killed.

It was a good start by the Administration, I thought—steady, measured, and accomplished with minimal casualties (only later would we discover the degree to which our failure to put sufficient military pressure on Al Qaeda forces at Tora Bora may have led to bin Laden's escape). And so, along with the rest of the world, I waited with anticipation for what I assumed would follow: the enunciation of a U.S. foreign policy for the twenty-first century, one that would not only adapt our military planning, intelligence operations, and homeland defenses to the threat of terrorist networks but build a new international consensus around the challenges of transnational threats.

This new blueprint never arrived. Instead what we got was an assortment of outdated policies from eras gone by, dusted off, slapped together, and with new labels affixed. Reagan's "Evil Empire" was now "the Axis of Evil." Theodore Roosevelt's version of the Monroe Doctrine—the notion that we could preemptively remove governments not to our liking—was now the Bush Doctrine, only extended beyond the Western Hemisphere to span the globe. Manifest destiny was back in fashion; all that was needed, according to Bush, was American firepower, American resolve, and a "coalition of the willing."

Perhaps worst of all, the Bush Administration resuscitated a brand of politics not seen since the end of the Cold War. As the ouster of Saddam Hussein became the test case for Bush's doctrine of preventive war, those who questioned the Administration's rationale for invasion were accused of being "soft on terrorism" or "un-American." Instead of an honest accounting of this military campaign's pros and cons, the Administration initiated a public relations offensive: shading intelligence reports to support its case, grossly understating both the costs and the manpower requirements of military action, raising the specter of mushroom clouds.

The PR strategy worked; by the fall of 2002, a majority of Americans were convinced that Saddam Hussein possessed weapons of mass destruction, and at least 66 percent believed (falsely) that the Iraqi leader had been personally involved in the 9/11 attacks. Support for an invasion of Iraq—and Bush's approval rating—hovered around 60 percent. With an eye on the midterm elections, Republicans stepped up the attacks and pushed for a vote authorizing the use of force against Saddam Hussein. And on October 11, 2002, twenty-eight of the Senate's fifty Democrats joined all but one Republican in handing to Bush the power he wanted.

I was disappointed in that vote, although sympathetic to the pressures Democrats were under. I had felt some of those same pressures myself. By the fall of 2002, I had already decided to run for the U.S. Senate and knew that possible war with Iraq would loom large in any campaign. When a group of Chicago activists asked if I would speak at a large antiwar rally planned for October, a number of my friends warned me against taking so public a position on such a volatile issue. Not only was the idea of an invasion increasingly popular, but on the merits I didn't consider the case against war to be cut-and-dried. Like most analysts, I assumed that Saddam had chemical and biological weapons and coveted nuclear arms. I believed that he had repeatedly flouted UN resolutions and weapons inspectors and that such behavior had to have consequences. That Saddam butchered his own people was undisputed; I had no doubt that the world, and the Iraqi people, would be better off without him.

What I sensed, though, was that the threat Saddam posed was not imminent, the Administration's rationales for war were flimsy and ideologically driven, and the war in Afghanistan was far from complete. And I was certain that by choosing precipitous, unilateral military action over the hard slog of diplomacy, coercive inspections, and smart sanctions, America was missing an opportunity to build a broad base of support for its policies.

And so I made the speech. To the two thousand people gathered in Chicago's Federal Plaza, I explained that unlike some of the people in the crowd, I didn't oppose all wars—that my grandfather had signed up for the war the day after Pearl Harbor was bombed and had fought in Patton's army. I also said that "after witnessing the carnage and destruction, the dust and the tears, I supported this Administration's pledge to hunt down and root out those who would slaughter innocents in the name of intolerance" and would "willingly take up arms myself to prevent such tragedy from happening again."

What I could not support was "a dumb war, a rash war, a war based not on reason but on passion, not on principle but on politics." And I said:

I know that even a successful war against Iraq will require a U.S. occupation of undetermined length, at undetermined cost, with undetermined consequences. I know that an invasion of Iraq without a clear rationale and without strong international support will only fan the flames of the Middle East, and encourage the worst, rather than the best, impulses of the Arab world, and strengthen the recruitment arm of Al Qaeda.

The speech was well received; activists began circulating the text on the Internet, and I established a reputation for speaking my mind on hard issues—a reputation that would carry me through a tough Democratic primary. But I had no way of knowing at the time whether my assessment of the situation in Iraq was correct. When the invasion was finally launched and U.S. forces marched unimpeded through Baghdad, when I saw Saddam's statue topple and watched the President stand atop the U.S.S. *Abraham Lincoln,* a banner behind him proclaiming "Mission Accomplished," I began to suspect that I might have been wrong—and was relieved to see the low number of American casualties involved.

And now, three years later—as the number of American deaths passed two thousand and the number of wounded passed sixteen thousand; after $250 billion in direct spending and hundreds of billions more in future years to pay off the resulting debt and care for disabled veterans; after two Iraqi national elections, one Iraqi constitutional referendum, and tens of thousands of Iraqi deaths; after watching anti-American sentiment rise to record levels around the world and Afghanistan begin to slip back into chaos—I was flying into Baghdad as a member of the Senate, partially responsible for trying to figure out just what to do with this mess.

The landing at Baghdad International Airport turned out not

to be so bad—although I was thankful that we couldn't see out
the windows as the C-130 bucked and banked and dipped its
way down. Our escort officer from the State Department was
there to greet us, along with an assortment of military personnel
with rifles slung over their shoulders. After getting our security
briefing, recording our blood types, and being fitted for helmets
and Kevlar vests, we boarded two Black Hawk helicopters and
headed for the Green Zone, flying low, passing over miles of
mostly muddy, barren fields crisscrossed by narrow roads and
punctuated by small groves of date trees and squat concrete shelters, many of them seemingly empty, some bulldozed down to
their foundations. Eventually Baghdad came into view, a sand-
colored metropolis set in a circular pattern, the Tigris River cutting a broad, murky swath down its center. Even from the air the
city looked worn and battered, the traffic on the streets intermit-
tent—although almost every rooftop was cluttered with satellite
dishes, which along with cell phone service had been touted by
U.S. officials as one of the successes of the reconstruction.

I would spend only a day and a half in Iraq, most of it in the
Green Zone, a ten-mile-wide area of central Baghdad that had
once been the heart of Saddam Hussein's government but was
now a U.S.-controlled compound, surrounded along its perimeter
by blast walls and barbed wire. Reconstruction teams briefed us
about the difficulty of maintaining electrical power and oil production in the face of insurgent sabotage; intelligence officers
described the growing threat of sectarian militias and their infiltration of Iraqi security forces. Later, we met with members of
the Iraqi Election Commission, who spoke with enthusiasm about
the high turnout during the recent election, and for an hour we
listened to U.S. Ambassador Khalilzad, a shrewd, elegant man
with world-weary eyes, explain the delicate shuttle diplomacy in
which he was now engaged, to bring Shi'ite, Sunni, and Kurdish
factions into some sort of workable unity government.

In the afternoon we had an opportunity to have lunch with

some of the troops in the huge mess hall just off the swimming pool of what had once been Saddam's presidential palace. They were a mix of regular forces, reservists, and National Guard units, from big cities and small towns, blacks and whites and Latinos, many of them on their second or third tour of duty. They spoke with pride as they told us what their units had accomplished— building schools, protecting electrical facilities, leading newly trained Iraqi soldiers on patrol, maintaining supply lines to those in far-flung regions of the country. Again and again, I was asked the same question: Why did the U.S. press only report on bombings and killings? There was progress being made, they insisted— I needed to let the folks back home know that their work was not in vain.

It was easy, talking to these men and women, to understand their frustration, for all the Americans I met in Iraq, whether military or civilian, impressed me with their dedication, their skill, and their frank acknowledgment not only of the mistakes that had been made but also of the difficulties of the task that still lay ahead. Indeed, the entire enterprise in Iraq bespoke American ingenuity, wealth, and technical know-how; standing inside the Green Zone or any of the large operating bases in Iraq and Kuwait, one could only marvel at the ability of our government to essentially erect entire cities within hostile territory, self-contained communities with their own power and sewage systems, computer lines and wireless networks, basketball courts and ice cream stands. More than that, one was reminded of that unique quality of American optimism that everywhere was on display—the absence of cynicism despite the danger, sacrifice, and seemingly interminable setbacks, the insistence that at the end of the day our actions would result in a better life for a nation of people we barely knew.

And yet, three conversations during the course of my visit would remind me of just how quixotic our efforts in Iraq still seemed—how, with all the American blood, treasure, and the best of intentions, the house we were building might be resting on quicksand. The first conversation took place in the early evening, when our delegation held a press conference with a group of foreign correspondents stationed in Baghdad. After the Q&A session, I asked the reporters if they'd stay for an informal, off-the-record conversation. I was interested, I said, in getting some sense of life outside the Green Zone. They were happy to oblige, but insisted they could only stay for forty-five minutes—it was getting late, and like most residents of Baghdad, they generally avoided traveling once the sun went down.

As a group, they were young, mostly in their twenties and early thirties, all of them dressed casually enough that they could pass for college students. Their faces, though, showed the stresses they were under—sixty journalists had already been killed in Iraq by that time. Indeed, at the start of our conversation they apologized for being somewhat distracted; they had just received word that one of their colleagues, a reporter with the *Christian Science Monitor* named Jill Carroll, had been abducted, her driver found killed on the side of a road. Now they were all working their contacts, trying to track down her whereabouts. Such violence wasn't unusual in Baghdad these days, they said, although Iraqis overwhelmingly bore the brunt of it. Fighting between Shi'ites and Sunnis had become widespread, less strategic, less comprehensible, more frightening. None of them thought that the elections would bring about significant improvement in the security situation. I asked them if they thought a U.S. troop withdrawal might ease tensions, expecting them to answer in the affirmative. Instead, they shook their heads.

"My best guess is the country would collapse into civil war within weeks," one of the reporters told me. "One hundred, maybe two hundred thousand dead. We're the only thing holding this place together."

That night, our delegation accompanied Ambassador Khalilzad for dinner at the home of Iraqi interim President Jalal Talabani. Security was tight as our convoy wound its way past a maze of barricades out of the Green Zone; outside, our route was lined with U.S. troops at one-block intervals, and we were instructed to keep our vests and helmets on for the duration of the drive.

After ten minutes we arrived at a large villa, where we were greeted by the president and several members of the Iraqi interim government. They were all heavyset men, most in their fifties or sixties, with broad smiles but eyes that betrayed no emotion. I recognized only one of the ministers—Mr. Ahmed Chalabi, the Western-educated Shi'ite who, as a leader of the exile group the Iraqi National Congress, had reportedly fed U.S. intelligence agencies and Bush policy makers some of the prewar information on which the decision to invade was made—information for which Chalabi's group had received millions of dollars, and that had turned out to be bogus. Since then Chalabi had fallen out with his U.S. patrons; there were reports that he had steered U.S. classified information to the Iranians, and that Jordan still had a warrant out for his arrest after he'd been convicted in absentia on thirty-one charges of embezzlement, theft, misuse of depositor funds, and currency speculation. But he appeared to have landed on his feet; immaculately dressed, accompanied by his grown daughter, he was now the interim government's acting oil minister.

I didn't speak much to Chalabi during dinner. Instead I was seated next to the former interim finance minister. He seemed impressive, speaking knowledgeably about Iraq's economy, its need to improve transparency and strengthen its legal framework to attract foreign investment. At the end of the evening, I mentioned my favorable impression to one of the embassy staff.

"He's smart, no doubt about it," the staffer said. "Of course, he's also one of the leaders of the SCIRI Party. They control the Ministry of the Interior, which controls the police. And the police, well . . . there have been problems with militia infiltration.

Accusations that they're grabbing Sunni leaders, bodies found the next morning, that kind of thing . . ." The staffer's voice trailed off, and he shrugged. "We work with what we have."

I had difficulty sleeping that night; instead, I watched the Redskins game, piped in live via satellite to the pool house once reserved for Saddam and his guests. Several times I muted the TV and heard mortar fire pierce the silence. The following morning, we took a Black Hawk to the Marine base in Fallujah, out in the arid, western portion of Iraq called Anbar Province. Some of the fiercest fighting against the insurgency had taken place in Sunni-dominated Anbar, and the atmosphere in the camp was considerably grimmer than in the Green Zone; just the previous day, five Marines on patrol had been killed by roadside bombs or small-arms fire. The troops here looked rawer as well, most of them in their early twenties, many still with pimples and the unformed bodies of teenagers.

The general in charge of the camp had arranged a briefing, and we listened as the camp's senior officers explained the dilemma facing U.S. forces: With improved capabilities, they were arresting more and more insurgent leaders each day, but like street gangs back in Chicago, for every insurgent they arrested, there seemed to be two ready to take his place. Economics, and not just politics, seemed to be feeding the insurgency—the central government had been neglecting Anbar, and male unemployment hovered around 70 percent.

"For two or three dollars, you can pay some kid to plant a bomb," one of the officers said. "That's a lot of money out here."

By the end of the briefing, a light fog had rolled in, delaying our flight to Kirkuk. While waiting, my foreign policy staffer, Mark Lippert, wandered off to chat with one of the unit's senior officers, while I struck up a conversation with one of the majors responsible for counterinsurgency strategy in the region. He was a soft-spoken man, short and with glasses; it was easy to imagine him as a high school math teacher. In fact, it turned out that be-

fore joining the Marines he had spent several years in the Philippines as a member of the Peace Corps. Many of the lessons he
had learned there needed to be applied to the military's work in
Iraq, he told me. He didn't have anywhere near the number of
Arabic-speakers needed to build trust with the local population.
We needed to improve cultural sensitivity within U.S. forces,
develop long-term relationships with local leaders, and couple
security forces to reconstruction teams, so that Iraqis could see
concrete benefits from U.S. efforts. All this would take time,
he said, but he could already see changes for the better as the
military adopted these practices throughout the country.

Our escort officer signaled that the chopper was ready to take
off. I wished the major luck and headed for the van. Mark came
up beside me, and I asked him what he'd learned from his conversation with the senior officer.

"I asked him what he thought we needed to do to best deal
with the situation."

"What did he say?"

"Leave."

THE STORY OF America's involvement in Iraq will be analyzed
and debated for many years to come—indeed, it's a story that's
still being written. At the moment, the situation there has deteriorated to the point where it appears that a low-grade civil war
has begun, and while I believe that all Americans—regardless of
their views on the original decision to invade—have an interest
in seeing a decent outcome in Iraq, I cannot honestly say that I
am optimistic about Iraq's short-term prospects.

I do know that at this stage it will be politics—the calculations of those hard, unsentimental men with whom I had dinner—and not the application of American force that determines
what happens in Iraq. I believe as well that our strategic goals at
this point should be well defined: achieving some semblance of

stability in Iraq, ensuring that those in power in Iraq are not hostile to the United States, and preventing Iraq from becoming a
base for terrorist activity. In pursuit of these goals, I believe it is in
the interest of both Americans and Iraqis to begin a phased withdrawal of U.S. troops by the end of 2006, although how quickly
a complete withdrawal can be accomplished is a matter of imperfect judgment, based on a series of best guesses—about the ability
of the Iraqi government to deliver even basic security and services
to its people, the degree to which our presence drives the insurgency, and the odds that in the absence of U.S. troops Iraq would
descend into all-out civil war. When battle-hardened Marine officers suggest we pull out and skeptical foreign correspondents
suggest that we stay, there are no easy answers to be had.

Still, it's not too early to draw some conclusions from our
actions in Iraq. For our difficulties there don't just arise as a result of bad execution. They reflect a failure of conception. The
fact is, close to five years after 9/11 and fifteen years after the
breakup of the Soviet Union, the United States still lacks a coherent national security policy. Instead of guiding principles, we
have what appear to be a series of ad hoc decisions, with dubious
results. Why invade Iraq and not North Korea or Burma? Why
intervene in Bosnia and not Darfur? Are our goals in Iran regime
change, the dismantling of all Iranian nuclear capability, the prevention of nuclear proliferation, or all three? Are we committed
to use force wherever there's a despotic regime that's terrorizing
its people—and if so, how long do we stay to ensure democracy
takes root? How do we treat countries like China that are liberalizing economically but not politically? Do we work through
the United Nations on all issues or only when the UN is willing
to ratify decisions we've already made?

Perhaps someone inside the White House has clear answers to
these questions. But our allies—and for that matter our enemies—
certainly don't know what those answers are. More important,
neither do the American people. Without a well-articulated strat

egy that the public supports and the world understands, America will lack the legitimacy—and ultimately the power—it needs to make the world safer than it is today. We need a revised foreign policy framework that matches the boldness and scope of Truman's post–World War II policies—one that addresses both the challenges and the opportunities of a new millennium, one that guides our use of force and expresses our deepest ideals and commitments.

I don't presume to have this grand strategy in my hip pocket. But I know what I believe, and I'd suggest a few things that the American people should be able to agree on, starting points for a new consensus.

To begin with, we should understand that any return to isolationism—or a foreign policy approach that denies the occasional need to deploy U.S. troops—will not work. The impulse to withdraw from the world remains a strong undercurrent in both parties, particularly when U.S. casualties are at stake. After the bodies of U.S. soldiers were dragged through the streets of Mogadishu in 1993, for example, Republicans accused President Clinton of squandering U.S. forces on ill-conceived missions; it was partly because of the experience in Somalia that candidate George W. Bush vowed in the 2000 election never again to expend American military resources on "nation building." Understandably, the Bush Administration's actions in Iraq have produced a much bigger backlash. According to a Pew Research Center poll, almost five years after the 9/11 attacks, 46 percent of Americans have concluded that the United States should "mind its own business internationally and let other countries get along the best they can on their own."

The reaction has been particularly severe among liberals, who see in Iraq a repeat of the mistakes America made in Vietnam. Frustration with Iraq and the questionable tactics the Administration used to make its case for the war has even led many on the left to downplay the threat posed by terrorists and nuclear proliferators; according to a January 2005 poll, self-identified conservatives were 29 points more likely than liberals to identify destroying Al Qaeda as one of their top foreign policy goals, and 26 points more likely to mention denying nuclear weapons to hostile groups or nations. The top three foreign policy objectives among liberals, on the other hand, were withdrawing troops from Iraq, stopping the spread of AIDS, and working more closely with our allies.

The objectives favored by liberals have merit. But they hardly constitute a coherent national security policy. It's useful to remind ourselves, then, that Osama bin Laden is not Ho Chi Minh, and that the threats facing the United States today are real, multiple, and potentially devastating. Our recent policies have made matters worse, but if we pulled out of Iraq tomorrow, the United States would still be a target, given its dominant position in the existing international order. Of course, conservatives are just as misguided if they think we can simply eliminate "the evildoers" and then let the world fend for itself. Globalization makes our economy, our health, and our security all captive to events on the other side of the world. And no other nation on earth has a greater capacity to shape that global system, or to build consensus around a new set of international rules that expand the zones of freedom, personal safety, and economic well-being. Like it or not, if we want to make America more secure, we are going to have to help make the world more secure.

The second thing we need to recognize is that the security environment we face today is fundamentally different from the one that existed fifty, twenty-five, or even ten years ago. When Truman, Acheson, Kennan, and Marshall sat down to design the architecture of the post–World War II order, their frame of reference was the competition between the great powers that had dominated the nineteenth and early twentieth centuries. In that world, America's greatest threats came from expansionist states like Nazi Germany or Soviet Russia, which could deploy large armies and powerful arsenals to invade key territories, restrict our access to critical resources, and dictate the terms of world trade.

That world no longer exists. The integration of Germany and Japan into a world system of liberal democracies and free-market economies effectively eliminated the threat of great-power conflicts inside the free world. The advent of nuclear weapons and "mutual assured destruction" rendered the risk of war between the United States and the Soviet Union fairly remote even before the Berlin Wall fell. Today, the world's most powerful nations (including, to an ever-increasing extent, China)—and, just as important, the vast majority of the people who live within these nations—are largely committed to a common set of international rules governing trade, economic policy, and the legal and diplomatic resolution of disputes, even if broader notions of liberty and democracy aren't widely observed within their own borders.

The growing threat, then, comes primarily from those parts of the world on the margins of the global economy where the international "rules of the road" have not taken hold—the realm of weak or failing states, arbitrary rule, corruption, and chronic violence; lands in which an overwhelming majority of the population is poor, uneducated, and cut off from the global information grid; places where the rulers fear globalization will loosen their hold on power, undermine traditional cultures, or displace indigenous institutions.

In the past, there was the perception that America could perhaps safely ignore nations and individuals in these disconnected regions. They might be hostile to our worldview, nationalize a U.S. business, cause a spike in commodity prices, fall into the Soviet or Communist Chinese orbit, or even attack U.S. embassies or military personnel overseas—but they could not strike us where we live. September 11 showed that's no longer the case. The very interconnectivity that increasingly binds the world together has empowered those who would tear that world down.

Terrorist networks can spread their doctrines in the blink of an eye; they can probe the world economic system's weakest links, knowing that an attack in London or Tokyo will reverberate in New York or Hong Kong; weapons and technology that were once the exclusive province of nation-states can now be purchased on the black market, or their designs downloaded off the Internet; the free travel of people and goods across borders, the lifeblood of the global economy, can be exploited for murderous ends.

If nation-states no longer have a monopoly on mass violence; if in fact nation-states are increasingly less likely to launch a direct attack on us, since they have a fixed address to which we can deliver a response; if instead the fastest-growing threats are transnational—terrorist networks intent on repelling or disrupting the forces of globalization, potential pandemic disease like avian flu, or catastrophic changes in the earth's climate—then how should our national security strategy adapt?

For starters, our defense spending and the force structure of our military should reflect the new reality. Since the outset of the Cold War, our ability to deter nation-to-nation aggression has to a large extent underwritten security for every country that commits itself to international rules and norms. With the only blue-water navy that patrols the entire globe, it is our ships that keep the sea lanes clear. And it is our nuclear umbrella that prevented Europe and Japan from entering the arms race during the Cold War, and that—until recently, at least—has led most countries to conclude that nukes aren't worth the trouble. So long as Russia and China retain their own large military forces and haven't fully rid themselves of the instinct to throw their weight around—and so long as a handful of rogue states are willing to attack other sovereign nations, as Saddam attacked Kuwait in 1991—there will be times when we must again play the role of the world's reluctant sheriff. This will not change—nor should it.

On the other hand, it's time we acknowledge that a defense budget and force structure built principally around the prospect of World War III makes little strategic sense. The U.S. military and defense budget in 2005 topped $522 billion—more than that of the next thirty countries combined. The United States' GDP is greater than that of the two largest countries and fastest-growing economies—China and India—combined. We need to maintain a strategic force posture that allows us to manage threats posed by rogue nations like North Korea and Iran and to meet the challenges presented by potential rivals like China. Indeed, given the depletion of our forces after the wars in Iraq and Afghanistan, we will probably need a somewhat higher budget in the immediate future just to restore readiness and replace equipment.

But our most complex military challenge will not be staying ahead of China (just as our biggest challenge with China may well be economic rather than military). More likely, that challenge will involve putting boots on the ground in the ungoverned or hostile regions where terrorists thrive. That requires a smarter balance between what we spend on fancy hardware and what we spend on our men and women in uniform. That should mean growing the size of our armed forces to maintain reasonable rotation schedules, keeping our troops properly equipped, and training them in the language, reconstruction, intelligence-gathering, and peacekeeping skills they'll need to succeed in increasingly complex and difficult missions.

A change in the makeup of our military won't be enough, though. In coping with the asymmetrical threats that we'll face in the future—from terrorist networks and the handful of states that support them—the structure of our armed forces will ultimately matter less than how we decide to use those forces. The United States won the Cold War not simply because it outgunned the Soviet Union but because American values held sway in the court of international public opinion, which included those who lived within communist regimes. Even more than was true during the Cold War, the struggle against Islamic-based terrorism will be not simply a military campaign but a battle for public opinion in the Islamic world, among our allies, and in the United States. Osama bin Laden understands that he cannot defeat or even incapacitate the United States in a conventional war. What he and his allies can do is inflict enough pain to provoke a reaction of the sort we've seen in Iraq—a botched and ill-advised U.S. military incursion into a Muslim country, which in turn spurs on insurgencies based on religious sentiment and nationalist pride, which in turn necessitates a lengthy and difficult U.S. occupation, which in turn leads to an escalating death toll on the part of U.S. troops and the local civilian population. All of this fans anti-American sentiment among Muslims, increases the pool of potential terrorist recruits, and prompts the American public to question not only the war but also those policies that project us into the Islamic world in the first place.

That's the plan for winning a war from a cave, and so far, at least, we are playing to script. To change that script, we'll need to make sure that any exercise of American military power helps rather than hinders our broader goals: to incapacitate the destructive potential of terrorist networks *and* win this global battle of ideas.

What does this mean in practical terms? We should start with the premise that the United States, like all sovereign nations, has the unilateral right to defend itself against attack. As such, our campaign to take out Al Qaeda base camps and the Taliban regime that harbored them was entirely justified—and was viewed as legitimate even in most Islamic countries. It may be preferable to have the support of our allies in such military campaigns, but our immediate safety can't be held hostage to the desire for international consensus; if we have to go it alone, then the American people stand ready to pay any price and bear any burden to protect our country.

I would also argue that we have the right to take unilateral military action to eliminate an *imminent* threat to our security— so long as an imminent threat is understood to be a nation, group, or individual that is actively preparing to strike U.S. targets (or allies with which the United States has mutual defense agreements), and has or will have the means to do so in the immediate future. Al Qaeda qualifies under this standard, and we can and should carry out preemptive strikes against them wherever we can. Iraq under Saddam Hussein did not meet this standard, which is why our invasion was such a strategic blunder. If we are going to act unilaterally, then we had better have the goods on our targets.

Once we get beyond matters of self-defense, though, I'm convinced that it will almost always be in our strategic interest to act multilaterally rather than unilaterally when we use force around the world. By this, I do not mean that the UN Security Council—a body that in its structure and rules too often appears frozen in a Cold War–era time warp—should have a veto over our actions. Nor do I mean that we round up the United Kingdom and Togo and then do what we please. Acting multilaterally means doing what George H. W. Bush and his team did in the first Gulf War—engaging in the hard diplomatic work of obtaining most of the world's support for our actions, and making sure our actions serve to further recognize international norms.

Why conduct ourselves in this way? Because nobody benefits more than we do from the observance of international "rules of the road." We can't win converts to those rules if we act as if they apply to everyone but us. When the world's sole superpower willingly restrains its power and abides by internationally agreed-upon standards of conduct, it sends a message that these are rules worth following, and robs terrorists and dictators of the argument that these rules are simply tools of American imperialism.

Obtaining global buy-in also allows the United States to carry a lighter load when military action is required and enhances the chances for success. Given the comparatively modest defense budgets of most of our allies, sharing the military burden may in some cases prove a bit of an illusion, but in the Balkans and

Afghanistan, our NATO partners have indeed shouldered their share of the risks and costs. Additionally, for the types of conflicts in which we're most likely to find ourselves engaged, the initial military operation will often be less complex and costly than the work that follows—training local police forces, restoring electricity and water services, building a working judicial system, fostering an independent media, setting up a public health infrastructure, and planning elections. Allies can help pay the freight and provide expertise for these critical efforts, as they have in the Balkans and Afghanistan, but they are far more likely to do so if our actions have gained international support on the front end. In military parlance, legitimacy is a "force multiplier."

Just as important, the painstaking process of building coalitions forces us to listen to other points of view and therefore look before we leap. When we're not defending ourselves against a direct and imminent threat, we will often have the benefit of time; our military power becomes just one tool among many (albeit an extraordinarily important one) to influence events and advance our interests in the world—interests in maintaining access to key energy sources, keeping financial markets stable, seeing international boundaries respected, and preventing genocide. In pursuit of those interests, we should be engaging in some hardheaded analysis of the costs and benefits of the use of force compared to the other tools of influence at our disposal.

Is cheap oil worth the costs—in blood and treasure—of war? Will our military intervention in a particular ethnic dispute lead to a permanent political settlement or an indefinite commitment of U.S. forces? Can our dispute with a country be settled diplomatically or through a coordinated series of sanctions? If we hope to win the broader battle of ideas, then world opinion must enter into this calculus. And while it may be frustrating at times to hear anti-American posturing from European allies that enjoy the blanket of our protection, or to hear speeches in the UN General Assembly designed to obfuscate, distract, or excuse inaction, it's just possible that beneath all the rhetoric are perspectives that can illuminate the situation and help us make better strategic decisions.

Finally, by engaging our allies, we give them joint ownership over the difficult, methodical, vital, and necessarily collaborative work of limiting the terrorists' capacity to inflict harm. That work includes shutting down terrorist financial networks and sharing intelligence to hunt down terrorist suspects and infiltrate their cells; our continued failure to effectively coordinate intelligence gathering even among various U.S. agencies, as well as our continued lack of effective human intelligence capacity, is inexcusable. Most important, we need to join forces to keep weapons of mass destruction out of terrorist hands.

One of the best examples of such collaboration was pioneered in the nineties by Republican Senator Dick Lugar of Indiana and former Democratic Senator Sam Nunn of Georgia, two men who understood the need to nurture coalitions before crises strike, and who applied this knowledge to the critical problem of nuclear proliferation. The premise of what came to be known as the Nunn-Lugar program was simple: After the fall of the Soviet Union, the biggest threat to the United States—aside from an accidental launch—wasn't a first strike ordered by Gorbachev or Yeltsin, but the migration of nuclear material or know-how into the hands of terrorists and rogue states, a possible result of Russia's economic tailspin, corruption in the military, the impoverishment of Russian scientists, and security and control systems that had fallen into disrepair. Under Nunn-Lugar, America basically provided the resources to fix up those systems, and although the program caused some consternation to those accustomed to Cold War thinking, it has proven to be one of the most important investments we could have made to protect ourselves from catastrophe.

In August 2005, I traveled with Senator Lugar to see some of this handiwork. It was my first trip to Russia and Ukraine, and

I couldn't have had a better guide than Dick, a remarkably fit seventy-three-year-old with a gentle, imperturbable manner and an inscrutable smile that served him well during the often interminable meetings we held with foreign officials. Together we visited the nuclear facilities of Saratov, where Russian generals pointed with pride to the new fencing and security systems that had been recently completed; afterward, they served us a lunch of borscht, vodka, potato stew, and a deeply troubling fish Jell-O mold. In Perm, at a site where SS-24 and SS-25 tactical missiles were being dismantled, we walked through the center of eight-foot-high empty missile casings and gazed in silence at the massive, sleek, still-active missiles that were now warehoused safely but had once been aimed at the cities of Europe.

And in a quiet, residential neighborhood of Kiev, we received a tour of the Ukraine's version of the Centers for Disease Control, a modest three-story facility that looked like a high school science lab. At one point during our tour, after seeing windows open for lack of air-conditioning and metal strips crudely bolted to door jambs to keep out mice, we were guided to a small freezer secured by nothing more than a seal of string. A middle-aged woman in a lab coat and surgical mask pulled a few test tubes from the freezer, waving them around a foot from my face and saying something in Ukrainian.

"That is anthrax," the translator explained, pointing to the vial in the woman's right hand. "That one," he said, pointing to the one in the left hand, "is the plague."

I looked behind me and noticed Lugar standing toward the back of the room.

"You don't want a closer look, Dick?" I asked, taking a few steps back myself.

"Been there, done that," he said with a smile.

There were moments during our travels when we were reminded of the old Cold War days. At the airport in Perm, for example, a border officer in his early twenties detained us for

three hours because we wouldn't let him search our plane, leading our staffs to fire off telephone calls to the U.S. embassy and
Russia's foreign affairs ministry in Moscow. And yet most of what
we heard and saw—the Calvin Klein store and Maserati show-
room in Red Square Mall; the motorcade of SUVs that pulled up
in front of a restaurant, driven by burly men with ill-fitting suits
who once might have rushed to open the door for Kremlin officials but were now on the security detail of one of Russia's bil-
lionaire oligarchs; the throngs of sullen teenagers in T-shirts and
low-riding jeans, sharing cigarettes and the music on their iPods
as they wandered Kiev's graceful boulevards—underscored the
seemingly irreversible process of economic, if not political, integration between East and West.

That was part of the reason, I sensed, why Lugar and I were
greeted so warmly at these various military installations. Our
presence not only promised money for security systems and fencing and monitors and the like; it also indicated to the men and
women who worked in these facilities that they still in fact mattered. They had made careers, had been honored, for perfecting
the tools of war. Now they found themselves presiding over remnants of the past, their institutions barely relevant to nations
whose people had shifted their main attention to turning a quick
buck.

Certainly that's how it felt in Donetsk, an industrial town in
the southeastern portion of Ukraine where we stopped to visit an
installation for the destruction of conventional weapons. The facility was nestled in the country, accessed by a series of narrow
roads occasionally crowded with goats. The director of the facility, a rotund, cheerful man who reminded me of a Chicago ward
superintendent, led us through a series of dark warehouse-like
structures in various states of disrepair, where rows of workers
nimbly dismantled an assortment of land mines and tank ord-
nance, and empty shell casings were piled loosely into mounds
that rose to my shoulders. They needed U.S. help, the director

explained, because Ukraine lacked the money to deal with all the weapons left over from the Cold War and Afghanistan—at the pace they were going, securing and disabling these weapons might take sixty years. In the meantime weapons would remain scattered across the country, often in shacks without padlocks, exposed to the elements, not just ammunition but high-grade explosives and shoulder-to-air missiles—tools of destruction that might find their way into the hands of warlords in Somalia, Tamil fighters in Sri Lanka, insurgents in Iraq.

As he spoke, our group entered another building, where women wearing surgical masks stood at a table removing hexogen— a military-grade explosive—from various munitions and placing it into bags. In another room, I happened upon a pair of men in their undershirts, smoking next to a wheezing old boiler, flicking their ashes into an open gutter filled with orange-tinted water. One of our team called me over and showed me a yellowing poster taped to the wall. It was a relic of the Afghan war, we were told: instructions on how to hide explosives in toys, to be left in villages and carried home by unsuspecting children.

A testament, I thought, to the madness of men.

A record of how empires destroy themselves.

THERE'S A FINAL dimension to U.S. foreign policy that must be discussed—the portion that has less to do with avoiding war than promoting peace. The year I was born, President Kennedy stated in his inaugural address: "To those peoples in the huts and villages of half the globe struggling to break the bonds of mass misery, we pledge our best efforts to help them help themselves, for whatever period is required—not because the Communists may be doing it, not because we seek their votes, but because it is right. If a free society cannot help the many who are poor, it cannot save the few who are rich." Forty-five years later, that mass misery still exists. If we are to fulfill Kennedy's promise—and serve our long-term security interests—then we will have to go beyond a more prudent use of military force. We will have to align our policies to help reduce the spheres of insecurity, poverty, and violence around the world, and give more people a stake in the global order that has served us so well.

Of course, there are those who would argue with my starting premise—that any global system built in America's image can alleviate misery in poorer countries. For these critics, America's notion of what the international system should be—free trade, open markets, the unfettered flow of information, the rule of law, democratic elections, and the like—is simply an expression of American imperialism, designed to exploit the cheap labor and natural resources of other countries and infect non-Western cultures with decadent beliefs. Rather than conform to America's rules, the argument goes, other countries should resist America's efforts to expand its hegemony; instead, they should follow their own path to development, taking their lead from left-leaning populists like Venezuela's Hugo Chávez, or turning to more traditional principles of social organization, like Islamic law.

I don't dismiss these critics out of hand. America and its Western partners did design the current international system, after all; it is our way of doing things—our accounting standards, our language, our dollar, our copyright laws, our technology, and our popular culture—to which the world has had to adapt over the past fifty years. If overall the international system has produced great prosperity in the world's most developed countries, it has also left many people behind—a fact that Western policy makers have often ignored and occasionally made worse.

Ultimately, though, I believe critics are wrong to think that the world's poor will benefit by rejecting the ideals of free markets and liberal democracy. When human rights activists from various countries come to my office and talk about being jailed or tortured for their beliefs, they are not acting as agents of American power. When my cousin in Kenya complains that it's impossible to find work unless he's paid a bribe to some official in the ruling party, he hasn't been brainwashed by Western ideas. Who doubts that, if given the choice, most of the people in North Korea would prefer living in South Korea, or that many in Cuba wouldn't mind giving Miami a try?

No person, in any culture, likes to be bullied. No person likes living in fear because his or her ideas are different. Nobody likes being poor or hungry, and nobody likes to live under an economic system in which the fruits of his or her labor go perpetually un-rewarded. The system of free markets and liberal democracy that now characterizes most of the developed world may be flawed; it may all too often reflect the interests of the powerful over the powerless. But that system is constantly subject to change and improvement—and it is precisely in this openness to change that market-based liberal democracies offer people around the world their best chance at a better life.

Our challenge, then, is to make sure that U.S. policies move the international system in the direction of greater equity, justice, and prosperity—that the rules we promote serve both our inter-ests and the interests of a struggling world. In doing so, we might keep a few basic principles in mind. First, we should be skep-tical of those who believe we can single-handedly liberate other people from tyranny. I agree with George W. Bush when in his second inaugural address he proclaimed a universal desire to be free. But there are few examples in history in which the freedom men and women crave is delivered through outside intervention. In almost every successful social movement of the last century, from Gandhi's campaign against British rule to the Solidarity movement in Poland to the antiapartheid movement in South Africa, democracy was the result of a local awakening.

We can inspire and invite other people to assert their free-doms; we can use international forums and agreements to set standards for others to follow; we can provide funding to fledg-ling democracies to help institutionalize fair election systems,

train independent journalists, and seed the habits of civic participation; we can speak out on behalf of local leaders whose rights
are violated; and we can apply economic and diplomatic pressure
to those who repeatedly violate the rights of their own people.

But when we seek to impose democracy with the barrel of a
gun, funnel money to parties whose economic policies are deemed
friendlier to Washington, or fall under the sway of exiles like
Chalabi whose ambitions aren't matched by any discernible local
support, we aren't just setting ourselves up for failure. We are
helping oppressive regimes paint democratic activists as tools of
foreign powers and retarding the possibility that genuine, home-
grown democracy will ever emerge.

A corollary to this is that freedom means more than elections.
In 1941, FDR said he looked forward to a world founded upon
four essential freedoms: freedom of speech, freedom of worship,
freedom from want, and freedom from fear. Our own experience
tells us that those last two freedoms—freedom from want and
freedom from fear—are prerequisites for all others. For half of
the world's population, roughly three billion people around the
world living on less than two dollars a day, an election is at best a
means, not an end; a starting point, not deliverance. These people
are looking less for an "electocracy" than for the basic elements
that for most of us define a decent life—food, shelter, electricity,
basic health care, education for their children, and the ability to
make their way through life without having to endure corruption, violence, or arbitrary power. If we want to win the hearts
and minds of people in Caracas, Jakarta, Nairobi, or Tehran,
dispersing ballot boxes will not be enough. We'll have to make
sure that the international rules we're promoting enhance, rather
than impede, people's sense of material and personal security.

That may require that we look in the mirror. For example, the
United States and other developed countries constantly demand
that developing countries eliminate trade barriers that protect
them from competition, even as we steadfastly protect our own

constituencies from exports that could help lift poor countries out of poverty. In our zeal to protect the patents of American drug companies, we've discouraged the ability of countries like Brazil to produce generic AIDS drugs that could save millions of lives. Under the leadership of Washington, the International Monetary Fund, designed after World War II to serve as a lender of last resort, has repeatedly forced countries in the midst of financial crisis like Indonesia to go through painful readjustments (sharply raising interest rates, cutting government social spending, eliminating subsidies to key industries) that cause enormous hardship to their people—harsh medicine that we Americans would have difficulty administering to ourselves.

Another branch of the international financial system, the World Bank, has a reputation for funding large, expensive projects that benefit high-priced consultants and well-connected local elites but do little for ordinary citizens—although it's these ordinary citizens who are left holding the bag when the loans come due. Indeed, countries that have successfully developed under the current international system have at times ignored Washington's rigid economic prescriptions by protecting nascent industries and engaging in aggressive industrial policies. The IMF and World Bank need to recognize that there is no single, cookie-cutter formula for each and every country's development.

There is nothing wrong, of course, with a policy of "tough love" when it comes to providing development assistance to poor countries. Too many poor countries are hampered by archaic, even feudal, property and banking laws; in the past, too many foreign aid programs simply engorged local elites, the money siphoned off into Swiss bank accounts. Indeed, for far too long international aid policies have ignored the critical role that the rule of law and principles of transparency play in any nation's development. In an era in which international financial transactions hinge on reliable, enforceable contracts, one might expect that the boom in global business would have given rise to vast legal reforms. But in fact countries like India, Nigeria, and China have developed two legal systems—one for foreigners and elites, and one for ordinary people trying to get ahead.

As for countries like Somalia, Sierra Leone, or the Congo, well, they have barely any law whatsoever. There are times when considering the plight of Africa—the millions racked by AIDS, the constant droughts and famines, the dictatorships, the pervasive corruption, the brutality of twelve-year-old guerrillas who know nothing but war wielding machetes or AK-47s—I find myself plunged into cynicism and despair. Until I'm reminded that a mosquito net that prevents malaria cost three dollars; that a voluntary HIV testing program in Uganda has made substantial inroads in the rate of new infections at a cost of three or four dollars per test; that only modest attention—an international show of force or the creation of civilian protection zones—might have stopped the slaughter in Rwanda; and that onetime hard cases like Mozambique have made significant steps toward reform.

FDR was certainly right when he said, "As a nation we may take pride in the fact that we are softhearted; but we cannot afford to be soft-headed." We should not expect to help Africa if Africa ultimately proves unwilling to help itself. But there are positive trends in Africa often hidden in the news of despair. Democracy is spreading. In many places economies are growing. We need to build on these glimmers of hope and help those committed leaders and citizens throughout Africa build the better future they, like we, so desperately desire.

Moreover, we fool ourselves in thinking that, in the words of one commentator, "we must learn to watch others die with equanimity," and not expect consequences. Disorder breeds disorder; callousness toward others tends to spread among ourselves. And if moral claims are insufficient for us to act as a continent implodes, there are certainly instrumental reasons why the United States and its allies should care about failed states that don't control their territories, can't combat epidemics, and are numbed by civil war and atrocity. It was in such a state of lawlessness that the Taliban took hold of Afghanistan. It was in Sudan, site of today's slow-rolling genocide, that bin Laden set up camp for several years. It's in the misery of some unnamed slum that the next killer virus will emerge.

Of course, whether in Africa or elsewhere, we can't expect to tackle such dire problems alone. For that reason, we should be spending more time and money trying to strengthen the capacity of international institutions so that they can do some of this work for us. Instead, we've been doing the opposite. For years, conservatives in the United States have been making political hay over problems at the UN: the hypocrisy of resolutions singling out Israel for condemnation, the Kafkaesque election of nations like Zimbabwe and Libya to the UN Commission on Human Rights, and most recently the kickbacks that plagued the oil-for-food program.

These critics are right. For every UN agency like UNICEF that functions well, there are other agencies that seem to do nothing more than hold conferences, produce reports, and provide sinecures for third-rate international civil servants. But these failures aren't an argument for reducing our involvement in international organizations, nor are they an excuse for U.S. unilateralism. The more effective UN peacekeeping forces are in handling civil wars and sectarian conflicts, the less global policing we have to do in areas that we'd like to see stabilized. The more credible the information that the International Atomic Energy Agency provides, the more likely we are to mobilize allies against the efforts of rogue states to obtain nuclear weapons. The greater the capacity of the World Health Organization, the less likely we are to have to deal with a flu pandemic in our own country. No country has a bigger stake than we do in strengthening international institutions—which is why we pushed for their creation in the first place, and why we need to take the lead in improving them.

Finally, for those who chafe at the prospect of working with our allies to solve the pressing global challenges we face, let me suggest at least one area where we can act unilaterally and improve our standing in the world—by perfecting our own democracy and leading by example. When we continue to spend tens of billions of dollars on weapons systems of dubious value but are unwilling to spend the money to protect highly vulnerable chemical plants in major urban centers, it becomes more difficult to get other countries to safeguard their nuclear power plants. When we detain suspects indefinitely without trial or ship them off in the dead of night to countries where we know they'll be tortured, we weaken our ability to press for human rights and the rule of law in despotic regimes. When we, the richest country on earth and the consumer of 25 percent of the world's fossil fuels, can't bring ourselves to raise fuel-efficiency standards by even a small fraction so as to weaken our dependence on Saudi oil fields and slow global warming, we should expect to have a hard time convincing China not to deal with oil suppliers like Iran or Sudan—and shouldn't count on much cooperation in getting them to address environmental problems that visit our shores.

This unwillingness to make hard choices and live up to our own ideals doesn't just undermine U.S. credibility in the eyes of the world. It undermines the U.S. government's credibility with the American people. Ultimately, it is how we manage that most precious resource—the American people, and the system of self-government we inherited from our Founders—that will determine the success of any foreign policy. The world out there is dangerous and complex; the work of remaking it will be long and hard, and will require some sacrifice. Such sacrifice comes about because the American people understand fully the choices before them; it is born of the confidence we have in our democracy. FDR understood this when he said, after the attack on Pearl Harbor, that "[t]his Government will put its trust in the stamina of the American people." Truman understood this, which is why he worked with Dean Acheson to establish the Committee for the Marshall Plan, made up of CEOs, academics, labor leaders, clergymen, and others who could stump for the plan across the country. It seems as if this is a lesson that America's leadership needs to relearn.

I wonder, sometimes, whether men and women in fact are capable of learning from history—whether we progress from one stage to the next in an upward course or whether we just ride the cycles of boom and bust, war and peace, ascent and decline. On the same trip that took me to Baghdad, I spent a week traveling through Israel and the West Bank, meeting with officials from both sides, mapping in my own mind the site of so much strife. I talked to Jews who'd lost parents in the Holocaust and brothers in suicide bombings; I heard Palestinians talk of the indignities of checkpoints and reminisce about the land they had lost. I flew by helicopter across the line separating the two peoples and found myself unable to distinguish Jewish towns from Arab towns, all of them like fragile outposts against the green and stony hills. From the promenade above Jerusalem, I looked down at the Old City, the Dome of the Rock, the Western Wall, and the Church of the Holy Sepulcher, considered the two thousand years of war and rumors of war that this small plot of land had come to represent, and pondered the possible futility of believing that this conflict might somehow end in our time, or that America, for all its power, might have any lasting say over the course of the world.

I don't linger on such thoughts, though—they are the thoughts of an old man. As difficult as the work may seem, I believe we have an obligation to engage in efforts to bring about peace in the Middle East, not only for the benefit of the people of the region, but for the safety and security of our own children as well.

And perhaps the world's fate depends not just on the events of its battlefields; perhaps it depends just as much on the work we do in those quiet places that require a helping hand. I remember seeing the news reports of the tsunami that hit East Asia in 2004—the towns of Indonesia's western coast flattened, the thousands of people washed out to sea. And then, in the weeks that followed, I watched with pride as Americans sent more than a billion dollars in private relief aid and as U.S. warships delivered thousands of troops to assist in relief and reconstruction. According to newspaper reports, 65 percent of Indonesians surveyed said that this assistance had given them a more favorable view of the United States. I am not naive enough to believe that one episode in the wake of catastrophe can erase decades of mistrust.

But it's a start.

Chapter 9

Family

B Y THE START of my second year in the Senate, my life had settled into a manageable rhythm. I would leave Chicago Monday night or early Tuesday morning, depending on the Senate's voting schedule. Other than daily trips to the Senate gym and the rare lunch or dinner with a friend, the next three days would be consumed by a predictable series of tasks—committee markups, votes, caucus lunches, floor statements, speeches, photos with interns, evening fund-raisers, returning phone calls, writing correspondence, reviewing legislation, drafting op-eds, recording podcasts, receiving policy briefings, hosting constituent coffees, and attending an endless series of meetings. On Thursday afternoon, we would get word from the cloakroom as to when the last vote would be, and at the appointed hour I'd line up in the well of the Senate alongside my colleagues to cast my vote, before trotting down the Capitol steps in hopes of catching a flight that would get me home before the girls went to bed.

Despite the hectic schedule, I found the work fascinating, if occasionally frustrating. Contrary to popular perceptions, only about two dozen significant bills come up for a roll-call vote on the Senate floor every year, and almost none of those are sponsored by a member of the minority party. As a result, most of my major initiatives—the formation of public school innovation districts, a plan to help U.S. automakers pay for their retiree health-care costs in exchange for increased fuel economy standards, an expansion of the Pell Grant program to help low-income students meet rising college tuition costs—languished in committee.

On the other hand, thanks to great work by my staff, I managed to get a respectable number of amendments passed. We helped provide funds for homeless veterans. We provided tax credits to gas stations for installing E85 fuel pumps. We obtained funding to help the World Health Organization monitor and respond to a potential avian flu pandemic. We got an amendment out of the Senate eliminating no-bid contracts in the post-Katrina reconstruction, so more money would actually end up in the hands of the tragedy's victims. None of these amendments would transform the country, but I took satisfaction in knowing that each of them helped some people in a modest way or nudged the law in a direction that might prove to be more economical, more responsible, or more just.

One day in February I found myself in particularly good spirits, having just completed a hearing on legislation that Dick Lugar and I were sponsoring aimed at restricting weapons proliferation and the black-market arms trade. Because Dick was not only the Senate's leading expert on proliferation issues but also the chairman of the Senate Foreign Relations Committee, prospects for the bill seemed promising. Wanting to share the good news, I called Michelle from my D.C. office and started explaining the significance of the bill—how shoulder-to-air missiles could threaten commercial air travel if they fell into the wrong hands, how small-arms stockpiles left over from the Cold War continued to feed conflict across the globe. Michelle cut me off.

"We have ants."

"Huh?"

"I found ants in the kitchen. And in the bathroom upstairs."

"Okay . . ."

"I need you to buy some ant traps on your way home tomorrow. I'd get them myself, but I've got to take the girls to their doctor's appointment after school. Can you do that for me?"

"Right. Ant traps."

"Ant traps. Don't forget, okay, honey? And buy more than one. Listen, I need to go into a meeting. Love you."

I hung up the receiver, wondering if Ted Kennedy or John McCain bought ant traps on the way home from work.

MOST PEOPLE WHO meet my wife quickly conclude that she is remarkable. They are right about this—she is smart, funny, and thoroughly charming. She is also very beautiful, although not in a way that men find intimidating or women find off-putting; it is the lived-in beauty of the mother and busy professional rather than the touched-up image we see on the cover of glossy magazines. Often, after hearing her speak at some function or working with her on a project, people will approach me and say something to the effect of "You know I think the world of you, Barack, but your wife . . . wow!" I nod, knowing that if I ever had to run against her for public office, she would beat me without much difficulty.

Fortunately for me, Michelle would never go into politics. "I don't have the patience," she says to people who ask. As is always the case, she is telling the truth.

I met Michelle in the summer of 1988, while we were both working at Sidley & Austin, a large corporate law firm based in Chicago. Although she is three years younger than me, Michelle was already a practicing lawyer, having attended Harvard Law straight out of college. I had just finished my first year at law school and had been hired as a summer associate.

It was a difficult, transitional period in my life. I had enrolled in law school after three years of work as a community organizer, and although I enjoyed my studies, I still harbored doubts about my decision. Privately, I worried that it represented the abandonment of my youthful ideals, a concession to the hard realities of money and power—the world as it is rather than the world as it should be.

The idea of working at a corporate law firm, so near and yet so far removed from the poor neighborhoods where my friends were still laboring, only worsened these fears. But with student loans rapidly mounting, I was in no position to turn down the three months of salary Sidley was offering. And so, having sublet the cheapest apartment I could find, having purchased the first three suits ever to appear in my closet and a new pair of shoes that turned out to be a half size too small and would absolutely cripple me for the next nine weeks, I arrived at the firm one drizzly morning in early June and was directed to the office of the young attorney who'd been assigned to serve as my summer advisor.

I don't remember the details of that first conversation with Michelle. I remember that she was tall—almost my height in heels—and lovely, with a friendly, professional manner that matched her tailored suit and blouse. She explained how work was assigned at the firm, the nature of the various practice groups, and how to log our billable hours. After showing me my office and giving me a tour of the library, she handed me off to one of the partners and told me that she would meet me for lunch.

Later Michelle would tell me that she had been pleasantly surprised when I walked into her office; the drugstore snapshot that I'd sent in for the firm directory made my nose look a little big (even more enormous than usual, she might say), and she had been skeptical when the secretaries who'd seen me during my interview told her I was cute: "I figured that they were just impressed with any black man with a suit and a job." But if Michelle was impressed, she certainly didn't tip her hand when we went to lunch. I did learn that she had grown up on the South Side, in a small bungalow just north of the neighborhoods where I had organized. Her father was a pump operator for the city; her mother had been a housewife until the kids were grown, and now worked as a secretary at a bank. She had attended Bryn Mawr Public Elementary School, gotten into Whitney Young Magnet School, and followed her brother to Princeton, where he had been a star on the basketball team. At Sidley she was part of the intellectual property group and specialized in entertainment law; at some point, she said, she might have to consider moving to Los Angeles or New York to pursue her career.

Oh, Michelle was full of plans that day, on the fast track, with no time, she told me, for distractions—especially men. But she knew how to laugh, brightly and easily, and I noticed she didn't seem in too much of a hurry to get back to the office. And there was something else, a glimmer that danced across her round, dark eyes whenever I looked at her, the slightest hint of uncertainty, as if, deep inside, she knew how fragile things really were, and that if she ever let go, even for a moment, all her plans might quickly unravel. That touched me somehow, that trace of vulnerability. I wanted to know that part of her.

For the next several weeks, we saw each other every day, in the law library or the cafeteria or at one of the many outings that law firms organize for their summer associates to convince them that their life in the law will not be endless hours of poring through documents. She took me to one or two parties, tactfully overlooking my limited wardrobe, and even tried to set me up with a couple of her friends. Still, she refused to go out on a proper date. It wasn't appropriate, she said, since she was my advisor.

"That's a poor excuse," I told her. "Come on, what advice are you giving me? You're showing me how the copy machine works. You're telling me what restaurants to try. I don't think the partners will consider one date a serious breach of firm policy."

She shook her head. "Sorry."

"Okay, I'll quit. How's that? You're my advisor. Tell me who I have to talk to."

Eventually I wore her down. After a firm picnic, she drove me back to my apartment, and I offered to buy her an ice cream cone at the Baskin-Robbins across the street. We sat on the curb and ate our cones in the sticky afternoon heat, and I told her about working at Baskin-Robbins when I was a teenager and how it was hard to look cool in a brown apron and cap. She told me that for a span of two or three years as a child, she had refused to eat anything except peanut butter and jelly. I said that I'd like to meet her family. She said that she would like that.

I asked if I could kiss her. It tasted of chocolate.

We spent the rest of the summer together. I told her about organizing, and living in Indonesia, and what it was like to body-surf. She told me about her childhood friends, and a trip to Paris she'd taken in high school, and her favorite Stevie Wonder songs.

But it wasn't until I met Michelle's family that I began to understand her. It turned out that visiting the Robinson household was like dropping in on the set of *Leave It to Beaver.* There was Frasier, the kindly, good-humored father, who never missed a day of work or any of his son's ball games. There was Marian, the pretty, sensible mother who baked birthday cakes, kept order in the house, and had volunteered at school to make sure her children were behaving and that the teachers were doing what they were supposed to be doing. There was Craig, the basketball-star brother, tall and friendly and courteous and funny, working as an investment banker but dreaming of going into coaching someday. And there were uncles and aunts and cousins everywhere, stopping by to sit around the kitchen table and eat until they burst and tell wild stories and listen to Grandpa's old jazz collection and laugh deep into the night.

All that was missing was the dog. Marian didn't want a dog tearing up the house.

What made this vision of domestic bliss all the more impressive was the fact that the Robinsons had had to overcome hardships that one rarely saw on prime-time TV. There were the usual issues of race, of course: the limited opportunities available to Michelle's parents growing up in Chicago during the fifties and sixties; the racial steering and panic peddling that had driven white families away from their neighborhood; the extra energy required from black parents to compensate for smaller incomes and more violent streets and underfunded playgrounds and indifferent schools.

But there was a more specific tragedy at the center of the Robinson household. At the age of thirty, in the prime of his life, Michelle's father had been diagnosed with multiple sclerosis. For the next twenty-five years, as his condition steadily deteriorated, he had carried out his responsibilities to his family without a trace of self-pity, giving himself an extra hour every morning to get to work, struggling with every physical act from driving a car to buttoning his shirt, smiling and joking as he labored—at first with a limp and eventually with the aid of two canes, his balding head beading with sweat—across a field to watch his son play, or across the living room to give his daughter a kiss.

After we were married, Michelle would help me understand the hidden toll that her father's illness had taken on her family; how heavy a burden Michelle's mother had been forced to carry; how carefully circumscribed their lives together had been, with even the smallest outing carefully planned to avoid problems or awkwardness; how terrifyingly random life seemed beneath the smiles and laughter.

But back then I saw only the joy of the Robinson house. For someone like me, who had barely known his father, who had spent much of his life traveling from place to place, his bloodlines scattered to the four winds, the home that Frasier and Marian Robinson had built for themselves and their children stirred a longing for stability and a sense of place that I had not realized was there. Just as Michelle perhaps saw in me a life of adventure, risk, travel to exotic lands—a wider horizon than she had previously allowed herself.

Six months after Michelle and I met, her father died suddenly of complications after a kidney operation. I flew back to Chicago and stood at his gravesite, Michelle's head on my shoulder. As the casket was lowered, I promised Frasier Robinson that I would take care of his girl. I realized that in some unspoken, still tentative way, she and I were already becoming a family.

THERE'S A LOT of talk these days about the decline of the American family. Social conservatives claim that the traditional family is under assault from Hollywood movies and gay pride parades. Liberals point to the economic factors—from stagnating wages to inadequate day care—that have put families under increasing duress. Our popular culture feeds the alarm, with tales of women consigned to permanent singlehood, men unwilling to make lasting commitments, and teens engaged in endless sexual escapades. Nothing seems settled, as it was in the past; our roles and relationships all feel up for grabs.

Given this hand-wringing, it may be helpful to step back and remind ourselves that the institution of marriage isn't disappearing anytime soon. While it's true that marriage rates have declined steadily since the 1950s, some of the decline is a result of more Americans delaying marriage to pursue an education or establish a career; by the age of forty-five, 89 percent of women and 83 percent of men will have tied the knot at least once. Married couples continue to head 67 percent of American families, and the vast majority of Americans still consider marriage to be the best foundation for personal intimacy, economic stability, and child rearing.

Still, there's no denying that the nature of the family has changed over the last fifty years. Although divorce rates have declined by 21 percent since their peak in the late seventies and early eighties, half of all first marriages still end in divorce. Compared to our grandparents, we're more tolerant of premarital sex, more likely to cohabit, and more likely to live alone. We're also far more likely to be raising children in nontraditional households; 60 percent of all divorces involve children, 33 percent of all children are born out of wedlock, and 34 percent of children don't live with their biological fathers.

These trends are particularly acute in the African American community, where it's fair to say that the nuclear family is on the verge of collapse. Since 1950, the marriage rate for black women has plummeted from 62 percent to 36 percent. Between 1960 and 1995, the number of African American children living with two married parents dropped by more than half; today 54 percent of all African American children live in single-parent households, compared to about 23 percent of all white children.

For adults, at least, the effect of these changes is a mixed bag. Research suggests that on average, married couples live healthier, wealthier, and happier lives, but no one claims that men and women benefit from being trapped in bad or abusive marriages. Certainly the decision of increasing numbers of Americans to delay marriage makes sense; not only does today's information economy demand more time in school, but studies show that couples who wait until their late twenties or thirties to get married are more likely to stay married than those who marry young.

Whatever the effect on adults, though, these trends haven't been so good for our children. Many single moms—including the one who raised me—do a heroic job on behalf of their kids. Still, children living with single mothers are five times more likely to be poor than children in two-parent households. Children in single-parent homes are also more likely to drop out of school and become teen parents, even when income is factored out. And the evidence suggests that on average, children who live with both their biological mother and father do better than those who live in stepfamilies or with cohabiting partners.

In light of these facts, policies that strengthen marriage for those who choose it and that discourage unintended births outside of marriage are sensible goals to pursue. For example, most people agree that neither federal welfare programs nor the tax code should penalize married couples; those aspects of welfare reform enacted under Clinton and those elements of the Bush tax plan that reduced the marriage penalty enjoy strong bipartisan support.

The same goes for teen pregnancy prevention. Everyone agrees that teen pregnancies place both mother and child at risk for all sorts of problems. Since 1990, the teen pregnancy rate has dropped by 28 percent, an unadulterated piece of good news. But teens still account for almost a quarter of out-of-wedlock births, and teen mothers are more likely to have additional out-of-wedlock births as they get older. Community-based programs that have a proven track record in preventing unwanted pregnancies—both by encouraging abstinence and by promoting the proper use of contraception—deserve broad support.

Finally, preliminary research shows that marriage education workshops can make a real difference in helping married couples stay together and in encouraging unmarried couples who are living together to form a more lasting bond. Expanding access to such services to low-income couples, perhaps in concert with job training and placement, medical coverage, and other services already available, should be something everybody can agree on.

But for many social conservatives, these commonsense approaches don't go far enough. They want a return to a bygone era, in which sexuality outside of marriage was subject to both punishment and shame, obtaining a divorce was far more difficult, and marriage offered not merely personal fulfillment but also well-defined social roles for men and for women. In their view, any government policy that appears to reward or even express neutrality toward what they consider to be immoral behavior—whether providing birth control to young people, abortion services to women, welfare support for unwed mothers, or legal recognition of same-sex unions—inherently devalues the marital bond. Such policies take us one step closer, the argument goes, to a brave new world in which gender differences have been erased, sex is purely recreational, marriage is disposable, motherhood is an inconvenience, and civilization itself rests on shifting sands.

I understand the impulse to restore a sense of order to a culture that's constantly in flux. And I certainly appreciate the desire of parents to shield their children from values they consider unwholesome; it's a feeling I often share when I listen to the lyrics of songs on the radio.

But all in all, I have little sympathy for those who would enlist the government in the task of enforcing sexual morality. Like most Americans, I consider decisions about sex, marriage, divorce, and childbearing to be highly personal—at the very core of our system of individual liberty. Where such personal decisions raise the prospect of significant harm to others—as is true with child abuse, incest, bigamy, domestic violence, or failure to pay child support—society has a right and duty to step in. (Those who believe in the personhood of the fetus would put abortion in this category.) Beyond that, I have no interest in seeing the president, Congress, or a government bureaucracy regulating what goes on in America's bedrooms.

Moreover, I don't believe we strengthen the family by bullying or coercing people into the relationships we think are best for them—or by punishing those who fail to meet our standards of sexual propriety. I want to encourage young people to show more reverence toward sex and intimacy, and I applaud parents, congregations, and community programs that transmit that message. But I'm not willing to consign a teenage girl to a lifetime of struggle because of lack of access to birth control. I want couples to understand the value of commitment and the sacrifices marriage entails. But I'm not willing to use the force of law to keep couples together regardless of their personal circumstances.

Perhaps I just find the ways of the human heart too various, and my own life too imperfect, to believe myself qualified to serve as anyone's moral arbiter. I do know that in our fourteen years of marriage, Michelle and I have never had an argument as a result of what other people are doing in their personal lives.

What we *have* argued about—repeatedly—is how to balance work and family in a way that's equitable to Michelle and good for our children. We're not alone in this. In the sixties and early seventies, the household Michelle grew up in was the norm— more than 70 percent of families had Mom at home and relied on Dad as the sole breadwinner.

Today those numbers are reversed. Seventy percent of families with children are headed by two working parents or a single working parent. The result has been what my policy director and work-family expert Karen Kornbluh calls "the juggler family," in which parents struggle to pay the bills, look after their children, maintain a household, and maintain their relationship. Keeping all these balls in the air takes its toll on family life. As Karen explained when she was director of the Work and Family Program at the New America Foundation and testified before the Senate Subcommittee on Children and Families:

> Americans today have 22 fewer hours a week to spend with their kids than they did in 1969. Millions of children are left in unlicensed day care every day—or at home alone with the TV as a babysitter. Employed mothers lose almost an hour of sleep a day in their attempt to make it all add up. Recent data show that parents with school age children show high signs of stress—stress that has an impact on their productivity and work—when they have inflexible jobs and unstable after-school care.

Sound familiar?

Many social conservatives suggest that this flood of women out of the home and into the workplace is a direct consequence of feminist ideology, and hence can be reversed if women will just come to their senses and return to their traditional homemaking roles. It's true that ideas about equality for women have played a critical role in the transformation of the workplace; in the minds of most Americans, the opportunity for women to pursue careers, achieve economic independence, and realize their talents on an equal footing with men has been one of the great achievements of modern life.

But for the average American woman, the decision to work isn't simply a matter of changing attitudes. It's a matter of making ends meet.

Consider the facts. Over the last thirty years, the average earnings of American men have grown less than 1 percent after being adjusted for inflation. Meanwhile, the cost of everything, from housing to health care to education, has steadily risen. What has kept a large swath of American families from falling out of the middle class has been Mom's paycheck. In their book *The Two-Income Trap*, Elizabeth Warren and Amelia Tyagi point out that the additional income mothers bring home isn't going to luxury items. Instead, almost all of it goes to purchase what families believe to be investments in their children's future—preschool education, college tuition, and most of all, homes in safe neighborhoods with good public schools. In fact, between these fixed costs and the added expenses of a working mother (particularly day care and a second car), the average two-income family has less discretionary income—and is less financially secure—than its single-earner counterpart thirty years ago.

So is it possible for the average family to return to life on a single income? Not when every other family on the block is earning two incomes and bidding up the prices of homes, schools, and college tuition. Warren and Tyagi show that an average single-earner family today that tried to maintain a middle-class lifestyle would have 60 percent less discretionary income than its 1970s counterpart. In other words, for most families, having Mom stay at home means living in a less-safe neighborhood and enrolling their children in a less-competitive school.

That's not a choice most Americans are willing to make. Instead they do the best they can under the circumstances, knowing that the type of household they grew up in—the type of household in which Frasier and Marian Robinson raised their kids—has become much, much harder to sustain.

BOTH MEN AND women have had to adjust to these new realities. But it's hard to argue with Michelle when she insists that the burdens of the modern family fall more heavily on the woman.

For the first few years of our marriage, Michelle and I went through the usual adjustments all couples go through: learning to read each other's moods, accepting the quirks and habits of a stranger underfoot. Michelle liked to wake up early and could barely keep her eyes open after ten o'clock. I was a night owl and could be a bit grumpy (mean, Michelle would say) within the first half hour or so of getting out of bed. Partly because I was still working on my first book, and perhaps because I had lived much of my life as an only child, I would often spend the evening holed up in my office in the back of our railroad apartment; what I considered normal often left Michelle feeling lonely. I invariably left the butter out after breakfast and forgot to twist the little tie around the bread bag; Michelle could rack up parking tickets like nobody's business.

Mostly, though, those early years were full of ordinary pleasures—going to movies, having dinner with friends, catching the occasional concert. We were both working hard: I was practicing law at a small civil rights firm and had started teaching at the

University of Chicago Law School, while Michelle had decided to leave her law practice, first to work in Chicago's Department of Planning and then to run the Chicago arm of a national service program called Public Allies. Our time together got squeezed even more when I ran for the state legislature, but despite my lengthy absences and her general dislike of politics, Michelle supported the decision; "I know it's something that you want to do," she would tell me. On the nights that I was in Springfield, we'd talk and laugh over the phone, sharing the humor and frustrations of our days apart, and I would fall asleep content in the knowledge of our love.

Then Malia was born, a Fourth of July baby, so calm and so beautiful, with big, hypnotic eyes that seemed to read the world the moment they opened. Malia's arrival came at an ideal time for both of us: Because I was out of session and didn't have to teach during the summer, I was able to spend every evening at home; meanwhile, Michelle had decided to accept a part-time job at the University of Chicago so she could spend more time with the baby, and the new job didn't start until October. For three magical months the two of us fussed and fretted over our new baby, checking the crib to make sure she was breathing, coaxing smiles from her, singing her songs, and taking so many pictures that we started to wonder if we were damaging her eyes. Suddenly our different biorhythms came in handy: While Michelle got some well-earned sleep, I would stay up until one or two in the morning, changing diapers, heating breast milk, feeling my daughter's soft breath against my chest as I rocked her to sleep, guessing at her infant dreams.

But when fall came—when my classes started back up, the legislature went back into session, and Michelle went back to work—the strains in our relationship began to show. I was often gone for three days at a stretch, and even when I was back in Chicago, I might have evening meetings to attend, or papers to grade, or briefs to write. Michelle found that a part-time job had a funny way of expanding. We found a wonderful in-home baby-sitter to look after Malia while we were at work, but with a full-time employee suddenly on our payroll, money got tight.

Tired and stressed, we had little time for conversation, much less romance. When I launched my ill-fated congressional run, Michelle put up no pretense of being happy with the decision. My failure to clean up the kitchen suddenly became less endearing. Leaning down to kiss Michelle good-bye in the morning, all I would get was a peck on the cheek. By the time Sasha was born—just as beautiful, and almost as calm as her sister—my wife's anger toward me seemed barely contained.

"You only think about yourself," she would tell me. "I never thought I'd have to raise a family alone."

I was stung by such accusations; I thought she was being unfair. After all, it wasn't as if I went carousing with the boys every night. I made few demands of Michelle—I didn't expect her to darn my socks or have dinner waiting for me when I got home. Whenever I could, I pitched in with the kids. All I asked for in return was a little tenderness. Instead, I found myself subjected to endless negotiations about every detail of managing the house, long lists of things that I needed to do or had forgotten to do, and a generally sour attitude. I reminded Michelle that compared to most families, we were incredibly lucky. I reminded her as well that for all my flaws, I loved her and the girls more than anything else. My love should be enough, I thought. As far as I was concerned, she had nothing to complain about.

It was only upon reflection, after the trials of those years had passed and the kids had started school, that I began to appreciate what Michelle had been going through at the time, the struggles so typical of today's working mother. For no matter how liberated I liked to see myself as—no matter how much I told myself that Michelle and I were equal partners, and that her dreams and ambitions were as important as my own—the fact was that when children showed up, it was Michelle and not I who was expected to make the necessary adjustments. Sure, I helped, but it was always on my terms, on my schedule. Meanwhile, she was the one who had to put her career on hold. She was the one who had to make sure that the kids were fed and bathed every night. If Malia or Sasha got sick or the babysitter failed to show up, it was she who, more often than not, had to get on the phone to cancel a meeting at work.

It wasn't just the constant scrambling between her work and the children that made Michelle's situation so tough. It was also the fact that from her perspective she wasn't doing either job well. This was not true, of course; her employers loved her, and everyone remarked on what a good mother she was. But I came to see that in her own mind, two visions of herself were at war with each other—the desire to be the woman her mother had been, solid, dependable, making a home and always there for her kids; and the desire to excel in her profession, to make her mark on the world and realize all those plans she'd had on the very first day that we met.

In the end, I credit Michelle's strength—her willingness to manage these tensions and make sacrifices on behalf of myself and the girls—with carrying us through the difficult times. But we also had resources at our disposal that many American families don't have. For starters, Michelle's and my status as professionals meant that we could rework our schedules to handle an emergency (or just take a day off) without risk of losing our jobs. Fifty-seven percent of American workers don't have that luxury; indeed, most of them can't take a day off to look after a child without losing pay or using vacation days. For parents who do try to make their own schedules, flexibility often means accepting part-time or temporary work with no career ladder and few or no benefits.

Michelle and I also had enough income to cover all the services that help ease the pressures of two-earner parenthood: reliable child care, extra babysitting whenever we needed it, take-out dinners when we had neither the time nor the energy to cook, someone to come in and clean the house once a week, and private preschool and summer day camp once the kids were old enough. For most American families, such help is financially out of reach. The cost of day care is especially prohibitive; the United States is practically alone among Western nations in not providing government-subsidized, high-quality day-care services to all its workers.

Finally, Michelle and I had my mother-in-law, who lives only fifteen minutes away from us, in the same house in which Michelle was raised. Marian is in her late sixties but looks ten years younger, and last year, when Michelle went back to full-time work, Marian decided to cut her hours at the bank so she could pick up the girls from school and look after them every afternoon. For many American families, such help is simply unavailable; in fact, for many families, the situation is reversed—someone in the family has to provide care for an aging parent on top of other family responsibilities.

Of course, it's not possible for the federal government to guarantee each family a wonderful, healthy, semiretired mother-in-law who happens to live close by. But if we're serious about family values, then we can put policies in place that make the juggling of work and parenting a little bit easier. We could start by making high-quality day care affordable for every family that needs it. In contrast to most European countries, day care in the United States is a haphazard affair. Improved day-care licensing and training, an expansion of the federal and state child tax credits, and sliding-scale subsidies to families that need them all could provide both middle-class and low-income parents some peace of mind during the workday—and benefit employers through reduced absenteeism.

It's also time to redesign our schools—not just for the sake of working parents, but also to help prepare our children for a more competitive world. Countless studies confirm the educational benefits of strong preschool programs, which is why even families who have a parent at home often seek them out. The same goes for longer school days, summer school, and after-school programs. Providing all kids access to these benefits would cost money, but as part of broader school reform efforts, it's a cost that we as a society should be willing to bear.

Most of all, we need to work with employers to increase the flexibility of work schedules. The Clinton Administration took a step in this direction with the Family and Medical Leave Act (FMLA), but because it requires only unpaid leave and applies only to companies with more than fifty employees, most American workers aren't able to take advantage of it. And although all other wealthy nations but one provide some form of paid parental leave, the business community's resistance to mandated paid leave has been fierce, in part because of concerns over how it would affect small businesses.

With a little creativity, we should be able to break this impasse. California has recently initiated paid leave through its disability insurance fund, thereby making sure that the costs aren't borne by employers alone.

We can also give parents flexibility to meet their day-to-day needs. Already, many larger companies offer formal flextime programs and report higher employee morale and less employee turnover as a result. Great Britain has come up with a novel approach to the problem—as part of a highly popular "Work-Life Balance Campaign," parents with children under the age of six have the right to file a written request with employers for a change in their schedule. Employers aren't required to grant the request, but they are required to meet with the employee to consider it; so far, one-quarter of all eligible British parents have successfully negotiated more family-friendly hours without a drop in productivity. With a combination of such innovative policy making, technical assistance, and greater public awareness, government can help businesses to do right by their employees at nominal expense.

Of course, none of these policies need discourage families from deciding to keep a parent at home, regardless of the financial sacrifices. For some families, that may mean doing without certain material comforts. For others, it may mean home schooling or a move to a community where the cost of living is lower. For some families, it may be the father who stays at home— although for most families it will still be the mother who serves as the primary caregiver.

Whatever the case may be, such decisions should be honored. If there's one thing that social conservatives have been right about, it's that our modern culture sometimes fails to fully appreciate the extraordinary emotional and financial contributions—the sacrifices and just plain hard work—of the stay-at-home mom. Where social conservatives have been wrong is in insisting that this traditional role is innate—the best or only model of motherhood. I want my daughters to have a choice as to what's best for them and their families. Whether they will have such choices will depend not just on their own efforts and attitudes. As Michelle has taught me, it will also depend on men—and American society—respecting and accommodating the choices they make.

"HI, DADDY."

"Hey, sweetie-pie."

It's Friday afternoon and I'm home early to look after the girls while Michelle goes to the hairdresser. I gather up Malia in a hug and notice a blond girl in our kitchen, peering at me through a pair of oversized glasses.

"Who's this?" I ask, setting Malia back on the floor.

"This is Sam. She's over for a playdate."

"Hi, Sam." I offer Sam my hand, and she considers it for a moment before shaking it loosely. Malia rolls her eyes.

"Listen, Daddy . . . you don't shake hands with kids."

"You don't?"

"No," Malia says. "Not even teenagers shake hands. You may not have noticed, but this is the twenty-first century." Malia looks at Sam, who represses a smirk.

"So what do you do in the twenty-first century?"

"You just say 'hey.' Sometimes you wave. That's pretty much it."

"I see. I hope I didn't embarrass you."

Malia smiles. "That's okay, Daddy. You didn't know, because you're used to shaking hands with grown-ups."

"That's true. Where's your sister?"

"She's upstairs."

I walk upstairs to find Sasha standing in her underwear and a pink top. She pulls me down for a hug and then tells me she can't find any shorts. I check in the closet and find a pair of blue shorts sitting right on top of her chest of drawers.

"What are these?"

Sasha frowns but reluctantly takes the shorts from me and pulls them on. After a few minutes, she climbs into my lap.

"These shorts aren't comfortable, Daddy."

We go back into Sasha's closet, open the drawer again, and find another pair of shorts, also blue. "How about these?" I ask.

Sasha frowns again. Standing there, she looks like a three-foot version of her mother. Malia and Sam walk in to observe the stand-off.

"Sasha doesn't like either of those shorts," Malia explains.

I turn to Sasha and ask her why. She looks up at me warily, taking my measure.

"Pink and blue don't go together," she says finally.

Malia and Sam giggle. I try to look as stern as Michelle might look in such circumstances and tell Sasha to put on the shorts. She does what I say, but I realize she's just indulging me.

When it comes to my daughters, no one is buying my tough-guy routine.

Like many men today, I grew up without a father in the house. My mother and father divorced when I was only two years old, and for most of my life I knew him only through the letters he sent and the stories my mother and grandparents told. There were men in my life—a stepfather with whom we lived for four years, and my grandfather, who along with my grandmother helped raise me the rest of the time—and both were good men who treated me with affection. But my relationships with them were necessarily partial, incomplete. In the case of my stepfather, this was a result of limited duration and his natural reserve. And as close as I was to my grandfather, he was both too old and too troubled to provide me with much direction.

It was women, then, who provided the ballast in my life—my grandmother, whose dogged practicality kept the family afloat, and my mother, whose love and clarity of spirit kept my sister's and my world centered. Because of them I never wanted for anything important. From them I would absorb the values that guide me to this day.

Still, as I got older I came to recognize how hard it had been for my mother and grandmother to raise us without a strong male presence in the house. I felt as well the mark that a father's absence can leave on a child. I determined that my father's irresponsibility toward his children, my stepfather's remoteness, and my grandfather's failures would all become object lessons for me, and that my own children would have a father they could count on.

In the most basic sense, I've succeeded. My marriage is intact and my family is provided for. I attend parent-teacher conferences and dance recitals, and my daughters bask in my adoration. And yet, of all the areas of my life, it is in my capacities as a husband and father that I entertain the most doubt.

I realize I'm not alone in this; at some level I'm just going through the same conflicting emotions that other fathers experience as they navigate an economy in flux and changing social norms. Even as it becomes less and less attainable, the image of the 1950s father—supporting his family with a nine-to-five job, sitting down for the dinner that his wife prepares every night, coaching Little League, and handling power tools—hovers over the culture no less powerfully than the image of the stay-at-home mom. For many men today, the inability to be their family's sole breadwinner is a source of frustration and even shame; one doesn't have to be an economic determinist to believe that high unemployment and low wages contribute to the lack of parental involvement and low marriage rates among African American men.

For working men, no less than for working women, the terms of employment have changed. Whether a high-paid professional or a worker on the assembly line, fathers are expected to put in longer hours on the job than they did in the past. And these more demanding work schedules are occurring precisely at the time when fathers are expected—and in many cases want—to be more actively involved in the lives of their children than their own fathers may have been in theirs.

But if the gap between the idea of parenthood in my head and the compromised reality that I live isn't unique, that doesn't relieve my sense that I'm not always giving my family all that I could. Last Father's Day, I was invited to speak to the members of Salem Baptist Church on the South Side of Chicago. I didn't have a prepared text, but I took as my theme "what it takes to be a full-grown man." I suggested that it was time that men in general and black men in particular put away their excuses for not being there for their families. I reminded the men in the audience that being a father meant more than bearing a child; that even those of us who were physically present in the home are often emotionally absent; that precisely because many of us didn't have fathers in the house we have to redouble our efforts to break the cycle; and that if we want to pass on high expectations to our children, we have to have higher expectations for ourselves.

Thinking back on what I said, I ask myself sometimes how well I'm living up to my own exhortations. After all, unlike many of the men to whom I was speaking that day, I don't have to take on two jobs or the night shift in a valiant attempt to put food on the table. I could find a job that allowed me to be home every night. Or I could find a job that paid more money, a job in which long hours might at least be justified by some measurable benefit to my family—the ability of Michelle to cut back her hours, say, or a fat trust fund for the kids.

Instead, I have chosen a life with a ridiculous schedule, a life that requires me to be gone from Michelle and the girls for long stretches of time and that exposes Michelle to all sorts of stress. I may tell myself that in some larger sense I am in politics for Malia and Sasha, that the work I do will make the world a better place for them. But such rationalizations seem feeble and painfully abstract when I'm missing one of the girls' school potlucks because of a vote, or calling Michelle to tell her that session's been extended and we need to postpone our vacation. Indeed, my recent success in politics does little to assuage the guilt; as Michelle told me once, only half joking, seeing your dad's picture in the paper may be kind of neat the first time it happens, but when it happens all the time it's probably kind of embarrassing.

And so I do my best to answer the accusation that floats around in my mind—that I am selfish, that I do what I do to feed my own ego or fill a void in my heart. When I'm not out of town, I try to be home for dinner, to hear from Malia and Sasha about their day, to read to them and tuck them into bed. I try not to schedule appearances on Sundays, and in the summers I'll use the day to take the girls to the zoo or the pool; in the winters we might visit a museum or the aquarium. I scold my daughters gently when they misbehave, and try to limit their intake of both television and junk food. In all this I am encouraged by Michelle, although there are times when I get the sense that I'm encroaching on her space—that by my absences I may have forfeited certain rights to interfere in the world she has built.

As for the girls, they seem to be thriving despite my frequent disappearances. Mostly this is a testimony to Michelle's parenting skills; she seems to have a perfect touch when it comes to Malia and Sasha, an ability to set firm boundaries without being stifling. She's also made sure that my election to the Senate hasn't altered the girls' routines very much, although what passes for a normal middle-class childhood in America these days seems to have changed as much as has parenting. Gone are the days when parents just sent their child outside or to the park and told him or her to be back before dinner. Today, with news of abductions and an apparent suspicion of anything spontaneous or even a tiny bit slothful, the schedules of children seem to rival those of their parents. There are playdates, ballet classes, gymnastics classes, tennis lessons, piano lessons, soccer leagues, and what seem like weekly birthday parties. I told Malia once that during the entire time that I was growing up, I attended exactly two birthday parties, both of which involved five or six kids, cone hats, and a cake. She looked at me the way I used to look at my grandfather when he told stories of the Depression—with a mixture of fascination and incredulity.

It is left to Michelle to coordinate all the children's activities, which she does with a general's efficiency. When I can, I volunteer to help, which Michelle appreciates, although she is careful to limit my responsibilities. The day before Sasha's birthday party this past June, I was told to procure twenty balloons, enough cheese pizza to feed twenty kids, and ice. This seemed manageable, so when Michelle told me that she was going to get goody bags to hand out at the end of the party, I suggested that I do that as well. She laughed.

"You can't handle goody bags," she said. "Let me explain the goody bag thing. You have to go into the party store and choose the bags. Then you have to choose what to put in the bags, and what is in the boys' bags has to be different from what is in the girls' bags. You'd walk in there and wander around the aisles for an hour, and then your head would explode."

Feeling less confident, I got on the Internet. I found a place that sold balloons near the gymnastics studio where the party would be held, and a pizza place that promised delivery at 3:45 p.m. By the time the guests showed up the next day, the balloons were in place and the juice boxes were on ice. I sat with the other parents, catching up and watching twenty or so five-year-olds run and jump and bounce on the equipment like a band of merry elves. I had a slight scare when at 3:50 the pizzas had not yet arrived, but the delivery person got there ten minutes before the children were scheduled to eat. Michelle's brother, Craig, knowing the pressure I was under, gave me a high five. Michelle looked up from putting pizza on paper plates and smiled.

As a grand finale, after all the pizza was eaten and the juice boxes drunk, after we had sung "Happy Birthday" and eaten some cake, the gymnastics instructor gathered all the kids around an old, multicolored parachute and told Sasha to sit at its center. On the count of three, Sasha was hoisted up into the air and back down again, then up for a second time, and then for a third. And each time she rose above the billowing sail, she laughed and laughed with a look of pure joy.

I wonder if Sasha will remember that moment when she is grown. Probably not; it seems as if I can retrieve only the barest fragments of memory from when I was five. But I suspect that the happiness she felt on that parachute registers permanently in her; that such moments accumulate and embed themselves in a child's character, becoming a part of their soul. Sometimes, when I listen to Michelle talk about her father, I hear the echo of such joy in her, the love and respect that Frasier Robinson earned not through fame or spectacular deeds but through small, daily, ordinary acts—a love he earned by being there. And I ask myself whether my daughters will be able to speak of me in that same way.

As it is, the window for making such memories rapidly closes. Already Malia seems to be moving into a different phase; she's more curious about boys and relationships, more self-conscious about what she wears. She's always been older than her years, uncannily wise. Once, when she was just six years old and we were taking a walk together along the lake, she asked me out of the blue if our family was rich. I told her that we weren't really rich, but that we had a lot more than most people. I asked her why she wanted to know.

"Well . . . I've been thinking about it, and I've decided I don't want to be really, really rich. I think I want a simple life."

Her words were so unexpected that I laughed. She looked up at me and smiled, but her eyes told me she'd meant what she said.

I often think of that conversation. I ask myself what Malia makes of my not-so-simple life. Certainly she notices that other fathers attend her team's soccer games more often than I do. If this upsets her, she doesn't let it show, for Malia tends to be protective of other people's feelings, trying to see the best in every situation. Still, it gives me small comfort to think that my eight-year-old daughter loves me enough to overlook my shortcomings.

I was able to get to one of Malia's games recently, when session ended early for the week. It was a fine summer afternoon, and the several fields were full of families when I arrived, blacks and whites and Latinos and Asians from all over the city, women sitting on lawn chairs, men practicing kicks with their sons, grandparents helping babies to stand. I spotted Michelle and sat down on the grass beside her, and Sasha came to sit in my lap. Malia was already out on the field, part of a swarm of players surrounding the ball, and although soccer's not her natural sport—she's a head taller than some of her friends, and her feet haven't yet caught up to her height—she plays with an enthusiasm and competitiveness that makes us cheer loudly. At halftime, Malia came over to where we were sitting.

"How you feeling, sport?" I asked her.

"Great!" She took a swig of water. "Daddy, I have a question."

"Shoot."

"Can we get a dog?"

"What does your mother say?"

"She told me to ask you. I think I'm wearing her down."

I looked at Michelle, who smiled and offered a shrug.

"How about we talk it over after the game?" I said.

"Okay." Malia took another sip of water and kissed me on the cheek. "I'm glad you're home," she said.

Before I could answer, she had turned around and started back out onto the field. And for an instant, in the glow of the late afternoon, I thought I saw my older daughter as the woman she would become, as if with each step she were growing taller, her shape filling out, her long legs carrying her into a life of her own.

I squeezed Sasha a little tighter in my lap. Perhaps sensing what I was feeling, Michelle took my hand. And I remembered a quote Michelle had given to a reporter during the campaign, when he'd asked her what it was like being a political wife.

"It's hard," Michelle had said. Then, according to the reporter, she had added with a sly smile, "And that's why Barack is such a grateful man."

As usual, my wife is right.

Epilogue

M Y SWEARING IN to the U.S. Senate in January 2005 completed a process that had begun the day I announced my candidacy two years earlier—the exchange of a relatively anonymous life for a very public one.

To be sure, many things have remained constant. Our family still makes its home in Chicago. I still go to the same Hyde Park barbershop to get my hair cut, Michelle and I have the same friends over to our house as we did before the election, and our daughters still run through the same playgrounds.

Still, there's no doubt that the world has changed profoundly for me, in ways that I don't always care to admit. My words, my actions, my travel plans, and my tax returns all end up in the morning papers or on the nightly news broadcast. My daughters have to endure the interruptions of well-meaning strangers whenever their father takes them to the zoo. Even outside of Chicago, it's becoming harder to walk unnoticed through airports.

As a rule, I find it difficult to take all this attention very seriously. After all, there are days when I still walk out of the house with a suit jacket that doesn't match my suit pants. My thoughts are so much less tidy, my days so much less organized than the image of me that now projects itself into the world, that it makes for occasional comic moments. I remember the day before I was

sworn in, my staff and I decided we should hold a press conference in our office. At the time, I was ranked ninety-ninth in sen-
iority, and all the reporters were crammed into a tiny transition
office in the basement of the Dirksen Office Building, across the
hall from the Senate supply store. It was my first day in the building; I had not taken a single vote, had not introduced a single
bill—indeed I had not even sat down at my desk when a very
earnest reporter raised his hand and asked, "Senator Obama,
what is your place in history?"

Even some of the other reporters had to laugh.

Some of the hyperbole can be traced back to my speech at
the 2004 Democratic Convention in Boston, the point at which
I first gained national attention. In fact, the process by which I
was selected as the keynote speaker remains something of a mystery to me. I had met John Kerry for the first time after the Illinois primary, when I spoke at his fund-raiser and accompanied
him to a campaign event highlighting the importance of job-
training programs. A few weeks later, we got word that the
Kerry people wanted me to speak at the convention, although it
was not yet clear in what capacity. One afternoon, as I drove
back from Springfield to Chicago for an evening campaign event,
Kerry campaign manager Mary Beth Cahill called to deliver the
news. After I hung up, I turned to my driver, Mike Signator.

"I guess this is pretty big," I said.

Mike nodded. "You could say that."

I had only been to one previous Democratic convention, the
2000 Convention in Los Angeles. I hadn't planned to attend that
convention; I was just coming off my defeat in the Democratic
primary for the Illinois First Congressional District seat, and was
determined to spend most of the summer catching up on work at
the law practice that I'd left unattended during the campaign (a
neglect that had left me more or less broke), as well as make up
for lost time with a wife and daughter who had seen far too little
of me during the previous six months.

At the last minute, though, several friends and supporters who were planning to go insisted that I join them. You need to make national contacts, they told me, for when you run again—and anyway, it will be fun. Although they didn't say this at the time, I suspect they saw a trip to the convention as a bit of useful therapy for me, on the theory that the best thing to do after getting thrown off a horse is to get back on right away.

Eventually I relented and booked a flight to L.A. When I landed, I took the shuttle to Hertz Rent A Car, handed the woman behind the counter my American Express card, and began looking at the map for directions to a cheap hotel that I'd found near Venice Beach. After a few minutes the Hertz woman came back with a look of embarrassment on her face.

"I'm sorry, Mr. Obama, but your card's been rejected."

"That can't be right. Can you try again?"

"I tried twice, sir. Maybe you should call American Express."

After half an hour on the phone, a kindhearted supervisor at American Express authorized the car rental. But the episode served as an omen of things to come. Not being a delegate, I couldn't secure a floor pass; according to the Illinois Party chairman, he was already inundated with requests, and the best he could do was give me a pass that allowed entry only onto the convention site. I ended up watching most of the speeches on various television screens scattered around the Staples Center, occasionally following friends or acquaintances into skyboxes where it was clear I didn't belong. By Tuesday night, I realized that my presence was serving neither me nor the Democratic Party any apparent purpose, and by Wednesday morning I was on the first flight back to Chicago.

Given the distance between my previous role as a convention gate-crasher and my newfound role as convention keynoter, I had some cause to worry that my appearance in Boston might not go very well. But perhaps because by that time I had become accustomed to outlandish things happening in my campaign, I didn't feel particularly nervous. A few days after the call from Ms. Cahill, I was back in my hotel room in Springfield, making notes for a rough draft of the speech while watching a basketball game. I thought about the themes that I'd sounded during the campaign— the willingness of people to work hard if given the chance, the need for government to help provide a foundation for opportunity, the belief that Americans felt a sense of mutual obligation toward one another. I made a list of the issues I might touch on—health care, education, the war in Iraq.

But most of all, I thought about the voices of all the people I'd met on the campaign trail. I remembered Tim Wheeler and his wife in Galesburg, trying to figure out how to get their teenage son the liver transplant he needed. I remembered a young man in East Moline named Seamus Ahern who was on his way to Iraq— the desire he had to serve his country, the look of pride and apprehension on the face of his father. I remembered a young black woman I'd met in East St. Louis whose name I never would catch, but who told me of her efforts to attend college even though no one in her family had ever graduated from high school.

It wasn't just the struggles of these men and women that had moved me. Rather, it was their determination, their self-reliance, a relentless optimism in the face of hardship. It brought to mind a phrase that my pastor, Rev. Jeremiah A. Wright Jr., had once used in a sermon.

The audacity of hope.

That was the best of the American spirit, I thought—having the audacity to believe despite all the evidence to the contrary that we could restore a sense of community to a nation torn by conflict; the gall to believe that despite personal setbacks, the loss of a job or an illness in the family or a childhood mired in poverty, we had some control—and therefore responsibility— over our own fate.

It was that audacity, I thought, that joined us as one people. It was that pervasive spirit of hope that tied my own family's story to the larger American story, and my own story to those of the voters I sought to represent.

I turned off the basketball game and started to write.

A FEW WEEKS later, I arrived in Boston, caught three hours' sleep, and traveled from my hotel to the Fleet Center for my first appearance on *Meet the Press.* Toward the end of the segment, Tim Russert put up on the screen an excerpt from a 1996 interview with the *Cleveland Plain-Dealer* that I had forgotten about entirely, in which the reporter had asked me—as someone just getting into politics as a candidate for the Illinois state senate— what I thought about the Democratic Convention in Chicago.

> The convention's for sale, right. . . . You've got these $10,000-a-plate dinners, Golden Circle Clubs. I think when the average voter looks at that, they rightly feel they've been locked out of the process. They can't attend a $10,000 breakfast. They know that those who can are going to get the kind of access they can't imagine.

After the quote was removed from the screen, Russert turned to me. "A hundred and fifty donors gave $40 million to this convention," he said. "It's worse than Chicago, using your standards. Are you offended by that, and what message does that send the average voter?"

I replied that politics and money were a problem for both parties, but that John Kerry's voting record, and my own, indicated that we voted for what was best for the country. I said that a convention wouldn't change that, although I did suggest that the more Democrats could encourage participation from people who felt locked out of the process, the more we stayed true to our origins as the party of the average Joe, the stronger we would be as a party.

Privately, I thought my original 1996 quote was better.

There was a time when political conventions captured the urgency and drama of politics—when nominations were determined by floor managers and head counts and side deals and arm-twisting, when passions or miscalculation might result in a second or third or fourth round of balloting. But that time passed long ago. With the advent of binding primaries, the much-needed end to the dominance of party bosses and backroom deals in smoke-filled rooms, today's convention is bereft of surprises. Rather, it serves as a weeklong infomercial for the party and its nominee—as well as a means of rewarding the party faithful and major contributors with four days of food, drink, entertainment, and shoptalk.

I spent most of the first three days at the convention fulfilling my role in this pageant. I spoke to rooms full of major Democratic donors and had breakfast with delegates from across the fifty states. I practiced my speech in front of a video monitor, did a walk-through of how it would be staged, received instruction on where to stand, where to wave, and how to best use the microphones. My communications director, Robert Gibbs, and I trotted up and down the stairs of the Fleet Center, giving interviews that were sometimes only two minutes apart, to ABC, NBC, CBS, CNN, Fox News, and NPR, at each stop emphasizing the talking points that the Kerry-Edwards team had provided, each word of which had been undoubtedly tested in a battalion of polls and a panoply of focus groups.

Given the breakneck pace of my days, I didn't have much time to worry about how my speech would go over. It wasn't until Tuesday night, after my staff and Michelle had debated for half an hour over what tie I should wear (we finally settled on the tie that Robert Gibbs was wearing), after we had ridden over to the Fleet Center and heard strangers shout "Good luck!" and "Give 'em hell, Obama!," after we had visited with a very gracious and funny Teresa Heinz Kerry in her hotel room, until finally it was just Michelle and me sitting backstage and watching the broadcast, that I started to feel just a tad bit nervous. I mentioned to Michelle that my stomach was feeling a little grumbly. She hugged me tight, looked into my eyes, and said, "Just don't screw it up, buddy!"

We both laughed. Just then, one of the production managers came into the hold room and told me it was time to take my position offstage. Standing behind the black curtain, listening to Dick Durbin introduce me, I thought about my mother and father and grandfather and what it might have been like for them to be in the audience. I thought about my grandmother in Hawaii, watching the convention on TV because her back was too deteriorated for her to travel. I thought about all the volunteers and supporters back in Illinois who had worked so hard on my behalf.

Lord, let me tell their stories right, I said to myself. Then I walked onto the stage.

I WOULD BE lying if I said that the positive reaction to my speech at the Boston convention—the letters I received, the crowds who showed up to rallies once we got back to Illinois—wasn't personally gratifying. After all, I got into politics to have some influence on the public debate, because I thought I had something to say about the direction we need to go as a country.

Still, the torrent of publicity that followed the speech reinforces my sense of how fleeting fame is, contingent as it is on a thousand different matters of chance, of events breaking this way rather than that. I know that I am not so much smarter than the man I was six years ago, when I was temporarily stranded at LAX. My views on health care or education or foreign policy are not so much more refined than they were when I labored in obscurity as a community organizer. If I am wiser, it is mainly because I have traveled a little further down the path I have chosen for myself, the path of politics, and have gotten a glimpse of where it may lead, for good and for ill.

I remember a conversation I had almost twenty years ago with a friend of mine, an older man who had been active in the civil rights efforts in Chicago in the sixties and was teaching urban studies at Northwestern University. I had just decided, after three years of organizing, to attend law school; because he was one of the few academics I knew, I had asked him if he would be willing to give me a recommendation.

He said he would be happy to write me the recommendation, but first wanted to know what I intended to do with a law degree. I mentioned my interest in a civil rights practice, and that at some point I might try my hand at running for office. He nodded his head and asked whether I had considered what might be involved in taking such a path, what I would be willing to do to make the Law Review, or make partner, or get elected to that first office and then move up the ranks. As a rule, both law and politics required compromise, he said; not just on issues, but on more fundamental things—your values and ideals. He wasn't saying that to dissuade me, he said. It was just a fact. It was because of his unwillingness to compromise that, although he had been approached many times in his youth to enter politics, he had always declined.

"It's not that compromise is inherently wrong," he said to me. "I just didn't find it satisfying. And the one thing I've discovered as I get older is that you have to do what is satisfying to you. In fact that's one of the advantages of old age, I suppose, that you've finally learned what matters to you. It's hard to know that at twenty-six. And the problem is that nobody else can answer that question for you. You can only figure it out on your own."

Twenty years later, I think back on that conversation and appreciate my friend's words more than I did at the time. For I am getting to an age where I have a sense of what satisfies me, and although I am perhaps more tolerant of compromise on the issues than my friend was, I know that my satisfaction is not to be found in the glare of television cameras or the applause of the crowd. Instead, it seems to come more often now from knowing that in some demonstrable way I've been able to help people live their lives with some measure of dignity. I think about what Benjamin Franklin wrote to his mother, explaining why he had devoted so much of his time to public service: "I would rather have it said, He lived usefully, than, He died rich."

That's what satisfies me now, I think—being useful to my family and the people who elected me, leaving behind a legacy that will make our children's lives more hopeful than our own. Sometimes, working in Washington, I feel I am meeting that goal. At other times, it seems as if the goal recedes from me, and all the activity I engage in—the hearings and speeches and press conferences and position papers—are an exercise in vanity, useful to no one.

When I find myself in such moods, I like to take a run along the Mall. Usually I go in the early evening, especially in the summer and fall, when the air in Washington is warm and still and the leaves on the trees barely rustle. After dark, not many people are out—perhaps a few couples taking a walk, or homeless men on benches, organizing their possessions. Most of the time I stop at the Washington Monument, but sometimes I push on, across the street to the National World War II Memorial, then along the Reflecting Pool to the Vietnam Veterans Memorial, then up the stairs of the Lincoln Memorial.

At night, the great shrine is lit but often empty. Standing between marble columns, I read the Gettysburg Address and the Second Inaugural Address. I look out over the Reflecting Pool, imagining the crowd stilled by Dr. King's mighty cadence, and then beyond that, to the floodlit obelisk and shining Capitol dome.

And in that place, I think about America and those who built it. This nation's founders, who somehow rose above petty ambitions and narrow calculations to imagine a nation unfurling

across a continent. And those like Lincoln and King, who ultimately laid down their lives in the service of perfecting an imperfect union. And all the faceless, nameless men and women, slaves
and soldiers and tailors and butchers, constructing lives for
themselves and their children and grandchildren, brick by brick,
rail by rail, calloused hand by calloused hand, to fill in the landscape of our collective dreams.

It is that process I wish to be a part of.

My heart is filled with love for this country.

Acknowledgments

THIS BOOK WOULD have not been possible without the extraordinary support of a number of people.

I have to begin with my wife, Michelle. Being married to a senator is bad enough; being married to a senator who is also writing a book requires the patience of Job. Not only did Michelle provide emotional support throughout the writing process, but she helped me arrive at many of the ideas that are reflected in the book. With each passing day, I understand more fully just how lucky I am to have Michelle in my life, and can only hope that my boundless love for her offers some consolation for my constant preoccupations.

I want to express as well my gratitude to my editor, Rachel Klayman. Even before I had won my Senate primary race, it was Rachel who brought my first book, *Dreams from My Father,* to the attention of Crown Publishers, long after it had gone out of print. It was Rachel who championed my proposal to write this book. And it has been Rachel who's been my constant partner in what's been the frequently difficult but always exhilarating effort of bringing this book to completion. At each stage of the editorial process, she's been insightful, meticulous, and unflagging in her enthusiasm. Often she's understood what I was trying to accomplish with the book before I did, and has gently but firmly brought me into line whenever I strayed from my own voice and slipped into jargon, cant, or false sentiment. Moreover, she's been incredibly patient with my unforgiving Senate schedule and periodic bouts of writer's block; more than once, she's had to sacrifice sleep, weekends, or vacation time with her family in order to see the project through.

In sum, she's been an ideal editor—and become a valued friend.

Of course, Rachel could not have done what she did without the full support of my publishers at the Crown Publishing Group, Jenny Frost and Steve Ross. If publishing involves the intersection of art and commerce, Jenny and Steve have consistently erred on the side of making this book as good as it could possibly be. Their faith in this book has led them to go the extra mile time and time again, and for that I am tremendously grateful.

That same spirit has characterized all the people at Crown who've worked so hard on behalf of this book. Amy Boorstein has been tireless in managing the production process despite very tight deadlines. Tina Constable and Christine Aronson have been vigorous advocates of the book and have deftly scheduled (and rescheduled) events around the demands of my Senate work. Jill Flaxman has worked diligently with the Random House sales force and with booksellers to help the book make its way into the hands of readers. Jacob Bronstein has produced—for the second time—an outstanding audio version of the book in less than ideal circumstances. To all of them I offer my heartfelt thanks, as I do to the other members of the Crown team: Lucinda Bartley, Whitney Cookman, Lauren Dong, Laura Duffy, Skip Dye, Leta Evanthes, Kristin Kiser, Donna Passannante, Philip Patrick, Stan Redfern, Barbara Sturman, Don Weisberg, and many others.

Several good friends, including David Axelrod, Cassandra Butts, Forrest Claypool, Julius Genachowski, Scott Gration, Robert Fisher, Michael Froman, Donald Gips, John Kupper, Anthony Lake, Susan Rice, Gene Sperling, Cass Sunstein, and Jim Wallis took the time to read the manuscript and provided me with invaluable suggestions. Samantha Power deserves special mention for her extraordinary generosity; despite being in the middle of writing her own book, she combed over each chapter as if it were hers, providing me with a steady flow of useful comments even as she cheered me up whenever my spirits or energy were flagging.

A number of my Senate staff, including Pete Rouse, Karen Kornbluh, Mike Strautmanis, Jon Favreau, Mark Lippert, Joshua DuBois, and especially Robert Gibbs and Chris Lu, read the manuscript on their own time and provided me with editorial suggestions, policy recommendations, reminders, and corrections. Thanks to all of them for literally going beyond the call of duty.

A former staffer, Madhuri Kommareddi, devoted the summer before she entered Yale Law School to fact-check the entire manuscript. Her talent and energy leave me breathless. Thanks as well to Hillary Schrenell, who volunteered to help Madhuri with a number of research items in the foreign policy chapter.

Finally, I want to thank my agent, Bob Barnett of Williams and Connolly, for his friendship, skill, and support. It's made a world of difference.

Index

Sources for the statistics in this book can be found at www.audacityofhope.com.

About the Author

Barack Obama is the junior U.S. Senator from Illinois. He began his career as a community organizer in some of Chicago's poorest communities and then attended Harvard Law School, where he was elected the first African American president of the *Harvard Law Review*. In 1992, he directed Illinois Project VOTE, which registered 150,000 new voters. From 1997 to 2004, he served as a three-term state senator from Chicago's South Side. In addition to his legislative duties, he has been a senior lecturer in constitutional law at the University of Chicago Law School, practiced civil rights law, and served on the board of directors of various charitable organizations.

Senator Obama lives in Chicago's Hyde Park neighborhood with his wife, Michelle, and daughters, Malia and Sasha.